# CONSIDER, CONSTRUCT, CONFIRM

## A New Framework in Teaching and Learning

## Timothy Goodwin

**Kendall Hunt**
publishing company

**Kendall Hunt**
publishing company

www.kendallhunt.com
*Send all inquiries to:*
4050 Westmark Drive
Dubuque, IA  52004-1840

Copyright © 2018 by Timothy Goodwin

ISBN 978-1-5249-4339-4

Published in the United States of America

# Contents

## PART 3 Student-Centered Curriculum Design

## Chapter 6 Thematic, Inquiry-Based Curriculum Design

## Chapter 7 Teaching From Questions

## Chapter 8 Designing Thematic, Inquiry-Based Units

## PART 4 Student-Centered Instruction

## Chapter 9 Enacting Instruction Based on Constructivist Learning Theory

# Acknowledgements

I would like to acknowledge the contribution of a number of individuals in the completion of this book. All of my colleagues in the Professional Education department at Bemidji State University have had to suffer through my writing of this book. Being a "verbal processor" means they have probably heard more than they cared to. Some might even say I have been insufferable! First, I would like to thank Dr. Linda Colburn. As we collaboratively developed the pedagogy course we taught, she repeatedly told me, "I think you've got a book here with your idea." She was persistent, so here it is. Without her prodding, encouragement, support, reviewing, and guidance, this book would not exist. Dr. Porter Coggins also deserves specific notice for always having a few minutes to listen to an idea and provide feedback. He never said no, nor did he ever provide anything but helpful, spot-on, positive encouragement. I have had the pleasure of collaborating with these two mentors on multiple projects and courses. I am a better teacher because of those opportunities. I would also like to thank my colleagues at my former teaching gig—Shattuck-St. Mary's School. It was while teaching at this 6-12 boarding school that I truly figured out how to teach from a foundation of constructivist learning theory and how to develop thematic, inquiry-based curriculum. It was there that I had the necessary space and opportunity to explore and invent pedagogical practices based on constructivist learning theory in my teaching. Lastly, gratitude to the publishing team at Kendall Hunt for the opportunity to see my ideas make it to print.

# About the Author

Photo Courtesy of Tracy Goodwin

Tim Goodwin has taught at Bemidji State University since 2013. During this time he has served as department chair and taught a variety of courses with an emphasis on pedagogy and science education. Tim has also taught secondary science for 20 years. He holds an M.A. and Doctorate in Education from Hamline University, and a Bachelor's degree in biology from St. Olaf College.

# Part 1

# A New Student-Centered Learning Cycle

This book provides a new framework for teaching and learning conceptualized through a learning cycle that emphasizes student-centered pedagogical practices. Part 1 consists of the introduction, then provides the philosophical foundation for teaching methods rooted in constructivist learning theory as an important foundation for teaching in the 21st century in *Chapter 1: An Argument for Constructivism*. After this foundation is provided, I will introduce a student-centered learning cycle that I call Consider, Construct, Confirm (CCC) in *Chapter 2: Constructivist Learning Cycle*. It is through this learning cycle that I provide a framework for student-centered planning and instruction rooted in constructivist learning theory. Part 2 explores student-centered classrooms. In this section, I will provide a description of the classroom climate and culture, and type of assessment necessary to foster student inquiry and discovery as the main mode of learning in a constructivist classroom. Part 3 builds on the foundation of the classroom climate necessary for student inquiry and outlines a methodology of developing thematic, inquiry-based curricula. Part 4 is about student-centered instruction. I will provide specific strategies for facilitating student inquiry.

Throughout the book, you will see the "Dig Deeper" graphic (Figure I.1) when I introduce a specific strategy that is explored more deeply later in the book. These allow you to jump to that specific item in a later chapter so you can further explore that technique in that moment if appropriate for you depending on how you are using this resource. This marker (Figure I.2) will mark the spot to find that further detailed discussion of that strategy or concept. You will also find this symbol (Figure I.3) to mark a concept that was discussed earlier or a connection of a concept to a previously discussed concept so you can easily go back and review if necessary, and then find your place and resume reading.

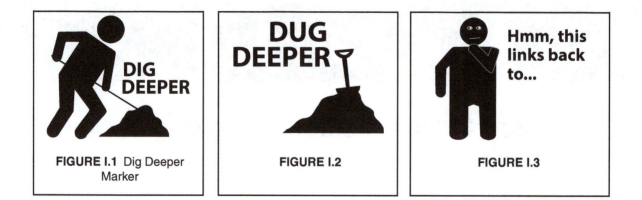

FIGURE I.1 Dig Deeper Marker

FIGURE I.2

FIGURE I.3

# Introduction

We are always *enacting* a story. This is more than just living one's life. To say one is enacting a story implies a sense of purpose; like walking barefoot on a beach, the footprints left behind tell us where we have been, which connect to the footprints we make as we walk, and then reveal the paths we can choose next. Past, present, and future link together as one enacts his or her own story. It is not a solo journey; it is a collective journey. *I* enact *my* story, but never in isolation. *We* enact *our* stories—together. Each of our individual stories, interconnected, become *our* story.

Brian McLaren (2014) titled a recent book, *We Make The Road By Walking* about finding and making one's purposeful spiritual journey. He begins with this paragraph:

> What we all want is pretty simple, really. We want to be alive. To feel alive. Not just to exist but to thrive, to live out loud, walk tall, breathe free. We want to be less lonely, less exhausted, less conflicted or afraid . . . more away, more grateful, more energized and purposeful. We capture this kind of mindful, overbrimming life in terms like *well-being*, shalom, *blessedness, wholeness, harmony, life to the full,* and *aliveness* (p. xv).

Though McLaren is writing about finding purpose in life through the lens of spirituality, his statement that we all search for meaning rings true for me—despite one's spirituality and religious affiliations. Before McLaren used this title, so too did two educators, Horton and Freire (1990) in a "talking book" which is a published transcript of their conversation about education topics and social change. Freire states the following:

> I think that one of the best ways for us to work as human beings is not only to know that we are uncompleted beings but to *assume* the uncompleteness. There is a little difference between knowing intellectually that we are unfinished and assuming the nature of being unfinished. We are not complete. We have to become inserted into a permanent process of searching. Without this we would die in life. It means that keeping curiosity is absolutely indispensable for us to continue to be or to become (p. 11).

We are never complete. We continue to enact our stories throughout our entire lives.

I began walking the road of my education career with these simple aspirations; I wanted to teach biology because I understood the world through that lens and I wanted to coach wrestling because (I thought at the time) it was through the collective battle of competition I made connections to my fellow athletes. It was the path I could easily visualize as it was my dad's journey as well. Quickly, however, my road forked and the path I walked no longer involved coaching athletes. I soon gravitated toward, and then often found, I was leading discussions about changing the way we teach. I found myself leading other educators. Then my footsteps slowed. More education. More writing. New characters added to the story. This opened new doors, as always happens if you continue walking. With each fork in the road I explored, and continue to explore, in conjunction with my colleagues and students, what it means to be a teacher, and what it means to be educated. All teachers walk this road, whether they acknowledge it or not. You teach as you live, and you live as you teach.

Each year, as a teacher, you have the opportunity to facilitate the formation of a new learning community (maybe even many). As we teachers each enact our story, we and all our students, learn from the other characters sharing the story. Each individual is enacting a story, cognizant of it or not, our most profound discoveries occur in the context of a learning community. So, what story are you enacting? How will you enact that story—the story that is *your* story and no one else's? And how will you make and walk this road with all of the students in your classroom?

This book is written for anyone, who like me, is passionate about teaching and learning. This book is about the craft of teaching. I've been a teacher all of my professional life. My entire career has been framed by the popular narrative and perception that public education is in crisis and in need of reform. Since the story of my career has been "set" in a world of education reform, I continually ask myself: Have I (we) done my (our) best? Sadly, I have no choice but to answer with a sheepish, "No, I don't think we have."

I know we can do better. I also recognize that despite years of legislated policy changes, successful reform has not taken root. Much of the reform efforts have been changes to what we teach (through content standards and testing), instead of a reform of how we teach. This book outlines a new framework for curriculum design and teaching, rooted in constructivist learning theory that just might help us, as individual teachers, make changes to the part of the system we can control—our own classrooms. We teachers and our students have the ability to rewrite our respective stories of what it means to learn and to be educated.

Let me use a metaphor to express where I see us educators currently in our efforts to reform education. Anyone who has golfed, or even just tried to golf, knows what a daunting task it is to hit a golf ball consistently straight. There are untold variables in each swing which makes striking that little white ball with that little club sitting at the end of a long flexible shaft almost impossible to do consistently for the recreational golfer. Most recreational golfers learn by watching others, maybe some instructional videos, and tips from friends or playing partners; but in the end, most individuals learn by getting out on the course and just figuring it out. It is a game after all and just practicing on the driving range is not satisfying. With some practice, many individuals develop enough consistency to (mostly) enjoy the game—despite potentially bad swing habits they have developed.

As the recreational golfer plays more and more, invests more money in better equipment, memberships, more green fees, etc., his or her expectations of proficiency with the game also increase. For most however, there is a point at which consistency in the swing plateaus and cannot be improved due to the self-learned habits creating a poor golf swing. Without a drastic increase in coaching, training, and practice, this is as good as it might get for the recreational golfer. With additional coaching, many discover vestigial flaws in their swing, left over from self-teaching and doing what *feels* natural in their swing. So engrained in muscle memory are these flaws, correcting them might take more practice than one has time for, or can afford. Not wanting to quit, most recreational golfers accept those limitations and adjust his or her strategy to compensate for the flaw.

The most common flaw compensated for, but not corrected, is a slice. This is when the angle of contact between the head of the club and the ball creates significant side-spin, causing it to arc away from the hitter on its flight (so a right-handed golfer slices to the right). Swinging harder and hitting it farther only compounds the flaw, increasing the slice. Instead of correcting the error in the swing, many learn how much slice to expect with a typical shot and compensate by aiming that much to the left.

Now, imagine this scene. You have the ball tee'd up and face a narrow fairway with a lake on the left and woods on the right. You're right handed and slice a bit to the right, and therefore, you aim to the left (out over the lake) to avoid hitting into the woods on the right.

"MAYBE I NEED TO SWING EVEN HARDER?!"

Wouldn't you know it, this time your swing is apparently perfect and your ball sails straight and far—and plunks down in the middle of the lake. You tee up a second ball and, out of frustration, you unconsciously grip a little tighter and swing a little harder. Muscle memory takes over your swing overriding what you know you should do to hit the ball straight. Anyone who has golfed knows the typical result. Now you *really* slice it and lose the ball in the woods off to the right. And so it goes.

In teaching, I propose that we are slicing it into the woods. Despite whatever training most of us have had, we are like the amateur golfer, relying on what *feels* right—vestiges of 16 or more years of sitting in a classroom, often as passive learners. This is especially true in the daily "grind" of teaching when push comes to shove (and with pressure to increase math and reading test scores, decreasing budgets, full classrooms, increased social needs of students, etc., there's a lot of "pushing and shoving" going on) the teacher falls back on his or her muscle memory. "Muscle memory" for teachers results in teaching something the way it was taught to you—even if that conflicts with what you know research says about how the brain constructs meaning, what works best for motivating students, and is the most effective assessment method.

Ignoring research and relying on "muscle memory" isn't limited to how we individual teachers teach. While we educators have learned a great deal about how children learn and how to meet their needs socially as they mature, the infrastructure of the physical, curricular, and organizational layout of most schools really has not changed much in the last 100 years. Now imagine yourself as a new teacher who knows all the research, but surrounded by colleagues primarily using didactic teaching methods, relying on a traditionally written textbook, and pressured to "cover" a long list of standards in this system that does not reflect the changing nature of our society and current research about children and learning. Or imagine yourself as the building administrator concerned with declining math and reading scores for your elementary students—these are the things we test for and the scores that get reported in the newspaper. Most teachers know we should be taking the time to allow students to do authentic, inquiry-based projects and assessments. Most know we should have fewer students per teacher to allow for more individualization, in-depth writing, and authentic assessment. Most know that all 12-year-olds are not at the same point in maturation and learning so should not all be lumped together and taught in the same way. But teaching differently would require more time and resources, and the spring math and reading tests are looming.

So what do we do? We increase practice for math and reading tests at the expense of the other subjects. We increase the pace at which we teach the content, requiring more didactic, stand-and-deliver instruction to at least *cover* the content. We eliminate the time for using individualized techniques for the students struggling to keep up, or bored students who understood the concept two months ago. To use a golfer phrase, we "grip it and rip it." Out of frustration we grip tighter and swing a little harder. We do what we have always done, but just faster and with more intensity—because that is what muscle memory tells us to do and what we know we can do to get through the curriculum, with the number of students we have in class, in time for the test. Of course it does not work. Test scores stagnate or even drop despite the increased focus on those two subjects. Student frustration and boredom increases and behavior management issues arise. We can either continue to compensate for our "slice" and aim a little more to the left (hoping we never actually hit it straight) so the ball will hit our target at least some of the time, or we can re-assess the fundamentals of our swing, forget the muscle memory, and re-learn to swing properly.

I've watched initiatives come and go, ideas take root, grow and then wither, and yet, through it all, *how* we teach is predominantly the same, though maybe now projected on an interactive white board. Whether you are a student in an education program, a brand new teacher, or a veteran teacher, this book is written as a conversation between me and you in an effort to foster a shift in teaching from a traditional, didactic model rooted in outdated essentialist ideals born of the industrial revolution, to a model that embraces how humans absorb and make meaning of their world.

The shift to understanding and implementing constructivist learning theory begins with the very nature of this book. The industry norm for a book of this type is to be written with a dispassionate, or authorless, voice. While the content in this style of writing might be accurate, the authors make the same mistake we teachers have made in education for too long—that learning is just about telling the audience (through lecture or reading) the information so they can memorize it and then send it back.

Ask anyone who their favorite teacher was and what made him/her their favorite and undoubtedly, one of the characteristics highlighted will be the teacher's passion about teaching the subject. If we know that passionate teachers are the most effective, why do we still use books about teaching (or any other subject) that remove the passion from the author's voice and the story or metaphor from the narrative? I'm passionate about teaching and learning, about education, the state of education, the future of education, and ultimately then the future of our democracy and the world in which we live. Ok, that's an awful lot, and I won't pretend this book can fix that. I do believe we teachers have a responsibility to create a classroom environment that is a calm refuge, like the eye of the hurricane in the current storm of education reform and a society undergoing continuous technological revolution. In doing so, maybe we can reform teaching and learning—one student at a time. So let's begin.

# Chapter 1

# An Argument for Constructivism

This book is about teaching practices aligned to constructivist learning theory. Through my lifetime of experience as a student and my career as a teacher, I, along with everyone else, has seen a variety of trends and practices come and go. We've also seen an incredible evolution in our understanding of how the human brain works, and how children grow and develop. While constructivism (as a learning theory) is relatively young, the foundation for many of the teaching practices aligned to constructivist learning theory date to the progressive movement in education from the early part of the 20th century. Those progressive practices, and more recent brain and child development research, bring us to the point now in the history of education that prompts me to believe I can make a strong argument for the need to use progressive teaching practices rooted in constructivist learning theory.

## My Turning Point as a Learner

Let me start with a bit of my story, specifically, my turning point as a teacher and the genesis of this book—though the actual writing of the book began years later. I share this story to provide you context for my framework of teaching and learning. About a decade ago I had an opportunity to attend a week-long, intensive seminar led by one of my academic heroes, Fritjof Capra (*The Tao of Physics, The Turning Point, Uncommon Wisdom, The Web of Life, The Hidden Connections, The Science of Leonardo*, Screenplay for film *Mindwalk*). His work significantly affected my thinking about environmental issues, ecology, teaching science, but most importantly, about . . . well, thinking. This seminar proved to be the genesis to applying holistic, or systemic thinking to the subjects I taught, and more importantly to how I understood and made sense of them. I cannot overstate the seismic nature of this shift on my teaching and continued learning.

Here's the setting, which is crucial to one's story, as setting and prior experiences determine how we make sense of new chapters added to the story we enact. I was the administrator for a fledgling, project-based charter school. I applied and was accepted as one of thirty participants to attend a seminar, Dialogues on Education for Sustainable Living, sponsored by the Center for Ecoliteracy, in California. Reservations were made, plane ticket purchased, and I prepped my little school to function without its sole administrator for a week during my absence. I was feeling pretty important at this point in time!

A couple of weeks prior to my flight from Minnesota to San Francisco, however, I awoke with a sharp pain shooting into my left leg, severe pain in my lower back and noticeable weakness in my lower left leg, ankle, and foot. Clearly, something had gone awry despite not being able to pinpoint any injury (or even strenuous activity that could account for this—which of course might actually account for the problem). After a few days of physical therapy, and only worsening symptoms, my doctor convinced me the MRI I initially refused was needed. Two days later I was on the surgeon's table having a partially ruptured disc repaired. Ten days after surgery, I hobbled my way onto a plane, sought assistance from a fellow passenger who loaded my carry-on into the overhead bin, and headed for the west coast. Needless to say I was wounded. I was a *very inexperienced* administrator leading a charter school in its infancy. I, and the school, were going through considerable growing pains. I can confidently say I was questioning everything—my teaching, my leadership skills, my understanding of what good teaching looked like, and even my choice of profession. I was not just feeling wounded physically, but also professionally, and even personally. Like the state of public education, I was also on the verge of crisis-mode.

The plane touched down in San Francisco, I found the retreat center's shuttle, and off I went with a few other attendees. After a few more stops, the van carried approximately 10 individuals out of the 30 attending the seminar. As I listened to introductions and conversations, I wanted to sink into the seams of the van seat. Except for Antarctica, nearly every continent was represented among this handful of people. Many had a terminal degree of some kind and multiple languages were being spoken. Suddenly, I was swimming in a much larger pond! This, and the curvy, up-and-down-roads of Northern California, was not helping my confidence—or my "wounds." After an hour of watching the hills north of San Francisco pass while I listened to these conversations, we arrived at

"I'M GONNA NEED A BIGGER BOAT"

the retreat center, dispersed out of the van to find our cabins and get situated, before making our way to the main building for dinner and introductions.

Not long after finding my cabin—a dorm-sized sleeping room, I took another pain pill and gingerly walked up toward the main building. I was thinking about meeting a hero. I had read his books, *The Tao of Physics*, *The Turning Point,* and most importantly for me, *The Web of Life*, and watched and re-watched the movie *Mindwalk*, based on the application of systems theory as described in his books. How would I introduce myself and not look like an idiot? After all, I was a wounded animal and in way over my head.

Twenty paces or so ahead of me was a taller man with curly gray hair. He passed through the double-door entrance and paused in the lobby to survey the surroundings, allowing me to close the gap. As all good introverts do, I also paused to survey the surroundings. You never know, a tiger or over-enthusiastic extrovert might be lurking somewhere ready to pounce. The man I had been following turned to me, extended his hand, and with a slight Austrian accent said, "Hi, I'm Fritjof." It was such a simple and un-assuming first encounter that my anxiety immediately eased (for the moment anyway). Not a tiger. Just a friendly housecat—though I would learn through the week's lectures, seminar discussions, and informal sharing of stories around a fire—a really, really, smart housecat. Just like me, this *flea* on that housecat by comparison, he was really just a fellow educator seeking answers to the same questions we all were chasing, which is ultimately, "how do we live in this world?" For me that meant, how do I live in this world *as a teacher*?

The point is this; our heroes should not scare us. The enormity of the task of "reforming" or at least improving education should not scare us. We can *all* do this work as teachers to heal the wounded system and we all belong at the table and in the conversation, whether a parent of school-age children, someone at the genesis of your teaching career, a new teacher, or a grizzled veteran teacher.

Capra's questions are broader than just education; his, instead, are about the global environmental crises we face, as well as, the systemic societal issues causing those crises and influencing efforts (or lack thereof) to address these crises. These environmental and societal structural issues form the foundation and backdrop for everything we do. Because these are all connected and based on how we interact with the world, he frames the crises as a "crisis of perception." What Capra means by this is that as a society, we continue to try and solve large issues from a reductionist (one piece at a time) philosophy—meaning we try and solve problems piecemeal. Therefore, we cannot perceive the interconnections *between* problems resulting in a myriad of unintended negative consequences from our efforts to affect positive change from a reductionist paradigm. Throughout Capra's work he is attempting to facilitate a paradigm shift in how we perceive our place on the planet so individuals can begin to understand our interconnectedness with all of the living and non-living systems. Capra argues that we must recognize and understand this interconnectedness to address our most complex issues. Since all are interconnected, changing one part of the system never happens in isolation, but always affects other parts of the system. We know we cannot change everything at once in a system, but Capra is trying to get us to understand the holistic nature of the system as a first step to a system's thinking paradigm instead of a reductionist paradigm.

Capra applies concepts of systems theory to understanding the nature of natural and societal systems. In this paradigm, a system in balance utilizes negative feedback loops to self-correct and maintain a constant state—like a thermostat automatically adjusts the heat in a house to maintain a constant temperature, or the human kidneys constantly adjust how much water and salt is filtered from the blood to maintain a constant salinity level. A system out of balance is experiencing positive feedback loops which push the system further and further from a balanced state. Global climate change is an example. The planet temperature warms, reducing how much carbon dioxide can be absorbed by the ocean, which leaves more $CO_2$ in the atmosphere, trapping more of the sun's heat, which then increases the atmospheric temperature, increasing ocean temp, further decreasing the oceans' capacity to absorb $CO_2$, thus adding to an increase in the Earth's temperature.

These examples of systemic negative and positive feedback loops are relatively easy to see. As you proceed, when considering education practices and policies, pause and try and identify how that issue fits into the education system as a functioning *system* governed by systems theory and then if that practice is contributing to negative or positive feedback loops in the system. Is it functioning to maintain a status quo or is it contributing to pushing the system further from equilibrium?

## The Education Crisis of Perception

Though broader in scope, Capra's way of thinking can be applied to the story all us teachers are enacting—education reform due to a national education crisis. Here too, just as in environmental crises, the approach has been reductionist—addressing one piece at a time, not taking into account counter-productive, unintended consequences and ripples throughout the rest of the system. I propose that education is in a similar "crisis of perception." To illustrate my point, let's consider an historical example of repeated science education-reform efforts—though the story of education reform (or lack thereof) can be applied across all of the subject areas.

In the early 20th century, John Dewey criticized science teachers for simply requiring students to accumulate facts. Dewey recommended shifting the focus from accumulating facts to teaching the process of inquiry. In the 1950s, Joseph Schwab again criticized science education for being taught as empirical, literal, and as irrevocable truths. He recommended emphasizing laboratory experiences during which students were left to ask questions, gather evidence and propose explanations based on evidence; in other words, he advocated for what we would now call inquiry-based learning. In the 1960s, with the country shaken by the late 1950s Soviet Union launch of Sputnik, sparking the space race, the spotlight was once again on public science education practices. F. James Rutherford criticized the profession for still not representing science as inquiry and added that science teachers must understand the history and philosophy of sciences in order to teach it as inquiry. In the 1980s, Project 2061, a long-term initiative by the American Association for the Advancement of the Sciences, provided a framework of science teaching. Want to take a guess at what they recommended? Students should start with questions, collect evidence, stop separating knowing from finding out, and deemphasize the memorization of technical vocabulary. This led to the National Science Education Standards in 1996 with a heavy emphasis on inquiry. The National Research Council, in 2000, told the same story. The Next Generation Science Standards were released a decade later with a heavy emphasis on inquiry. Nearly a full century of critiques and reform efforts of the profession has yielded the same critiques and recommendations over and over again. What again is the colloquial definition of insanity?

Here we are, nearly two decades into the 21st century, and still reforming. Years after the passing of No Child Left Behind (NCLB) has been widely recognized as a failure, or at least with undesirable unintended consequences, we reformed the reform with the Race to the Top initiative and then rewrote the NCLB law calling it the Every Student Succeeds Act but the paradigm has not really changed.

Since *The Nation at Risk* report in the early 1980s, reform has included more and more standards to define what facts are to be learned, more and more testing to reward those schools that test well (and punish those that do not), more school choices, and ironically the unintended consequence of more, not less, racial and economic segregation. Despite multiple efforts from various starting points on the political spectrum, we have seen very little change and/or improvement in graduation rates, test scores, public satisfaction, and student achievement (at least based on the measures we are using). Through all of these reforms, "most elementary and secondary schools today take an empiricist/reductionist approach in their curriculum planning" (Fosnot 1989). Changes upon changes, we are more or less the same.

So what is the problem? We have a crisis of perception. We continue to address education reform from the same paradigm over and over again. That same reductionist—one piece at a time—approach Capra criticized for addressing our larger environmental problems is also used in education reform because that is how we have, and continue to, train individuals in our society to think, ironically, largely by the public education system. With each new critique and poor report about student achievement, we dig deeper into the machinery of education and begin replacing parts. We are operating from a failed perceptual model of reductionism. Students aren't keeping up in science—so we invent an acronym called STEM—but do not really change much of *how* we teach science. Test scores are flat so we write tougher standards—but use the same methods of teaching math and reading. We push the system harder and harder, replacing a gear here and a piston there but the engine can only turn its pistons so fast. We fail to recognize, just like when we tug at a strand of a living system with all of its interconnections, all of that system is affected, all the components of the education system are also interconnected. And they are not just connected to one another, they also interconnect with the rest of the social systems in which that engine operates. This is why a paradigm shift in education is so difficult, maybe even seemingly impossible.

CLEARLY THE PROBLEM IS A BUSTED TAILLIGHT

So how do you change the paradigm? The paradigm shift begins with training ourselves and the next generation to think differently. While simplistic answers may get politicians elected, simplistic answers will not fix what ails us. One cannot fix a system without understanding the system. The best he or she can do is treat symptoms. We need to retrain ourselves to see the systems before we take them apart to replace the mechanisms within those systems. Currently, we educate our children to live in the world by breaking the world into tiny bits and feeding it back to them one piece at a time. We then expect them to naturally put those tiny bits together, seeing the connections between the bits when they complete their education. But how can they when never taught to even see the connections, let alone understand the positive and negative feedback mechanisms that are foundational to systems theory? We need to flip this methodology 180°. Show the systems, the connections and the interrelationships first, and then help students to pull those systems apart and understand the "gears" and "pulleys" of that system in context of the larger system.

If we can accomplish this, then just maybe, we can have a populace that is not reliant upon a select few to engineer our way out of the next crisis—be it environmental, political, educational, or economic. Maybe, just maybe, we can have a populace that chooses political leaders who offer solutions resulting from discussion and debate over the merits and impact on the collective good for generations to come instead of simply scoring a "political win" and regaining political power over the other party, often at the expense of the collective good.

I began my paradigm shift in that seminar led by Capra, which was necessary for me to then understand what it meant to be constructivist teacher. It took some more years and more schooling during which I experienced constructivist teaching for the first time *as a student* to have it sink in to my practices as a teacher. And honestly, I still have to work at it. As you will find (or already have found) too. Teaching from a constructivist learning theory paradigm is difficult, maybe Sisyphean, as that traditional-teaching-model boulder is continually pulled back down the hill by gravity to squish us. But everything we know about how children learn tells us teachers that yes, shifting to teaching practices rooted in constructivist learning theory is a necessary part of reforming education. As individual teachers, we can control what and how we teach in our classrooms, even in the context of state-mandated curriculum and testing, so that is where I will focus the energy of our conversation in this book.

I belonged at that seminar led by Capra in 2007, despite my initial trepidation and feelings of inadequacies, because I was seeking answers and was ready to learn, even though my credentials didn't stack up to many of the participants. My lack of education and experience were hurdles I had to get over, but those hurdles did not discount my ability to ask questions and to learn, they just informed my starting point as a learner. It is the same with your teaching and your student's learning. The story I am enacting was altered not just by those that taught me in that seminar, but also my fellow students and the setting of the seminar. Throughout our educational journey we wander and wonder with our fellow teachers and our students. We are all, always simultaneously teachers and students. We all are ready to learn, though we do that learning within the context of our own starting point—our own story. None of us are a blank page waiting for the teacher to fill with information and write our story. We all bring a setting for our story through our prior knowledge, experiences, triumphs and even wounds. As we learn we are just adding more anecdotes, characters, and chapters to the story we write and enact. Our job as teachers (or future job if a prospective teacher), despite all that is happening around us in terms of school policy, legislation, and society, is to provide students the experiences they need to write and enact *their own story*.

# Teaching in the Age of Standards

Recently I broke down and got lunch at a fast food place. I know, I know. Ick. I won't say which franchise to protect their identity and my dignity. I was struck by what the cashier said when handing me my meal in a bag. She didn't say, "Enjoy your meal." Instead she said, "Enjoy the rest of your day." There was no pretense here. I was not really going to enjoy the meal.

Most of us "break down" and eat fast food. We know it is not good for us. We know it is not really that good either. Yet we do it—when in a hurry, when traveling, when the pantry is bare, and a trip to the grocery store is not in the cards. We also do it because we know exactly what we are going to get. The standards are set and we know the hamburger from McDonalds in Minneapolis is going to taste just like the hamburger in Atlanta. That is the strength of fast food. However, its strength is also its weakness. It is standardized and predictable. There is no creativity involved.

In our efforts to increase rigor and "teacher-proof" education, we have adopted a litany of education content standards. What works in Minneapolis schools must also work in Atlanta schools right? During the span of my career we have successfully standardized the content of the curriculum. Attempts to teacher-proof the education system have made education predictable and, well quite frankly, boring.

When I started teaching, I had complete academic freedom. Probably too much. Most teachers today have very little academic freedom in what they teach. Probably too little. Some do not even have any academic freedom in regards to how they teach and how they assess their students. If the paradigm for the craft of teaching is simply a matter of any person opening a book and assigning an assignment, giving a lecture, and then providing the mandated objective test, then yes this paradigm might work. This kind of people-proofing of an industry, be it food, retail, engineering, or art only results in one thing however—predictability and mediocrity. Then I ask, why do we want this for our education system?

We continue to operate under a great lie that has become accepted as "truth" in modern education: educators require a set of standards to know what to teach and when to teach it. Within the span of my career, the politics and profession of education has moved from local decision-making about curriculum, to accepted state-sponsored, mandated-by-law curriculum, in the form of content standards measured by standardized tests. While we now argue politically from left to right about the content of state-mandated standards and standardized tests, we no longer even debate the validity of the very existence of standards, or any unintended consequences of such mandates. This is Mother Culture as Daniel Quinn (1994) described in his novel *Ishmael*, at its finest, quietly whispering in our ears telling us this is the way it has been and always shall be.

Imagine our greatest scientists, artists and thinkers in today's education setting. Would they have a chance to shine, to explore their passions, to fail safely and learn from mistakes, to dream and to create, or would they be studying for A.P. exams and taking SAT prep courses? Would they have graduated burned out, and sick of learning before entering their first years of college or graduate school? Would they have taken the safe route to get training for a good job and sacrificed dreaming up the theory of relativity, the transistor, or even iPods?

Our efforts to standardize the curriculum have not closed the achievement gap, nor have they "teacher-proofed" the curriculum against mediocrity. In fact, I believe they have increased mediocrity, because the introduction of the standards has shut down the "art" of teaching. Roland Barth said in a talk I attended at the Progressive Education Network National Conference in 2007, (I'm paraphrasing as best I can remember), "The job of the administrator is to provide a safe place for teachers to fail. If you do that, then the good ones will rise to the top as they try innovative and creative ways to teach, reach, and inspire children. They will then create classroom environments where students will take risks, are creative, and innovative." We will never "people-proof" an industry that relies so heavily on people and the relationships that are formed between students and teachers. If we want to "teacher-proof" the curriculum we need to provide better teachers, and then place those teachers a setting in which they can be innovative and creative. Instead we are putting teachers behind the metaphorical fast food counter, saying "enjoy the rest of your day."

This is part of the crisis of perception introduced earlier we face in education. We currently teach in a school system that is based on a very "essentialist" philosophy—that what students need to know is clearly identified by society, and that the role of the

teacher is to simply transmit that information to the next generation. This has been a constant in American education. Within the span of my career, however, we have shifted to a state-sponsored, *mandated*, set of ideas. This might seem to be a subtle shift, but the impact has been profound. Many teachers, especially new teachers, teach with the standards hanging over their head like the sword of Damocles. We know that when students are operating from a fear of failure they do not fully explore their creativity and potential. The same is true for teachers. Can an education system such as we have today, mandated in statute, and prepackaged to remove any chance for an emergent curriculum, produce the next Galileo, Newton, Einstein, Shakespeare, Plato, Gates, or Steve Jobs? Would the very state and democratic system of freedom to pursue happiness envisioned by the minds of such divergent thinkers as Adams and Jefferson come to pass from today's education system? I'm almost afraid to ask the question because the answer might undermine everything we teachers do professionally.

## Reclaiming Leadership

It is tempting to blame a flawed system and give up in frustration. However, if teachers do a better job, through more effective teaching methods, then parents, politicians, and policymakers will support public education with resources and prestige. This will create a positive feedback loop. Positive feedback loops overcome the inertia that keeps a system stuck at the status quo and drive the system away from equilibrium and cause systemic change. More resources and more prestige equal better teaching and learning conditions, increasing success of students and satisfaction from parents, prompting more support, and so on. Until the perception changes and politicians are satisfied, they will continue to pass legislation with the intent of reforming or improving public education—even though those piece-meal reform efforts, largely measured by standardized testing, do not yield the desired results—creative problem solvers and critical thinkers.

Piaget (1978) has argued that success on school tasks is not analogous to real understanding, yet, because teachers are usually trained to assess only competency on tasks, understanding is frequently sacrificed. What we do as teachers then, often does not empower and inspire a life of learning and inquiry. Fosnot (1989) describes an empowered learner as:

> one who is an autonomous, inquisitive thinker—one who questions, investigates, and reasons. An empowered teacher is a reflective decision maker who finds joy in learning and in investigating the teaching/learning process—one who views learning as construction and teaching as a facilitating process to enhance and enrich development . . . If change is to occur in teacher education, the new models advanced must be based on what we know about teaching and learning, and they must aim at producing teachers who are decision makers, researchers, and articulate change agents" (pp. xi–xiii).

As teachers, and the experts in the classroom, it is time to reclaim our leadership role in what we teach and how we teach it. We teachers need to reclaim leadership to facilitate learning that aligns with constructivist learning theory. I have the lofty goal of helping you as a teacher, and then by extension, your students ignite (or reignite) a love for learning. All individuals love to learn. That is why babies crawl and put everything in their mouth—to figure things out. As children progress through school, engagement and excitement for learning decreases, seemingly at an inverse relationship to the number of years in school. It is up to us teachers to fix that decline in engagement.

## Digging Deeper into Constructivism

When I was maybe eight years old, I recall a time in a park with my family and some extended family. I was playfully wrestling with my dad, and in the midst of "battle," playfully said, "Dad, you bastard." Wow, did that stop the fun. I possibly saw the word on the cover of a 1974 novel by John Jakes titled *The Bastard* that was a best-seller at the time. Context is everything. And so it is with learning as well. We do not learn anything in a vacuum—even as newborns. Everything has a context. A basic tenet of constructivism is knowledge cannot exist outside of our minds; knowledge is the result of construction of meaning by individuals based on his or her experience, not the result of discovery (Yilmaz Spring 2008). That is not to say that everything is relative. $2 + 2 = 4$, however, how one makes meaning of it *is* relative. The impact of this conceptualization of learning is that knowledge is not passively received, but always the result of an individual interpreting and constructing meaning of information provided by experience (Maclellan and Soden 2004), though the experience might be a passive transmission of information by a teacher. However, you as the teacher cannot be confident that even though you told the student something it was understood and contextualized the way you intended.

According to Piaget, as summarized by Brooks and Brooks, ". . . knowledge comes neither from the subject nor the object, but from the unity of the two . . ." (1993, 5). Again, I don't mean simple measurable, quantifiable facts, such as the mass of on object, or the effect of gravity on an object. Facts are of course important, but as a society we need students who don't just know the facts, but know what to do with those facts in the context of their lives. Currently, "the implicit assumption that permeates the thinking of educational institutions as well as mainstream society, namely that knowledge is a case of having more facts and information, that more knowledge changes behavior, and that people need facts and information first in order to think" (Fosnot 1989, 4). It might be necessary here to differentiate between facts, knowledge, and theory.

I find it easiest to think of the difference between *facts* and *truths* or *knowledge* in the context of the scientific method. Science provides us with theories, which are not "just a theory" but the result of many measured experiments producing the same results. The theory of gravity, however, is not a fact. The facts of gravitation theory are measurable observations such as objects have an acceleration rate of 9.81 m/s$^2$ on earth. The *theory* of gravity explains how and why—which is much more complex and involves the curvature of space–time as described by Einstein's theory of relativity. This is a theory. It's a good theory and the current, best explanation. But it is still *just* a theory, and it could be changed, improved, modified, or completely discarded at some point in the future with new observed, measured facts. So it is with constructing meaning for a learner. The facts may be unchanged, but his/her contextualization of those facts is dependent on the prior knowledge and past and present experiences of the learner. According to Brooks and Brooks, "coming to know is an adaptive process that organizes one's experiential world; it does not discover an independent, pre-existing world outside the mind of the knower" (Brooks and Brooks 1993, 27).

According to Brooks and Brooks (1993) "constructivism is not a theory about teaching. It's a theory about knowledge and learning . . . The theory defines knowledge as temporary, developmental, socially and culturally mediated, and thus, nonobjective . . . Learning from this perspective is understood as a self-regulated process of resolving inner cognitive experience, collaborative discourse, and reflection" (p. vii). Constructivist learning theory is informed by ideas of individuals such as John Dewey, William James, Jean Piaget, Lev Vygotsky, Jerome Bruner, and Ernst von Glasserfeld (Yilmaz Spring 2008). Teaching utilizing pedagogical methods rooted in constructivism requires that you as the teacher provide students with opportunities to make sense of their world through reflection of their interaction with ideas and objects by incorporating new lived experiences and ideas with what he or she has previously come to understand (Brooks and Brooks 1993; Fosnot 1989). Piaget posited that individual's need to reach equilibrium when confronted with contradictions between previous experience and new experiences and ideas. This need for cognitive equilibrium is a controversial idea from Piaget. Others such as Bruner and Chomsky theorize that language and prior experience provide the framework for construction of meaning more than a desire to resolve any disequilibrium (Brooks and Brooks 1993). All acknowledge that "meaningful learning occurs through reflection and resolution of cognitive conflict and this serves to negate earlier, incomplete levels of understanding" (Fosnot 1989, 3). Learning is not just a case of the student acquiring knowledge dispensed by you, the teacher. In that model of teaching, you cannot ensure the student has actually assimilated that information. The learner must construct the knowledge with you serving as the mediator and facilitator. Through these adaptive processes of assimilating the information into (and then adjusting when necessary) one's world-view, the learner adapts and alters old concepts. This is when true cognitive development occurs and true learning occurs (Fosnot 1989). This is the foundation of constructivism as a learning theory.

The implication of this learning theory on pedagogy is that teaching should be about providing students opportunities to develop deep understanding of ideas, best done through authentic tasks, as opposed to memorization of information. The memorization of a teacher's description of an idea (mostly through the act of passive listening and note-taking) results not in deep understanding, but in mimetic parroting of another's construction of meaning about a topic. This does not allow for the evolution and deepening of ideas by individuals, and then by extension, societies. When you think about this process, it is the antithesis of authenticity. Just imagine that you are memorizing what is taught to you and the teacher who is doing the teaching memorized it from the one who taught him or her . . . . and on and on; where is the thinking in this? Mimetic passing of information is rooted in an essentialist philosophy. More in line with constructivist learning theory is to present ideas ". . . as wholes, on the other hand, [and require] students to make meaning by breaking the wholes into parts that they can see and understand. Students initiate this process to make sense of the information; they construct the process and the understanding rather than having it done for them" (Brooks and Brooks 1993, 47). Constructivist pedagogy is built, then, on the following assumptions (Yilmaz Spring 2008, 167–168):

- Learning is an active process
- Learning is an adaptive activity

- Learning is situated in the context in which it occurs.

- Knowledge is not innate, passively absorbed, or invented but constructed by the learner.

- All knowledge is personal and idiosyncratic

- All knowledge is socially constructed

- Learning is essentially a process of making sense of the world

- Experience and prior understanding play a role in learning

- Social interaction plays a role in learning

- Effective learning requires meaningful, open-ended, challenging problems for the learner to resolve.

Ultimately then, pedagogy rooted in constructivist learning theory results in "the creation of classroom environments, activities, and methods that are grounded in a constructivist theory of learning, with goals that focus on individual students developing deep understandings of the subject matter of interest and habits of mind that aid in future learning" (Yilmaz Spring 2008, 165 qouting Richardson 2003).

## Applying Constructivism to a Classroom

This sounds nice and all, but how might it play out in a classroom? First, teachers recognizing that learning is developmental, need to allow students to ask and answer their own questions through hypoth

 DIG DEEPER into student-designed project-based learning on p. 223

esizing, testing, and self-organizing ideas and explanations. This requires challenging, open-ended questions for students to explore and then learn from contradictions and mistakes—meaning, the teacher needs to create an environment where mistakes are honored and respected, not avoided and even result in punishment or shaming. The classroom needs to be a community where reflection by the individual happens through collective dialogue and individual processing and reflection (Fosnot 1996). Ultimately, this requires the teacher provides students with context and *big ideas* to consider and make meaning of instead of just a memorization of disconnected facts of information; this requires a shift in teaching away from an essentialist and behaviorist paradigm where teaching as telling, testing for recall, and rewarding (or punishing) for successful recall of information. Pedagogy rooted in constructivist learning theory allows for the creation of new understandings and an emergence of new ideas and cognitive structures beyond parroting the understanding of a teacher, textbook author, or the committee that wrote legislated standards.

We can see the difference between the traditional classroom and constructivist classroom using Figure 1.1 which is an adaptation of Brooks and Brooks (1993, 17) side-by-side comparison of the two. As you review this comparison below, reflect on what you have experienced as a student and/or what you have provided for your students as a teacher. Then ask which from the chart below describe the learning experiences during which you had your greatest "aha moments" as a learner.

| Traditional Classrooms | Constructivist Classrooms |
|---|---|
| Curriculum presented from part to whole with basic skill emphasis. | Curriculum is presented whole to part with big concepts emphasized. |
| Strict adherence to highly valued fixed curriculum. | Student questions highly valued. |
| Lessons primarily from textbooks and workbooks for activities. | Lessons utilize primary sources of data and manipulative materials. |
| Students are viewed as "blank slates" unto which teacher imparts information. | Students are viewed as thinkers with emerging theories about the world. |
| Instruction primarily didactic with teacher disseminating information to students. | Teacher and students interact to explore and inquire about the world around the students. |
| Teacher validates student learning with recitation of information. | Teacher starts with students' present conceptions about topic for use in subsequent lessons. |
| Assessment of student learning is viewed as seperate from teaching and occurs almost entirely through testing. | Assessment of student learning is interwoven with teaching and occurs through teacher observations of students at work and through student exhibitions and portfolios. |
| Students primarily work alone. | Students primarily work in groups. |

**FIGURE 1.1** A Look at School Environments

A constructivist learning environment allowing for student-centered learning must include, for example, multimedia resources, peer feedback, and Socratic dialogue, scaffolding of skills and information exploration through role playing, simulation, storytelling, case studies, hypothesizing and explaining, and shared ownership. This provides students with multiple modes of discovery and representation of ideas, perspective, relative contexts, authentic learning, allowing for self-awareness and construction of meaning (Dagar 2016). According to Brooks and Brooks (1993, 103–117) constructivist teachers:

1. Encourage and accept student autonomy and initiative
2. Use raw data and primary sources along with manipulative, interactive, and physical materials.

3. When framing tasks, use cognitive terminology such as 'classify,' 'analyze,' 'predict,' and 'create.'

4. Allow student responses to drive lessons, shift instructional strategies, and alter content.

5. Inquire about students' understanding of concepts before sharing their own understanding of those concepts.

6. Encourage students to engage in dialogue, both with the teacher and with one another.

7. Encourage student inquiry by asking thoughtful, open-ended questions and encouraging students to ask questions of each other

8. Seek elaboration of students' initial responses

9. Engage students in experiences that might engender contradictions to their initial hypothesis and then encourage discussion

10. Allow wait time after posing questions

11. Provide time for students to construct relationships and create metaphors

12. Nurture students' natural curiosity through frequent use of the learning cycle model.

Now let's face some reality. We teachers are working in primarily an essentialist world in which we are responsible for students' learning of specific content standards and performing at expected levels on standardized tests. I've heard teachers complain, "I can't be creative or take the time for students to explore a topic deeply and cover all of the standards." I challenge this notion. I challenge it ethically, on grounds that if we know something to be better for children and do not pursue that course of action we are acting with negligence, and I challenge the premise that students cannot meet state-standardized curriculum content and perform well on tests *while* learning in a constructivist classroom. This complaint is built on a misunderstanding of constructivism, assuming it involves abdication of responsibility by the teacher for content and instead letting students just learn what they want, when they want. Granted, this *could* be a constructivist classroom. However, it might also be a classroom where a student only learns how to successfully dribble a soccer ball for a year. Yes, he or she has truly made meaning about something important to himself or herself, but this too, of course, would be negligence on the part of the teacher. Providing a structured curriculum and set of topics *and* inquiry that leads to construction of meaning do not have to be mutually exclusive. The teacher can provide relevance for students and "create educational environments that permit students to assume the responsibility that is rightfully and naturally theirs. Teachers do this by encouraging self-initiated inquiry, providing the materials and supplies appropriate for the learning tasks, and sensitively mediating teacher/student and student/student interactions" (Brooks and Brooks 1993, 49). This requires a balance between the teacher providing students with the questions to ask and helping students to explore the questions they *should* be asking (Noddings 2007). If we teachers do not take up this challenge, then we are complicit in participating in an education system that is the equivalent of "fast food."

Shifting to constructivist learning theory is difficult for many because they cannot even envision what constructivism looks like as they have not experienced it as a student. Therefore, most teach the way they were taught. This deficiency is in existence even though most teachers have been trained in the developmental theory of Piaget, Vygotsky, Bruner, and other "constructivists." Because they only heard about it, but have not had a lived experience with it they did not really learn it. They don't *own* it. They did not construct meaning about it. New teachers, hit with the stress of that first teaching job rely on the practices they truly understand, i.e., traditional, didactic instruction they have experienced for 16 years of schooling and not what they are told about how it *should* be. Add to this pressure to cover all of the standards, and being immersed in school systems and curricula that pay lip service to constructivism but do not fully embrace it, it is no wonder that changing how we teach is so difficult. I do believe it is possible if we can change our perceptual model of teaching to one that consists of practices rooted in constructivist learning theory.

# Chapter 2

# Constructivist Learning Cycle

If you ever memorized something for a test and then soon forgot it, I would argue that you did not actually learn it. Instead, you just rented that factoid long enough to answer a test question. Our goal as teachers, however, should be to create conditions so our students can move beyond *renting* the information to *owning* it. Owning it means for the learner to align the new information or skill to his or her own lived experiences and then internalize and incorporate it into his or her own worldview. This is construction of knowledge. For this to occur, students have to learn about something by experiencing it the way that the brain is wired to take in and assimilate information and skills—through play. In school we call this inquiry.

## The Idea of the Learning Cycle

Inquiry and learning (ownership, not renting) is cyclical, not linear. The brain is not a blank slate, or for a more modern metaphor—a blank hard drive, to be filled or written on by you as the teacher. For years teachers have operated with this nice, simple equation in mind (Figure 2.1).

**FIGURE 2.1**  Linear Equation for Teaching and Learning

Too bad it is wrong. The process of learning is an iterative journey, looping back on itself, starting and stopping, with side trips, set-backs, and unexpected discoveries. It is not a destination. Each step on the journey results in ever-increasing knowledge.

First and foremost, constructivism is built on the work of Piaget and Dewey who argued that learning must be built on or connected to students' prior knowledge or experiences (Noddings 2007). According to Piaget, knowledge is a result of the confluence of the subject and the object, meaning that our knowledge about an object is built upon our (the subjects) experiences with that object (Brooks and Brooks 1993). This equates to what Thomas Kuhn (1962) called a paradigm shift in his work, *The Structure of Scientific Revolutions*. For a person to make a paradigm shift he or she must be able to take in new information, make sense of it through his or her own particular lens and then adjust that lens or worldview moving forward. This is the same thing as construction of knowledge—meaning internalizing it into one's worldview and experiences as Dewey and Piaget might have described.

These ideas of paradigm shifting, making meaning, constructing knowledge, can all be understood in the context of systems theory. Recall that foundational to systems theory is the concept of positive and negative feedback loops and that positive and negative, in this setting, do not mean good and bad. They instead refer to the directional force on a system from a perturbation (a force causing a system to be thrown out of equilibrium). A positive feedback loop will then cause a system to continue further out of equilibrium to the point where it changes completely or collapses. A negative feedback loop returns the system back to equilibrium (or its original state). Applied to learning, then, what we are really talking about is the presence of a feedback loop in the learning process. Individuals begin with ideas, information, metaphors, etc., to describe a phenomena. Then, they take in new information, and *if* they learn something, that new information provides a feedback loop to cause them to change their paradigm (make a shift), add a new paradigm, or confirm their existing paradigm (Figure 2.2). No matter which is the result, growth has occurred on the part of the student and his or her understanding and application of a concept.

The idea of representing learning as cyclical is not new. Multiple variations of learning cycles have been proposed, especially in conjunction with inquiry-based learning. One example of this cycle includes the concepts of *connecting* interests and previous knowledge with observations, *wondering* about those observations and investigating those "wonderings" and then *constructing* a way to investigate those questions through experimentation, data collection, hypothesizing, and analysis to come to a final answer (NYC Department of Education 2009, 20–21). Another model uses the terms *exploration, term/concept introduction*, and *concept application*.

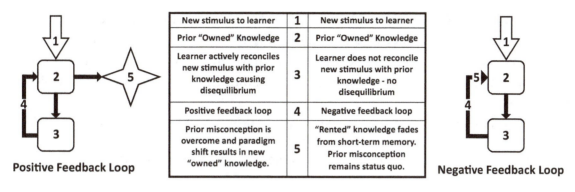

| | |
|---|---|
| New stimulus to learner | **1** |
| Prior "Owned" Knowledge | **2** |
| Learner actively reconciles new stimulus with prior knowledge causing disequilibrium | **3** |
| Positive feedback loop | **4** |
| Prior misconception is overcome and paradigm shift results in new "owned" knowledge. | **5** |

| | |
|---|---|
| New stimulus to learner | |
| Prior "Owned" Knowledge | |
| Learner does not reconcile new stimulus with prior knowledge - no disequilibrium | |
| Negative feedback loop | |
| "Rented" knowledge fades from short-term memory. Prior misconception remains status quo. | |

**Positive Feedback Loop**          **Negative Feedback Loop**

**FIGURE 2.2**  Systems Theory Feedback Loops Applied to Learning

One widely used learning cycle from Biological Sciences Curriculum Study (BSCS), is called the "5E Model of Learning Cycle." It includes the following phases (Dass 2015):

- Engagement (asking questions and defining problems)

- Exploration (creating hypothesis and testing those through the process of experimentation and data collection)

- Explanation (constructing answers and explanations, or solutions to a problem based on the data—and then explaining it)

- Elaboration (applying the knowledge learned in the investigation to new situations)

- Evaluation (assessment of the students' knowledge).

Honestly, I have never found that any of these learning cycles translate well from the theoretical and into guiding the daily work of teachers—lesson planning and teaching. I agree with Singer and Moscovici (2008) and their criticism of these previous cycles as holding too rigidly to the scientific method (which isn't nearly so rigid and structured in actual practice) and a sense of finality. Additionally, the application of these models often shifts away from true inquiry, using instead teacher prescribed questions, hypotheses and/or procedures for methods of investigations. Having taught high school science for many years I can attest to this being a combination of two factors. One is a limited understanding of constructivism in practice, and two, is a limitation of time and resources in the classroom. As a teacher with a classroom of students, it is usually not pragmatic to allow students the freedom to do true inquiry and manage the necessary supplies for such inquiry and allow for potential deviation away from planned for mandated standards/content topics. Instead of actually solving an authentic problem then, the students in reality are simply trying to find the hidden answer the teacher already knows. While there is an element of inquiry in this process, and undoubtedly this should be more engaging for the student than listening to a lecture, it still may not have much authentic value to the student. In the end, the student may still just be renting the information for the benefit of pleasing the teacher.

Another model involves a three phase cycle (Singer and Moscovici 2008):

- Immersion (providing provocative problem or situation to students to explore and investigate)
- Structuring (provide means to synthesize and generalize what is discovered during the immersion and then opportunity to explain and connect and correlate their version of understanding of phenomena to new examples and counterexamples)
- Applying (practice and extend new knowledge to explorations of the concepts and patterns to other situations and use to drive further research and questioning).

This model has appeal as it supports inquiry-based learning, but this too is missing the critical component of reflection which is necessary to resolve any disequilibrium or cognitive dissonance experienced throughout the learning cycle in relation to prior knowledge. Therefore, the proper feedback loop to close the cycle is often overlooked in the teacher's lesson plans.

All of these models are most prominently used in science classes. This is because the discipline of science is based on inquiry—despite that we science teachers have historically struggled to teach it that way. Although the idea of learning cycles comes from the science discipline, the idea of learning as a cyclical process is not limited to science content. Indeed, if true learning involves construction of meaning, and this is best accomplished through the inquiry process, then the inquiry process can and should be applied to all learning.

I argue that if you have learned something, truly learned it making a paradigm shift so that you *own* it, internalizing the meaning of that concept into your understanding of the world around you and can apply that concept in your lived experiences, you have completed learning that is by definition constructivism. Anything *truly learned* is the result of constructivism, which involved some aspect of inquiry.

When I was very young my parents took me to the ocean for the first time. The story of this experience, as told by my parents, is they arrived at the beach and they and my older brother immediately ran down the beach to explore the crashing waves of the pacific surf. I wanted nothing to do with it. It took a long time and many tears for me to finally be coaxed down to the water. This new experience with water was at complete odds with my previous experience with water. My experience with water at the age of five was that it came from a tap, filled bathtubs, or was calm and still in lakes and rivers. This water was nothing of the sort. The spray and mist in the air was salty. And it was loud. Probably deafening to my five-year-old ears. There was significant cognitive dissonance between my prior experience with water, my expectations for going to the beach (just a lake you couldn't see the other side of) and my new lived experience of water in the ocean. I eventually did overcome the fear, make sense of this new kind of water, and enjoyed playing in the ocean. Lived experiences lead to *owned* knowledge.

## The Consider, Construct, Confirm Learning Cycle

I am proposing a learning cycle model that I think is both easier to use on a daily basis as a teacher and also contains a stronger emphasis on allowing for students to *close the loop* by incorporating more purposeful reflection on learning. This allows more paradigm shifts as defined by Kuhn, or instances of *owning* it as I describe it. I call this cycle: the Consider, Construct, Confirm (CCC) learning cycle (Figure 2.3). The learning process in the *Consider* phase begins with students considering what they know about a topic or skill. This can happen in a variety of ways and is accomplished with varying degrees of teacher-centered or student-centered activities. Next is the *Construct* phase of the cycle in which students work with the new knowledge. It is necessary that students have a "lived experience" with the new knowledge or skill. Therefore, this requires more hands-on or authentic learning activities that should be student-centered, and not rely on didactic instruction from the teacher. Didactic instruction does have a place, but should be reserved for explanation of procedures and tasks as opposed to concepts. Concept exploration is best done through inquiry and requires application by the learner to make meaning. Last is the *Confirm* phase of the cycle. This is the portion of the learning cycle often overlooked by teachers and curriculum designers. During this phase, students complete the feedback loop and wrestle with any cognitive dissonance or rectify the

**FIGURE 2.3** CCC Learning Cycle

disequilibrium caused by comparing new understandings based on new lived experience in class to prior understandings (based on prior knowledge and lived experiences). "Constructivist teachers challenge students to justify and defend their [own] positions so that [the student] can change their conceptual framework (e.g., beliefs, assumptions, and conceptions)" (Yilmaz 2008). This requires students to make sense of what they have learned, so I call this process "sense-making." Children must be given a structured method to have the opportunity (as a regular part of the class-

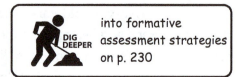

DIG DEEPER into formative assessment strategies on p. 230

room activities) to complete sense-making tasks so they can construct new understandings and make meaning. Constructivist learning is, according to Fosnet (1996), "[a] self-regulatory process of struggling with the conflict between existing personal models of the world and discrepant new insights, constructing new representations and models of reality as human meaning-making venture with culturally developed tools and symbols, and further negotiating such meaning through cooperative social activity, discourse, and debate" (p. ix).

It is during this purposeful time of reflection on what was learned, how it was learned, and how that compares to initial ideas that students create cognitive equilibrium as Piaget has described by dealing with any cognitive dissonance with what they previously thought about a concept and what their new experience revealed about a concept. Brooks and Brooks (1993) write about this process stating, "We construct through reflection upon our interactions with objects and ideas . . . Each sense of our world by synthesizing new experiences into what we have previously come to understand . . . when confronted with such initially discrepant data or perceptions, we either interpret what we see to conform to our present set of rules for explaining and ordering our world, or we generate a new set of rules that better accounts for what we perceive to be occurring" (p. 4).

In addition to comparing a new piece of information or skill to prior knowledge, students must understand the context of the new information which might happen at any point in the learning cycle but most commonly in the consider or confirming phase. Paul Simon sang in the song Kodachrome, "I think back on all the crap I learned in high school." Unfortunately, this sentiment registers with most students. What we often learned felt like "random crap." Context was not provided. Even information taken in passively, must be mentally acted upon to "file it away" into an appropriate context so that it has meaning (Brooks and Brooks 1993). Students who routinely scored well in traditional, didactic learning models (say the top 10–20%) have always done this even if we as teachers did not provide the time, space, and direction to complete this mental activity. Those students, just might have been teacher-proof. If the subject "naturally" made sense to them, fit their prior worldview, or was simply an area of passion, maybe all they needed from the teacher was essentially a table of contents of the ideas in a lecture. Then, on their own, they could make meaning by processing what they heard from the teacher or read in a book and file that new information away in the context of their previous understanding. The shift that can occur using the CCC learning cycle is for a teacher to purposefully facilitate this mental activity for *all* students so *all* students have the opportunity to make meaning, not just those that have the where-with-all to ponder, process, dig deeper, dialogue, and study it on their own outside of class—though certainly those actions should be encouraged as well!

For students to effectively have a place to "file away" this information there has to be context for learning the information. I would suspect that no teacher actually thinks they are teaching "random crap" but I bet most students think every teacher requires them to learn at least some random crap. Another aspect of sense making and *owning it* then is understanding how what they have learned fits into a bigger picture.

Traditionally, the American education curriculum has operated from a reductionist viewpoint. The general curricular design is to present students with an approach where each subject or skill is broken into its component parts and presented in that manner. Imagine two scenarios to completing a jigsaw puzzle. In one scenario you look at the box to see the picture and size of the puzzle so you know what you are making and how big of a surface you'll need. This helps you to know the context and approximate placement of the differently colored puzzle pieces and what to expect for the perimeter of the edge pieces. Or, you can complete the puzzle without looking at the picture and knowing what to expect in the size of the puzzle. Granted, some people prefer to do it the second way as that presents more of a challenge. However, our job as teachers is to make it as *easy* as possible for students to learn as *much* as possible. What students are learning and  why they are learning it should not be a mystery nor where they invest their intellectual inquiry energy. Therefore, curriculum design and lesson design should provide students with not just a chance to discover tidbits of information, but understand that information in the context of a bigger picture, objective, or question that is being addressed. "When concepts are presented as wholes, on the other hand, students seek to make meaning by breaking the wholes into parts that they can see and understand. Students initiate this process to make sense of the information; they construct the process and the understanding rather than having it done for them" (Brooks and Brooks 1993, 47).

I will use the CCC learning cycle throughout this book. I will use it to frame all aspects of what a teacher does in a classroom: course planning, unit planning, and finally (and most importantly) lesson planning. Utilizing this model can ensure students have the opportunity to construct new knowledge through inquiry-based learning experiences, organized around thematic units of study.

# Part 2

# Student-Centered Classroom Culture

A Rita Pierson (Pierson 2013) TED talk, *Every Kid Needs a Champion* was very moving to me. In it she states, "Kids, don't learn from people they don't like." Of course I'm not saying, and she wasn't advocating for teachers to have a goal of being popular with students. She was highlighting the importance of advocacy for your students.

Part 2 is about just that, ways you can partner with students to build a learning environment where all students feel safe to engage in learning. Chapter 3 is about strategies of engaging students in learning. To effectively keep students engaged requires understanding about motivation, and in particular, understanding means by which a teacher can tap into students' intrinsic motivation and the importance of empathy so that you can better understand and connect with your students. Chapter 4 builds on this with strategies aimed at developing trusting and respectful relationships with students to foster a healthy, inviting learning community. Lastly, the section concludes with a chapter about assessment and grading. At first look, this might seem out of place, but the reality is the requirement for conducting assessment and grading (in some form) is a fundamental component of the teacher-student relationship. This power differential created by this relationship requires careful attention in the context of classroom climate and culture.

# Chapter 3

# Engaging Students in Learning

All teachers want students fully engaged in learning. The first step to fully engaged students is understanding your own engagement as a teacher. Thinking about what motivates and engages individual teachers, I generalize two kinds of teachers. Some are driven to teach by a passion about a desire to share that subject. Others teach because they enjoy working with kids; they could, and would, teach anything. To further generalize, the former tend to be secondary teachers and the latter tend to be elementary teachers. However, I believe that great teachers get their motivation from *both* purposes.

I freely admit that I am predominantly the first type of teacher. I see the world through a biology lens and find purpose in sharing my biological view and love for the natural world. I'm trying to grow as a teacher—still making the road as I walk, if you will, and purposefully trying to make a connection with every student in my classroom. My dad, also a life-long biology teacher (I know, I know . . .), advised this when I started teaching, "Try and have one conversation each day with a different student about something other than school." It is a simple, yet effective tactic to make a connection and invite students into the learning community. Your responsibility as a teacher is to foster maximum engagement of as many of your students as possible. Using simple strategies to get to know them as individuals, not just as students is a first step. That's a tall order requiring you to know the students as well as you know the content—maybe even better. Students feed off the tone set by the teacher. For students to be engaged in learning, you have to be fully engaged in not just the lesson but also fully engaged in teaching *them* as individual persons.

## Active Student Engagement

Teaching the students who come ready to learn and ready to fully engage is easy. However, students operating around the margins require much more purposeful teacher attention. These students might be those who have not fit in, have been bullied, and/or carry baggage into the classroom preventing them from engaging with other students. Consequently, they do their best to remain hidden in plain sight, quietly trying to get through the day unnoticed and unscathed. Shane Koyczan (2013) speaks eloquently about this at the TED2013 conference with his performance titled "To This Day . . . for the bullied and beautiful." Here are two excerpts. Speaking specifically about being bullied and finding yourself as a child Koyczan says:

> We were told . . . 'Stand up for yourself.' And that's hard to do if you don't know who you are. We were expected to define ourselves at such an early age, and if we didn't do it, others did it for us. Geek, Fatty. Slut. Fag. And at the same time we were being told what we were, we were being asked, 'What do you want to be when you grow up?' I always thought that was an unfair question. It presupposes that we can't be what we already are. We were kids . . . when we finally decide to smash all the things we thought we used to be, and if you can't see anything beautiful about yourself, get a better mirror . . .

Your job as teacher is to reach these students as well, to draw them out from the margins and create a safe space for them to engage with you, their peers, and the content. I do wonder how many of these kids I have not seen and not reached out to during my career as a 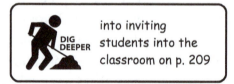 teacher. It pains me to think of that failure on my part. It is also motivation for me to do better with my next set of students by asking myself this question: In what way can I serve as a better mirror for them to see themselves in a new way, instead of possibly limiting their hopes and dreams?

Many children start off so excited to *get* to go to school only to have that excitement replaced by angst of *having* to go school. What happens to cause that shift? I clearly recall the excitement I experienced before my first day of kindergarten. I sang, over and over, a little song that expressed the joy of getting to go to school for "real." I don't remember the song specifically, as I have few clear memories of my early elementary years. I'm awed and amazed by individuals that recount specific memories of early childhood. For me, they are dream-like flashes and glimpses at most; but the emotions involved with that first day linger still, even after the specific memories have faded. We teachers must like school because we choose to continue to go to school for the *rest of our lives*. Therefore, many teachers have to consciously work to empathize with our students who dread each school day.

A 2012 Gallup Poll found that almost eight in ten elementary students qualify as engaged. By middle school years this number drops to six out of ten, and four out of ten by high school. Something is not right here. Overt expressions of exuberance and joy may naturally wane as we age or become too cool for such expressions (literally too cool for school!), but for too many students, the prospect of starting a new year just brings . . . nothing. Or worse, it brings dread.

Four-plus decades later, I don't literally sing a whimsical, made up song one might expect to hear from Winnie-the-Pooh as each new school year approaches. Though I don't have dread, I do have anxiety and nerves. I have anxiety dreams. You know the ones. I'm at school but can't find my locker, or am approaching the end of a term and realize I never attended one of my classes. When anxiety is really high, I experience those scenarios, but also only dressed in my underwear. Sorry for that imagery.

A colleague of mine wisely concluded that if we are nervous about the first day of class we must still care. You don't get anxious about things that are not important. Therefore, some anxiety and nervousness is healthy as a teacher and as a student. I would prefer that we approach the commencement of another school year with an excitement for possibilities instead of dread. Maybe we *should* sing a happy song like that silly old bear.

> The first days of
> SCHOOL – tiddely – pom
> Brings the world
> ANEW – tiddely – pom
> Brings the world
> ANEW – tiddely – pom
> For teachers and students
> Together.

Teachers and students working together results in a micro-society in the classroom. Teaching from a mindset of teacher as facilitator allows the teacher and students to be part of a micro-society that promotes autonomy, mutual reciprocity of social relations, and empowers students to make meaning and construct new knowledge. A mindset of authoritarianism or autocracy does not (Fosnot 1996).

Children come into the world full of questions. Yet often their questioning nature gets muted or even silenced as kids progress through a traditional education system. There is a conspicuous absence of displays of curiosity and natural wonder in many classrooms. McTighe and Wiggins (2013) write:

> If we value open yet disciplined inquiry, if we seek thoughtful, not thoughtless, responses to questions, then we must shape the environment accordingly. That shaping requires us to ensure a safe and inviting space for thinking out loud while making it clear that certain habits, beliefs, actions, and contributions can undermine the aim of free thought and collaborative inquiry (pp. 42–43).

It is the teacher's responsibility to make it safe for students to ask questions, seek answers, wonder aloud while exploring ideas through individual and collaborative investigation, open and safe dialogue and discussion, and unabashed wonderment.

Here's an exercise you can do to begin to explore the culture of a classroom. Find a classroom to visit and complete the following exercise. Conduct an ethnographic observa-

"POOH BEAR? ARE YOU IN THERE?"

tion to observe its culture. This is different than observing a teacher's lesson plan or act of teaching. Instead of focusing on the individual teacher, observe an entire classroom session (period, lesson, full day, etc.) as an ethnographer (one who studies culture). Begin by being present in the classroom before the students arrive and staying until the lesson, class period, or day is completed. And then just watch all that happens from the rituals and routines of arrival through the activities and then the departure of the students. Put on a "wide-angle lens" and observe not just teacher actions and lesson-plan details, but instead all of the interactions: student—students, students—teacher, who comes and goes, how students engage (or don't) with each other, the teacher, and the lesson, etc. Just note all that occurs and don't try and analyze specific actions in the moment. As soon as you zoom in your "lens" on one thing you will miss other interactions. Then, once concluded, go through the observations using that data to determine what each observation tells you about the culture of the classroom and the type of interactions between individuals. You will be amazed with all that is occurring which otherwise often goes unnoticed. Whether you are cognizant of it or not, there is a culture underpinning all that occurs in the classroom. Until you recognize what that culture is and acknowledge your role in establishing that classroom climate, there will always be a separation between you and your students, so much so, that the evolution of the classroom climate and culture will evolve out of your control.

What you will see are varying degrees of engagement among the students (and teacher as well). I identify five levels of engagement (Figure 3.1). The highest level of engagement is when students are intrinsically motivated to be actively and completely engaged. These students are fully present and participating. They would continue to do the lesson, activity, or project even if the teacher was not present, the lesson ended, or the assignment was done. In this situation, the intrinsic motivation for the work outweighs any extrinsic motivation.

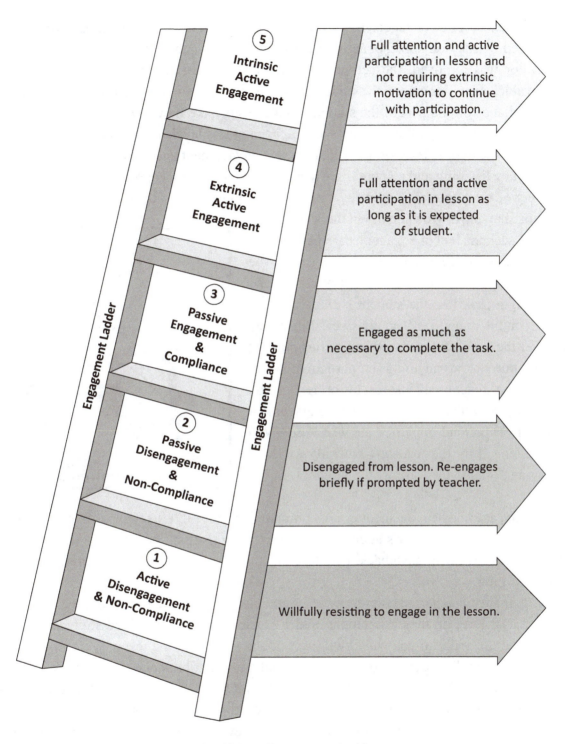

**FIGURE 3.1** Engagement Ladder

The next level of engagement is when students are actively engaged, but extrinsically motivated. The lesson, topic, or activity, is fully engaging in the moment, but if the extrinsic motivator was removed, the activity would soon wain and be replaced by other more "enjoyable" activities among the students. This level of engagement is an example of a kind of compliance on the part of the student. Make no mistake however, you should feel successful if the majority of the students are engaged at this level. This is a laudable goal.

I label the middle level of the ladder passive engagement and compliance. Students are engaged by listening and responding when spoken to or asked a question, but not willingly offering or providing any enthusiasm or positive momentum to the completion of the lesson nor showing any ownership in the learning.

The second level of engagement is passive disengagement or noncompliance. This might be more common to see in a secondary classroom. This might look like the student sitting, slumped quietly at his or her desk, hoody sweatshirt pulled up over the head, arms crossed and staring straight ahead, but not at anything in particular. More overtly, the student may just rest his or her head on the table. A student at this level of engagement will at least pretend to participate when prompted or challenged by the teacher—but only as minimally as possible to ward off the attention of the teacher.

"IF ONLY THIS THING WAS AN INVISIBILITY CLOAK"

Lastly, active disengagement or noncompliance is willful refusal to participate. Despite (or in spite of) the teacher's attempts to prompt participation, the student refuses. And if pushed, he or she will push back, resulting in a disciplinary situation disrupting other students learning.

If you are a teacher, or soon-to-be teacher, I suspect it is safe to say you were rarely at level one or level on the engagement ladder—at least not for sustained stretches of your schooling. It's doubtful you would willingly attend school for the rest of your professional life if you were disengaged from school throughout your childhood. I also think it is safe to say that most of us can fully appreciate what level three looks like. Most, unfortunately, have plenty of experience at that engagement level throughout our schooling experiences. The ideal, of course, is to have all your students at level five, but that is an unrealistic goal. There may be moments where this occurs, and you could walk out of the classroom, or arrive late, and all the students would be actively progressing on the lesson. A realistic goal is to achieve this at times, while recognizing that it is more realistic in the traditional school setting to get a majority of your students at least to level four. Level three is acceptable, but if the norm, I suspect you and your students are not really enjoying your time together as a learning community.

For students to be engaged above a level of three, they need a reason and a desire to do so. Therefore, the first step is to welcome students into the space. You might stand at the door and great each student as they enter. Give high fives, make jokes, and ask about their day; engage with them as individuals, not students, customers, or your charges. This may not need to happen every day or literally at the door, but doing something showing students you are happy to see them is crucial. That's a good place to start, but then you must provide them a reason to engage with you and your lesson. Student engagement requires a classroom culture that is safe. When students are connected in socially positive and productive ways through shared conversations and behaviors in the classroom they are more likely to participate actively (Cappella et al. 2013). Too often, we teachers design the school day as preparation for adult life instead of recognizing learning is "a process of living and not a preparation for future living" (Brooks and Brooks 1993, p. 9). For many students, this means what they are learning, and why they are learning it, is only in service to an abstract future, not a concrete present. For many, this provides no practical reason for engagement. This is especially true for early elementary students who are not developmentally capable of such abstract projections. Without a more immediate purpose to the learning that is pertinent to who they are in his or her current state of development, wonderings, questions, or suppositions, the students " . . . will find the lessons bereft of meaning, regardless of how charismatic the teacher or attractive the materials might be" (Brooks and Brooks 1993, 69).

"GOOD TO SEE YOU TODAY!"

## Motivating Students

What then motivates students to be engaged? As a teacher we want all of our students to be as engaged as possible for as much as possible. School is an artificial setting because students lack significant autonomy over their actions unlike the autonomy they possess during unstructured play time. Because of this, teachers must often motivate students to climb up

the engagement ladder and actively participate in lessons. We know that extrinsic motivators work; at least conventional wisdom is
that they work in the immediate. Common
sense tells us that if you want someone to
do something better, faster, more efficiently,
etc. then the bigger the reward you offer to
complete the task, the better, faster, more
efficiently it will get done, right? Well, sur-
prisingly, it just isn't true that contingent

"I DON'T SMELL LIKE A HORSE DO I?"

motivators ("if you do this, then I will give you that . . . ") are all that effective. Contingent
motivators can be effective in the short-term for tasks that are rote-learning type of tasks—
maybe completing a set of practice math problems, but when it comes to motivating individuals to creatively solve problems, the contingent motivators can actually have the
opposite effect. Daniel Pink (2009) describes this kind of extrinsic motivation as Motivation 2.0. The underlying assumption is that the work being asked of the participant is inher-
ently unenjoyable to do. This assumption requires the teacher to use contingent rewards; if
you do "this," then I will give you "that" (usually a grade or score in the case of school).
If-then rewards only work if the recipient of the reward forfeits their autonomy. Study after
study has found that extrinsic (especially contingent) motivators can effectively motivate
students for short-term, rote-learning tasks. However, extrinsic motivators ultimately can
reduce long-term engagement and productivity—even in tasks that individuals enjoyed
doing before the contingent, extrinsic motivator was implemented (Pink 2009).

It is evident that when children are intrinsically
motivated to complete a task, they will be more
engaged and learn more—even things the teacher did
not anticipate. Whereas, if children are completing
tasks due to extrinsic motivation, they will complete
what is necessary, but nothing more.

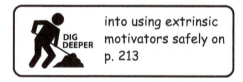

DIG DEEPER into using extrinsic motivators safely on p. 213

It is useful then to explore the characteristics of individuals who naturally possess intrinsic
motivation to see how that might impact what teachers do in the classroom. Pink (2009) identifies 3 inherent elements of intrinsically motivated individuals. The first element is a sense of
autonomy over the task. "The opposite of autonomy is control. And since they sit at different
poles of the behavioral compass, they point us toward different destinations. Controls leads to
compliance; autonomy leads to engagement" (Pink 2009, 108). Teachers must determine to
what degree they can allow students to exercise autonomy over elements of a task.

The second element of intrinsically motivated individuals is a desire to get better and better at something—or mastery. The tricky thing with mastery is that achieving mastery is impossible to fully realize. There is always room for improvement. Intrinsically motivated individuals work to achieve mastery goals in the sense that they are motivated to improve at something and increase their competence. For intrinsically motivated individuals the joy is in the *pursuit* of mastery as much or more than actually the achieving of mastery. Conversely, extrinsically motivated individuals are motivated to demonstrate competence at something. Struggles and failure are a real problem for these individuals—so much so that for many it can shut down attempts to complete a goal. Therefore, performance-oriented goals can actually cause avoidance of challenging tasks (Dweck and Leggett 1988). The implication for teachers is clear. The more we can tap into children's intrinsic motivation, the more challenging tasks they will attempt.

According to Pink (2009), the third element of intrinsic motivation is purpose as "[T]he most deeply motivated people—not to mention those who are most productive and satisfied—hitch their desires to a cause larger than themselves" (p. 131). If your purpose to complete a task is for the reward (or to avoid punishment), then you will take the safest, fastest route to completing the minimum necessary to get the reward or avoid the punishment. If your purpose is to complete a task or learn something that you as an individual care about, or connects to a larger goal you believe in, then you have a better chance of working towards mastery, and going beyond minimum expectations of a teacher because you aren't doing it for him or her (even if it started as a class assignment), but you are doing it for yourself or even for an ideal greater than the individual.

All humans love to learn (at least some things). All humans love to be good at things—again, at least at some things. All humans develop passions for something. Many children develop a love for books and reading. Others, a love for art and drawing. Others, a love for solving math problems. Why is it that many of these children might then refuse to do homework in these subjects by the time they reach middle school?

If I, as the adult, have to bribe you with a reward (be it actual physical reward or a good grade) or threaten you with punishment (taking away a physical object or privilege, or give a poor grade) to do something, what does that communicate about the task? Take the precocious child who is an early reader.

"YOU RUINED HARRY POTTER"

By the time he or she gets to middle school, incentivized reading programs have clearly communicated that "you must not want to really read, so I have to reward you to do it." Rewards (or punishment) as our primary motivation tactic run the risk of actually reducing a student's motivation. Pink (2009) provides these Seven Deadly Flaws of Carrots and Sticks (p. 57):

1. They can extinguish intrinsic motivation.
2. They can diminish performance.
3. They can crush creativity.
4. They can crowd out good behavior.
5. The can encourage cheating, shortcuts, and unethical behavior.
6. They can become addictive.
7. They can foster short-term thinking.

In fact, the higher the stake of the grade, the less likely a student will take a risk. Why take a risk on a project, assignment, paper, etc., and potentially risk damaging a grade in a class? Therefore, the higher the stakes in terms of a course grade on the final project as opposed to the *pursuit* of mastery, the more conservative the student will be when deciding what to attempt (if given options by the teacher).

The errant thinking about student motivation is thinking of it as a separate, specific act, or set of tricks or tactics that a teacher must use to motivate students to climb the engagement ladder. This is a predominant paradigm among many teachers, but ultimately a self-defeating one. The assumption is that students have to be motivated and/or tricked into learning. Humans like to learn. Humans like to be good at things. The disconnect for many students is the what and when of what the teacher is "selling." And the students aren't "buying it."

First and foremost, the *teacher* needs to be fully engaged and motivated. Feelings are infectious. Try this thought exercise. Imagine you are camping with friends and spent the day hiking in the woods. You are sitting around the campfire at the end of the day enjoying toasted marshmallows (dipped in Bailey's Irish Cream—much better than s'mores!) and you discover a wood tick at the base of your hairline. Pretty soon all your camp-mates are sure that every little tickle on their skin must be a tick crawling on them. This is the work of "mirror neurons." As empathic beings we pick up on other's feelings. Reflect on the qualities of your best or favorite teacher and I would be willing to bet, passionate about the subject/learning or enthusiastic is one of the top traits. Teacher enthusiasm arouses students' attention, which then facilitates student achievement (Marzano and Pickering 2011).

Enthusiastic verbal and nonverbal cues along with humor are essential to arousing student engagement, and getting students engaged is the first step to "motivating" students. Welcome them in.

Relying on charm, wit, enthusiasm, or energy, might be adequate for getting the students' attention, but usually not for keeping them engaged and motivated to learn. If so, then it is still a teacher-centered paradigm, which always requires external motivators. Again, fine for short-term, rote learning tasks, but not for life-long learning skills and knowledge *ownership*. For ownership, students need purpose. Essential to long-term, authentic motivation is treating students with respect, listening to their opinions, and giving students options and encouragement to work on issues they might find interesting and important. If you are still of the mindset that I (as the teacher) need to wow and entertain students for them to be engaged then you are still stuck on the teacher-centered paradigm. Of course I'm not advocating that you can be monotone and lack any dynamics in your teaching. As a teacher you can motivate students to situational interest which Marzano and Pickering (Marzano and Pickering 2011) describe as:

> a short-term psychological state as opposed to a longer-term interest in a topic, like hockey for instance. Teachers face a plethora of challenges in capturing students' attention because they are competing with thoughts about last night's basketball game or a girlfriend. Research points to four ways to maintain situational interest: (1) using game-like activities, (2) initiating friendly controversy, (3) using unusual information, and (4) using effective questioning strategies.

Motivating students situationally is an absolutely necessary skill of any teacher and is certainly valuable methodology to move students up the engagement ladder. However, if our ultimate goal is to get students to the top of the engagement ladder, situational motivation, activating mirror neurons, being a stand-up comic, will only get students so far up the engagement ladder.

Shifting from the teacher-centered paradigm in which the idea of the teacher as entertainer emanates, to a child-centered paradigm isn't "just about making education pleasing or entertaining to students, but it needs to be relevant, meaningful, and connected to their current position in life, not just about future needs and aims for the child" (Noddings 2007, 32). Students will internalize the value of learning if you can "provide explanations for why certain activities that are not intrinsically fun are nevertheless relevant and critical to learning (Furrer, Skinner, and Pitzer 2014, 105–106) and to connect to the students' current situation in life—not just an abstract future need such as success in college or future employment.

To move beyond situational interest, Marzano and Pickering identify criteria for a learning activity to be of intrinsic interest to a student. The learning activity needs to coincide with his or her own personal goals, sense of self, and the student needs to also feel that classroom activities are appropriately complex (2011). I am not advocating that what students do in the class has to be completely generated by their own interests or questions. The teacher has a responsibility to guide students' learning in particular subjects. The teacher's role is to motivate students by guiding students to answer the questions they *should* ask. This is a component of the true art of a master teacher—being able to work with students to generate questions of value to the students. Often-times, teachers will attempt to create a student-centered course by generating a series of essential questions to frame the content of the course. In fact, subsequent chapters will be about how to do this. If the questions are not of interest to the students' current life situation, then, the teacher still will need to use extrinsic motivators and the students will not reach the top of the engagement ladder. At times this cannot be avoided! But our goal should be to use authentic, valuable essential questions students want to know the answer to, and then your role becomes helping students discover the answer as opposed to telling students to discover the answer, or worse yet, telling students the answer.

For students to reach the top of the engagement ladder and intrinsic motivation requires what Bruhn, Hirsch, and Vogelgesang (2017) call the three Cs of motivating instruction: challenge, context, and control.

### Challenge

Instruction needs to be neither too easy nor too hard. The *goldilocks tasks* are just the right level of difficulty. If the task is perceived as too difficult, especially by struggling students, students will disengage, possibly even actively disengage (level 1). Conversely, if the task is too easy, students quickly become bored with the task. Providing a range of materials and options matched to students' knowledge and skills is crucial to providing learning tasks in which students will be intrinsically motivated to engage (Bruhn et al. 2017).

### Context

As stated before, context is everything. Students are more likely to be intrinsically motivated to engage in learning activities if deemed personally relevant. Activating students' prior knowledge and experience related to a topic (part of the Consider phase of the previously described learning cycle), can help students to contextualize and comprehend what they are learning (Bruhn et al. 2017). If students lack background or prior knowledge, then they lack mental images, or metaphors (think existing file folders) in which to put this new information. The teacher then needs to help the students develop the proper vocabulary to place this new information in a context (Bruhn et al. 2017). This will be explored in further detail in coming chapters.

### *Control*

I recently said to a colleague, "You might have noticed I don't do well when things happen that are beyond my control." She laughed and said (very sarcastically) "No, you?" We all want control and autonomy over our actions. A sense of autonomy and control are essential for a student to take that last step and reach the top rung of the engagement ladder. This is of course the great challenge for the teacher aspiring to provide a student-centered classroom rooted in constructivist learning theory. How does a teacher allow choice, while still meeting required district curriculum objectives or state-mandated standards—and do so with a variety of students at different levels of maturation, with different skills, backgrounds, and, interests? This is why teaching is hard work! As a teacher you can provide students choices on the order in which to complete tasks, or a menu of tasks or texts, aligned to a particular objective or essential question. Another methodology for providing choices is to give students options for how to present the information learned. Additionally, students' sense of control can be supported by teaching students the skill of self-management. Students can become autonomous learners if given the opportunities to use self-management strategies such as goal-setting, self-monitoring, self-instruction, strategy instruction, and self-evaluation (Bruhn et al. 2017). Students involved in self-management have a voice in the challenge of the assignment, thus making it more likely the assignment will be a *goldilocks task* described earlier.

In the end, as a teacher, you can use coercion, rewards, punishment, entertainment, enthusiasm and shiny objects to motivate students to learn, but if this is the only reason students are completing learning tasks, then it is unlikely they will ever reach the top of the engagement ladder. Our goal as teachers is for students to discover their own passion for learning and what areas ignite that passion to learn more. Certainly, you must use "shiny objects," be enthusiastic, and provide a fun and an enjoyable place to learn, but the goal is to provide students opportunities to find the intrinsic value in learning while learning what we as a society deem as crucial skills and content to perpetuate our culture.

# Empathy

Having empathy for your students and knowing their interests, background, and skills is necessary for providing students with an opportunity to climb the engagement ladder. As a teacher you model empathy and empathy is crucial to a functioning, healthy society—so no pressure! Jeremy Rifkin (2009) defines empathy as "the mental process by which one person enters into another's being and comes to know how they feel and think . . . Unlike sympathy, which is more passive, empathy conjures up active engagement—the willingness of an observer to become part of another's experience, to share the feelings of the experience" (p. 12). Knowing strategies to get to know your students and express empathy for them is a foundational skill to being a constructivist teacher. As teachers we must seek information about who our students are, their interests, what they care about (Knight 2013). This can be done in formal questionnaires, writing, or in informal one-on-one conversations, among other methods of simply getting to know the students in your charge.

Having empathy for students allows you to have insights into the students' points of view. "Each student's point of view is an instructional entry point that sits at the gateway of personalized education. Teachers who operate without awareness of their students' points of view often doom students to dull, irrelevant experiences, even failure" (Brooks and Brooks 1993, 60) which can lead to active disengagement and then disruptive behavior. The immediate response of the teacher is of course to correct the behavior and minimize the disruption to the rest of the students, but it is important to empathize with the student and understand the origin of

into classroom management on p. 211

the behavior in addition to correcting it with extrinsic classroom management techniques. While necessary, know that techniques relying on extrinsic motivators ultimately wrest a sense of control from the student and do come at a cost, so must be used judiciously. This might lead to more disengagement. Students who are actively disengaged, more than any others, might need to see and experience empathic relationships with the teacher more than any other. "Negative behaviors as a response to difficult situations on the part of the student is a learned skill to cope with a situation. The teacher should acknowledge the skill the student has developed and then redirect it. This leads to an increase in the student's perceived empathy from the teacher" (Beaty-O'Ferrall, Green, and Hanna 2010, 3). Students who do not experience quality relationships—relationships built on empathy—are more likely to become disaffected from school. Empathetic relationships in the classroom community (teacher to student and student to teacher) is foundational to students' engagement, academic success, performance, and healthy socialization (Furrer, Skinner, and Pitzer 2014).

I believe that empathetic relationships are built on trust and gratitude—maybe all relationships. Trust and gratitude go together. When you have gratitude toward someone or something you also have trust in it. It is worth asking ourselves on a regular basis for what we are grateful. In what do we trust? I first thought about the interaction between trust and gratitude while journaling during a canoe-camping trip in the Boundary Waters Canoe Area Wilderness in Northern Minnesota. The wind was blowing hard enough that we were essentially bound to camp for an afternoon as it was unsafe to venture away from the island campsite by canoe. This gave me an opportunity to read about the interplay between trust and gratitude in the book *Active Hope* (2012) by Joanna Macy and Chris Johnstone. I recall one campmate chopping wood for that night's fire. I was grateful for his efforts. Another was in his hammock reading my first book *Within These Woods*. I was grateful for his attentiveness. My ego thanked him as well. I was grateful for the wind, slowing me down enough to read about this in *Active Hope*.

Gratitude and trust. Two sides of the same coin possibly. How do these two concepts inform who I am as a spouse, father, and teacher? How do these become chapters in the story that we each enact? When I was teaching at a private school I was initially taken aback by students who would thank me at the end of each class. It could be that they were thankful the lesson was finally over, or maybe it was rote learned politeness and respect for an elder, and therefore not entirely sincere. I'll choose to think it was genuine, and expressing this gratitude was an expression demonstrating trust in me as a teacher. However, at least I hope this was the case. It is easy to think of this as a one-way street from student to teacher, that the student has to have trust in the teacher. The very act of teaching requires tremendous trust on the part of the *teacher* in his or her student(s). Inspired teaching requires the teacher to make himself or herself vulnerable to the student. This is an act of trust. Maybe it was for that willingness to be vulnerable for which my students were expressing gratitude. The stronger this symbiotic relationship enabling healthy back and forth of trust and gratitude between the student and the teacher the more likely each is to take a risk and try new things: innovative ways of teaching on the part of the teacher and willingness to engage in challenging academic projects and tasks on the part of the student.

In our classrooms, there must be empathy expressed among all members of the learning community. This requires gratitude and trust among the members of the community. As teachers we can embed opportunities to build trust and gratitude, and therefore develop empathy for other's experiences and views throughout the school day not just in the content of the lesson (through selected literature for example exemplifying these characteristics) but also in the structure of the classroom and the modeling of the teacher. Ashoka (Ashoka's Start Empathy Initiative n.d.) writes about the importance of empathy beyond simply a motivation/engagement teaching strategy:

Empathy is the little-known giant. Empathy is hardwired into our brain and when harnessed, plays a crucial role in innovation, change-making, and solving systemic problems. The textbook definition of empathy is 'the ability to understand what someone else is feeling,' but when put into practice, empathy means so much more: it means being able to grasp the many sides of today's complex problems and the capacity to collaborate with others to solve them; it means being as good at listening to the ideas of others as articulating your own; it means being able to lead a team one day, and participate as a team member the next. Cognitive empathy expands our social imagination beyond our own direct experience. It is what gives us the will and the tools to be effective change-makers. Empathy in action is foundational in our ability to resolve conflict and make decisions with no precedents and drive positive change.

Like it or not, we teachers have a greater responsibility than just teaching the academics. While the teaching of traditional academic subjects might be our primary goal, students also develop many necessary socialization skills including empathy and collaboration from what teachers model and the types of learning experiences provided.

I believe this is more important now than ever, as we are educating in an age of "fear." Let me provide an example to make my point. A few years ago I was with my family in a national park attending a park ranger presentation. I have fond memories of these as a child in the early to mid-1970s. The presentation I saw with my daughter was reminiscent of my child-hood experiences. It was mostly information about the park, the animals and plants—a general presentation about the complexity and beauty of the ecosystem and geology. The updated version of the presentation included a disturbing new element. The concluding message this time was a dire warning that all of this splendor was in danger of being lost and we needed the next generation to step up and rescue it. I didn't think much of it at the time until I started noticing the same message in nature programs such as "Nature" or "Nova" on PBS, and at other parks, information boards at science museums, etc. That's an awful big load to put on the shoulders of an eight-year-old.

We are educating in an age of fear—fear about pollution in our air and water, global warming, terrorism, active shooters necessitating lock-down

"DON'T WORRY, WE GOT THIS"

drills, endangered species—even an entire endangered planet. My blood pressure rises just writing that sentence. How many adults are paralyzed by these fears? How can our children not be?

Buddhism teaches to stand with a strong back and a soft front. The strong back is needed to stand up and face difficulties of the world, but the soft front is needed to embrace the world. I fear the next generation(s) will not have the soft front unless we can purposefully and specifically model empathy. Will they retreat into hard-shelled cocoons in order to protect themselves from the onslaught of burdens put upon them by our generation?

Twenty-first century students have access to the global information network like previous generations never did. This is an awesome gift but also a heavy burden. As educators, it is paramount that we maintain our soft front so, we can teach with compassion and empathy, as children of younger and younger ages are cognizant of the global village and not just their local "tribe."

There-in might be the answer. Not only do we need to teach *with* compassion and empathy, I believe we must *teach* compassion and empathy. Social theorist, Jeremy Rifkin gave a talk at the Royale Society for the Arts, and wrote a book of the same title, *The Empathic Civilzation: The Race to Global Consciousness in a World in Crisis* (2009) in which he posits an interesting idea about empathy. Consider this: 50,000 years ago the empathy one felt was to his or her blood ties or clan. Anyone further away than shouting distance was outside an individual's sphere of concern, or empathy. As time progressed, the world became smaller as the individual's tribes grew. Agriculture, written communication, and religion expanded one's empathy beyond clans to tribes. Nation-states formed and one's empathy was extended to those sharing national identity which at times superseded tribes. Here in the first part of the 21st century, social networking has the potential to expand empathy beyond national borders. Consider the nearly instantaneous global response to a natural disaster. Images and information spread within minutes! The rest of the world offers to help within hours! According to Rifkin, we are naturally inclined for empathy and this can be stronger than inclinations for our own individual survival at the cost of others (Rifkin 2009).

Despite this natural empathy for those in our tribe (be they family, clan, race, entire species, all life on the planet) we still struggle as a society with empathy and how to have constructive, difficult conversations around difficult societal issues and events. This brings us back to trust and gratitude, and building the skill of empathy within the safe environment of a classroom. Here too, social media plays a big role since as much as it can be used to bring people together, it can also be used to sow seeds of mistrust and ingratitude, leading to further division.

On June 17, 2015, Dylan Roof walked into Emanual African Methodist Episcopal Church in downtown Charleston South Carolina, participated in an open Bible study and then opened gunfire killing nine individuals. His motive was purely racial as he later freely admitted he wanted to "agitate race relations" (Sanchez and O'Shea 2016). This is certainly an example of a difficult issue and situation requiring difficult conversations. The political left and right immediately took sides and the story morphed depending on who was analyzing and recounting it. Over the next days that followed I listened to the pundits expertly contort themselves and their viewpoint to find any motive other than race to explain this heinous act. Was this an attempt to avoid difficult conversations, a difficult truth and conversation, or a need to turn the conversation back on to something they could relate to such as their own Christianity? Empathy based on trust and gratitude; I found little if any of those characteristics or social skills expressed in the conversations that followed that awful crime. In what ways can we, in difficult times, use well-practiced empathy to build trust and gratitude, thus opening the opportunity for difficult conversations and then potential mutual understanding and solutions?

Maybe teaching our children compassion and empathy and how to express trust and gratitude towards the global "tribe" of which we are all a part is the role that teachers can play in providing the next generation the necessary skills they will need to face the bombardment of fearful news reports. Without these skills, the risk is that self-preservation will kick in and drive decision making—both individual and societal. Fostering empathy and compassion might actually be more life-affirming, empowering, and necessary for our individual survival.

# Chapter 4

# Co-Constructing Classroom Culture and Norms

I once observed an exchange between a student and one of my colleagues in which the student turned in a late assignment to my colleague. She accepted the assignment with a very gracious and sincere smile and a couple of questions.

"Did you get it done the way you wanted? Are you satisfied with it?"

"Oh yes!" the student responded. "I'm much happier with it now. Thank you for the extra time."

I've worked with others who would not have accepted the late work or would have only done so with a reduction in points, credit, or grade—and possibly reacted in such a way as to ensure the student felt adequate shame or guilt for missing an assignment deadline.

"Accountability," he or she would argue. "How will students learn to meet deadlines and be accountable?"

From my perspective, the former's approach establishes the teacher as the advocate of the student's learning journey and the latter establishes the teacher as the adversary. The cynic might argue the former is an enabler and the latter is pushing the students to achieve their best. I do not believe the two have to be mutually exclusive.

Which response would you prefer if you were the student, or if it was your own child? I would prefer a setting that encourages and supports completion of tasks to the highest of the students' abilities, resulting in work they have pride in—not just by a seemingly arbitrary deadline. Of course, as an

advocate for students, you also should recognize dangerous procrastination which detracts from learning, and therefore hold students accountable to deadlines that are not arbitrary.

If you have established a culture of advocacy as opposed to one of adversary, then the only struggles students encounter should be on understanding the content of the curriculum, not the teacher and his or her expectations. Then, the "tough love" sometimes required for such things as missed deadlines won't feel personal or arbitrary from the student's perspective. So, are you your students' advocate or adversary?

## Developing Trusting and Respectful Relationships with Students

If preparing students for active citizenship in a participatory democracy is one purpose of public education, then, how the classroom functions and promotes equity is crucial to that aim. The enculturation of democratic values from a traditional or essentialist paradigm often involves the teacher transmitting and passing on this skill in a form of rote learned ideals. A more constructivist approach, advocated for by John Dewey, is that a culture transmits its values to children by providing them with age appropriate experiences in democratic living and processes (Noddings 2007). Therefore, the whole school (or at least your classroom if that is all that can be managed in your particular situation) should be organized in a manner allowing students experiences in which they "learn through practic[ing] how to promote their own growth, that of others, and that of the whole society" (Noddings 2007, 39).

A classroom is indeed a microcosm of the greater society in which it is situated. For that microcosm to function at peak efficiency for learning, as well as model a society built on trust, gratitude, and mutual empathy among its members, the teacher must purposefully and actively establish trusting and respectful relationships.

Bronfenbrenner's (1979) peer ecology rooted in ecological systems theory can be useful in imagining how to achieve this goal in the classroom (Figure 4.1). All individuals are nested within social settings such as families, classrooms, schools, communities, etc. By interacting with each other within any of these settings, called "proximal processes," children influence one another in a social microsystem.

Doyle (2006), provides an ecological perspective on the classroom environment. Within the classroom there are several competing, overlapping, and interacting factors already in place when the students arrive in the classroom, and then even more after those students arrive. First, Doyle (2006) posits, the classroom is a crowded place where many

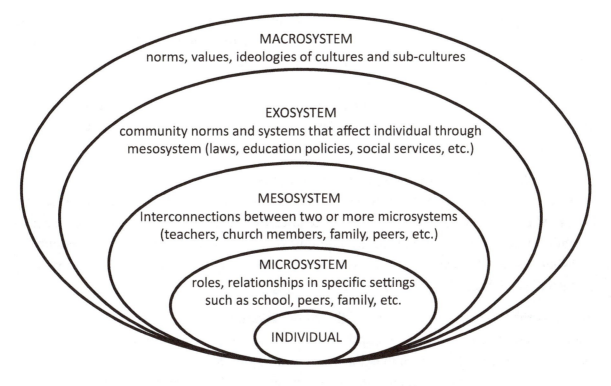

**FIGURE 4.1**   Bronfenbrenner's Peer Ecology

people must access a restricted supply of resources, creating a multidimensional environment. Second, many factors are playing out simultaneously and third, many of these individual needs of the students and the teacher are often requiring immediate attention, or at least those individuals needing the attention certainly feel a sense of immediacy. Fourth, the classroom ecosystem, because it is made up of so many intricate social and physical factors can be highly unpredictable. Fifth, the classroom provides little space to hide, so all individuals' needs are playing out publicly, and sixth, all of these factors build up a common set of experiences, routines and norms, establishing the shared history of the ecosystem which influence the future evolution of that classroom ecosystem.

Within these microsystems, students experience and learn how to navigate interpersonal ties, social status, hierarchy, and interpret peer social behaviors. The teacher is an individual who has the ability to oversee and affect the classroom peer ecology (Hendrickx et al. 2016). You as the teacher set the tone for peer interactions by the behaviors and nature of interactions you model. Obviously, if you show and model supportive, positive interactions versus interactions based on conflict or negativity, your classroom is more likely to be filled with positive peer interactions based on mutual support (Hendrickx et al. 2016). If students see you as their advocate, you are more likely to be able to facilitate a classroom that is a social microsystem where individual members willingly participate in peer-advocacy as opposed to a competitive culture were peers become adversaries.

Students (we all for that matter) have a need to be connected to others or to belong to larger social groups, while also having the opportunity to express their own autonomy of person-hood.

> In the classroom, teachers and peers are social partners who can meet (or undermine) a student's needs via three pathways: (1) relatedness is promoted by warmth or undermined by rejection; (2) competence is promoted by structure or undermined by chaos; and (3) autonomy is promoted by autonomy support or undermined by coercion. When a student's needs are met, he or she is more likely to be engaged in classroom activities (Furrer, Skinner, and Pitzer 2014).

If you as the teacher can express warmth and invite opinions and involvement in the classroom social microsystem while supporting students struggling with academic or social issues, the more likely it is the that students will feel safe at school.

In your teacher role, you are the model for interpersonal interactions within the classroom, first and foremost the students must feel that you like them (Hendrickx et al. 2016). This is about how you speak to, and behave with, the students. You must ensure

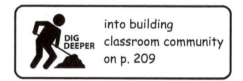

DIG DEEPER into building classroom community on p. 209

fair and equitable treatment of all students and show interest in, and affection toward, all of the students. Greeting students at the door and making specific eye-contact while initiating conversations about topics other than academic progress in the class go a long way toward communicating respect for the student as an individual. This allows you as the teacher to begin to know the student as a child or person as opposed to simply as a student (Marzano and Pickering 2011). By *knowing* them, you can then be more effective in offering any individualization to their education appropriate for the specific lesson. And *knowing* someone is the foundation for trust, gratitude, and empathy which are necessary characteristics of respectful relationships.

Therefore, if respectful peer relationships, which allow for peer advocacy, are to exist, students have to "have opportunities to talk and listen to each other, provide emotional support, share learning experiences, and develop respect" (Furrer et al. 2014). This allows for a climate of comfort and mutual support to exist in the classroom. Collaboration among classmates in this manner leads to improved student attention to academic materials and success. The more a teacher shows support for students, the more likely students themselves will support one another. Conversely, when a teacher exhibits behaviors of conflict with individual students, or students perceive favoritism towards individual students, they are more likely to demonstrate behaviors showing dislike for one another (Hendrickx et al. 2016). Classrooms with a hierarchical culture will consist of divisions of students between popular students and those that are marginalized. Classrooms with rigid and hierarchical status structures have more instances of peers acting aggressively toward one another. A more egalitarian classroom culture results in more students connected in friendship (Cappella et al. 2013).

## Facilitating Classroom Community

I have always approached classroom management with the mindset that the best classroom management "tool" is a curriculum that engages students in purposeful, inquiry-based learning. I recall an incident very early in my teacher career that illustrates this point. My seventh grade life science class was working on a multi-day project. During the second or third day of the project, one of my students came to me at the beginning of class and said, "Can we just get started right away—you don't have to, like, tell us anything or talk to us about anything today do you?" Point taken. I was talking too much and actually distracting them from something they wanted to do—something that I had assigned which allowed the majority of the students in the class to reach the top of the engagement ladder. Each day that I took 10 of the 50 minutes to retell instructions, the ladder just sunk deeper into the soft ground as they tried to climb it. I had hit the *goldilocks task*. They were now doing it because of intrinsic motivation and I was in the way with my yammering on and on. My

energy was better spent moving amongst the groups, providing individual formative assessment, instead of blanket observations and instructions each of which might have only applied to a different portion of the class. While more efficient for me, it was inefficient for them, and most likely quite ineffective as well. While I was still operating in a teacher-centered paradigm, they had left me behind and shifted to a student-centered paradigm—and I hadn't even noticed it! Sometimes, the teacher needs to shut up and get out of the way. Fortunately, I had a polite 13-years old to teach me that lesson.

Okay, so recognizing that finding the *goldilocks task* and the actively engaged, intrinsically motivated student is not the norm, the teacher must take an active role in classroom management. However, as purposeful curriculum planning is necessary for coherent and meaningful lessons, purposeful classroom space, and practices/routines are essential for effective "classroom management." Done well, classroom management is invisible. My colleague uses this five-P mantra: "**p**roper **p**reparation **p**revents **p**oor **p**erformance" (Colburn 2017).

The first thing to plan for as a teacher is how to create a space where students feel safe and welcomed. This is done purposefully to foster trusting and respectful peer-to-peer and teacher-to-student relationships. I have found it most effective to include students in establishing the norms for the community, then doing the continual work to keep the students (and the teacher) focused on those norms. Therefore, it is important to establish regular routines. You know this is done well when the teacher can be late to class and the students have started working by the time the teacher arrives. The classic movie scene of the students loudly talking, music blaring, and paper airplanes flying, until the teacher walks into the classroom is not a scene you ever want to witness as a teacher. Students need to have "structured interactions, in which teachers set high standards, clear expectations, and reasonable limits for students' behaviors and performance and consistently follow through on their demands. Optimal structure includes teachers' confidence in students' underlying abilities as well as helping students figure out how to reach high levels of understanding and performance" (Furrer et al. 2014).

Maintaining supportive relationships with all students may not always be easy for teachers—especially with students who are passively or actively disengaged with the lessons. However, I have found when faced with a specific discipline incident interrupting the class at large from progressing, peers will almost always empathize with their peer more than they will with you the teacher. What this means is that, "handling" a difficult or struggling student can have lasting impact (positive or negative) on the nature of your relationship with the rest of your students. From how you manage this situation, students will determine if you are their advocate or their adversary. While you obviously must intervene with a child who is actively disengaged to stop the disruptive behavior (and hopefully correct and redirect), it is imperative that the teacher not shame a student or place that student in

JOHNNY EXPERIENCES THE
DREADED TEACHER FACE INVERSION

a situation where they are "backed into a corner" either metaphorically or literally. The student in question is left with only two choices—retreat or fight back. Neither is really a good option. His or her peers will empathize because tomorrow it could be them! The "teacher needs to be aware of the supportive and conflictive interactions that are visible and/or audible to the other students in the classroom. So, the combination of a private reprimand aimed at decreasing disruptive behavior and a public expression of support another time might serve both classroom management and peer ecology, and thus individual students' development, best" (Hendrickx et al. 2016, 32).

Of course, the best way to "deal" with a discipline issue is to avoid it. Well-established routines (the development of the social contract being one) is essential to making classroom management invisible. The use of clearly understood routines which are a combi-

into managing misbehavior on p. 212

nation of teacher-directives and student-participated-in social norms are crucial for students to be able to self-regulate. The biggest challenges in classroom management often come from students being unable to self-regulate. Routines help students successfully self-regulate.

Educators can help students act with empathy and kindness with the following types of routines in place according to Ashoka (Ashoka's Start Empathy Initiative n.d.):

1. Student-generated rules of kindness for how to interact.
2. Implementation of strategies students can choose to regain control of emotions and actions.
3. Set of strategies students can use to self-mediate conflict among peers.

If part of the purpose of education is to meet the needs of all students and fostering them "coming to know [that] one's world is a function about one's world . . . [and] caring about one's world is fostered by communities of learners involved in trying to answer similar but not necessarily identical problems" (Brooks and Brooks 1993, 39). Then the question is how can the teacher facilitate this participatory, supportive environment into the daily routines of a classroom? Foundational to a classroom that is equitable, engaging, and supportive, is the use of specific routines. Students in classrooms with more routines and organized structures providing a predictable setting are more on task and engaged than in classrooms lacking routines and organization (Emmer and Stough 2001).

Some years ago I was trained in "Developmental Designs™," which is the middle school iteration of the more well-known classroom management training titled "Responsive Classroom™." The most valuable lesson from that training for me was how to facilitate the creation of a social contract previously mentioned. I've successfully used or witnessed the use of this method with classrooms ranging from kindergarten to college, and isolated classes within a school to whole schools. The process I have developed, which is based on my Developmental Designs™, training begins by asking students to think about (and preferably write down) the conditions that they need to exist for them to be successful. It is important for students to include in these conditions, the elements that they bring to the classroom so they are not just focused on behaviors of their peers and teachers. Next, students pair up to share their lists and create a combined list of a few statements they both agree on as conditions they both need to be successful in the class. Then, pairs combine to form groups of four, repeat the process and combine to form groups of 8 and repeat the process of creating a list all can agree to. After this, the teacher calls the whole class together and going around the room asks each group to provide one of their conditions. I proceed from group to group so, one at a time, each can provide a new statement, add on to an existing statement already heard, or pass if all of their ideas are already represented on the class list. Once a master list is created in rough form, then comes the task of editing and wordsmithing to creating a single list representing all students' (and you as the teacher's) conditions. Depending on the age and size of the class, this final wordsmithing can be done as a whole group, by a committee of students, or even the teacher. Once the list is agreed upon, it is posted prominently in the classroom and all students are encouraged to sign the poster. With each group that I have conducted this exercise I have found there are of course many similarities from year to year, group to group. There are always statements about personal responsibility and showing respect for one another. Sometimes there are statements that move beyond simple behaviors and instead establish the foundation of the *kind of learning* students want to occur. My favorite is one that was generated for a whole school social contract: "we will support one another in our creativity." Beautiful.

The writing of the social contract is just a foundation for the learning community. Your role as the teacher is then to lead the necessary conversations to define what those conditions look like in the classroom. This provides the necessary details for the age appropriate routines you will establish. Developing social norms in this manner provides space for all students to have a voice in the learning community. For this to work and provide the foundation of the learning community, the students' voices have to be honored and this process must be done sincerely by the teacher. If there are nonnegotiables to the classroom norms that you have as the teacher (and that don't emerge from the students' conditions) then you must be up front about those expectations. Providing students a sincere opportunity to help establish the community is a crucial first step in helping students *be* a part of the community.

To be part of a community, one has to be known. Ashoka (Ashoka's Start Empathy Initiative n.d.) describes an elementary school that guides students to create a photo collage about themselves. The collage could include photos of family members and/or photos that show the student's interests and activities in which he or she participates. The parents provide family photos and a photo of the child if possible to serve as the center of the collage. The teacher can also take the photo if family photos are not accessible. My preference, instead of a photo, is to have the students create their own self-portrait instead—even an abstract kind of self-portrait that symbolizes one's passions—the child who loves soccer and illustrates his or her face as part of a drawing of a soccer ball. The teacher than can guide the student to

finding or creating images which radiate out from the center to visually show the student's family heritage, culture, passions, interests, and favorite activities and things. As students work together and learn about one another, they can help each other find images that fit that individual student. Therefore, not only does the completed collage communicate that the student is known to some degree and is an important part of the classroom, the process of completing the collage facilitates students getting to know one another and honors the cultural heritage and diversity of the students.

I have a colleague that starts every class with what she calls "morning meeting." It doesn't matter at what time of the day the class actually begins. Conducting morning meeting in a circle is ideal. There is power in circling up so everyone can see everyone else's face. If it is age appropriate, space appropriate, and subject appropriate, a circle where all can see one another to begin the day is better than all students in rows with eyes on the teacher.

Whether the class starts at 8 am or 3 pm, the need is the same—students need to begin each class with enthusiasm for what is to come. This certainly feels like beginning with a fresh new day or morning—even if not actually morning. In addition to communicating what is to come, the other aspect of a morning meeting is to establish (and continue to nurture) students knowing one another and accepting one another despite any differences. The goal of this isn't just about classroom management and preventing conflict or disruptive behaviors, it is also about establishing camaraderie in working towards a shared goal—each other's learning. In elementary classrooms, especially self-contained classrooms, utilizing the morning meeting to have a unique greeting each day, a quick team-building game, or simply an opportunity for students to share with one another or the class what they are thinking about that morning can go along ways toward developing a classroom founded in advocacy as opposed to adversary.

The majority of my teaching career has been working with older students, and therefore, having students for a specific (45- to 75-minute) period of time during the day. I personally don't begin my classes with something I call "morning meeting." However, I do have the day's activities clearly displayed on the board or projection screen before students arrive so as they can check in and see what is happening that day as they get situated. In addition to this utilitarian function of organizing the day, I will often provide a "Quick-Write" or "QuickDiscuss" topic for students to complete during the first five minutes of class as other students get settled, complete established start-up routines, or I complete necessary tasks such as taking attendance. The topics usually serve to preview the day's topic and allow students to access prior knowledge about that topic, but also engage with one another.

Additionally, I like to organize the class into a variety of groupings. For example, each student might be assigned a color group, animal group, and interest area group. This allows me to easily post on the board if they are to begin in a seat of their choice, 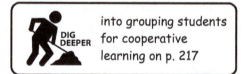 into grouping students for cooperative learning on p. 217 or with one of their groups. This is helpful for quickly getting students into new groupings so they work with a variety of peers throughout the course of the term.

No matter the strategies used, the important thing is that students feel welcomed into the classroom community, are known and know their peers, have ownership in the goals of the community, and kinship or shared purpose with their classmates.

## Physical Space

Modern humans' brains evolved approximately 200,000–300,000 years ago, based on the most recent fossil evidence. For most of our species' existence, we lived as hunter-gatherers in maximum group sizes around 150 individuals. This persisted until 10–15 thousand years ago. From that time forward, our societies have evolved at a rapid pace—much more quickly than the biological evolution of our brains. Therefore, we are educating hunter-gatherer brains, but now in a modern society based on agricultural histories, which changed us from nomadic social groups to sessile, agricultural groupings.

Social group size (class and school size for this discussion) really does matter. All teachers know this. Give a teacher too many students, and the best he or she can do is lecture to the masses, but not interact with the individual in a meaningful way. Too few students, and he or she does not have enough learners to create a community of learners that interact, encourage, and teach one another. I have long felt that classes of 15–20 students were the size with which I felt the most effective as a teacher, or a total of 45–60 students to have con-

*"I CAN'T FIGURE OUT HOW TO MAKE THIS THING TWEET!"*

tact with throughout a typical day with whom I would have to get to know during the course of a term (or year). The norm in public secondary schools is five sections of 30–40 students, or 150–200 students a day that a teacher interacts with and must get to know throughout the term. I've been in the experience of teaching 150 or more students in a given day and felt that was my limit to how many I could work with and effectively "know." Though I could identify this many, effectively teaching and assessing with writing assignments and projects, required smaller numbers just for logistical reasons. My personal experience as a student and my professional experience as a teacher tells me that classes should be smaller, for logistical and social reasons, and schools themselves should be smaller as well— hundreds of students housed together, not thousands. Turns out there might be some research to support my "gut."

Evolutionary psychologist, Dunbar (1995), has discovered a link in primates between brain size and average preferred social group size—the larger the brain, the larger the acceptable social group size. The more neural connections, the greater the ability to manage intricacies of neural information required for social group interactions. In apes and old world monkeys (those endemic to Africa), most species effectively lived in groups of 5–50. Comparing brain size of the different species of primates and effective social group size, and then extrapolating and adding humans to this chart, the predicted, highly functioning social group size for humans is around 150 (Dunbar 1995; Goncalves, Perra, and Vespignani 2011). Interestingly, this size matches natural human group sizes, from military companies to Hutterite farming communities and even average size of hunter-gatherer bands. It also matches my (and probably many teachers) experience as well.

While we may be able to remember up to 2000 people, according to Dunbar's research, the maximum number of social interactions an individual can reasonably maintain max out at around 150 individuals. In hunter-gatherer bands, this translates into groups, splitting when they approach this maximum size of 150 individuals. In schools, this translates into smaller social groups, clubs, sports teams, classes, and unfortunately then cliques. If the maximum number of individuals one can know is around 150, then when put into groups larger than that, the individual *must* dehumanize one another. To not do so would be too overwhelming for our senses. Imagine trying to maneuver through an urban setting, or a crowded school hallway with many hundreds or thousands of individuals passing on the street or hallway, and trying to maintain complex social interactions with all persons you encounter. You would never get anywhere. The only option is, to at best acknowledge the presence of most of the other individuals, but for the most part you must ignore other individuals—you must relegate them to be part of the background. To do otherwise would simply be too overwhelming with too many social interactions to mentally process.

There appears to then be a mismatch between our human brains which evolved over thousands of millennia in sparsely populated hunter-gatherer groups and the now densely populated, noisy, modern world in which we live. This background overstimulation might be the cause for such high rates of mental illness—the highest rate of which occurs in the most developed and urbanized environments as well. The most prescribed drugs in the United States are anti-depressants. Maybe being forced to sit still in too-large of social groups is just too much to ask of many of our children? If so, what ramifications does this have for how we design schools, classrooms, and curricula? Maybe we educators need a better education in our evolutionary biological and cultural history as we continue to reform our schools for the future. To do otherwise, might simply exacerbate the problem and marginalize more and more students, requiring more and more medical intervention.

It's not just the number of people surrounding us that affect us, but so too does the design of the physical space. A number of years ago, I was teaching at a district working to pass a bond referendum to remodel some of the high school classrooms. The arguments for it were what you would expect—not enough space, too old of space, outdated technology, etc. The argument against it (beyond not wanting to pay more property taxes) was that "it was good enough for me, why isn't it good enough for today's kids?" This, of course, is a specious argument. Imagine you are house-hunting and you find a home that has the perfect floor plan, the perfect location, and is the right size for your family, but the kitchen hasn't been updated for 40 years. If you could afford it, wouldn't you figure the cost of remodeling into the purchase of the home? Most house hunters would not say, "Well, if that hard, patterned carpet, olive-green refrigerator spewing heat out the back, and microwave with the rotary dial were good enough for my parents, then it is good enough for me and my family!" Of course not. How many for-profit businesses keep recycling the same office furniture for 50+ years? The space you are in matters. It affects your mood, your productivity, your interactions, and so on. Kids are not immune from this. Space matters. It is necessary to be purposeful with your space and develop the expertise to utilize the space in a way that fosters inquiry and collaboration.

What happens in the classroom space is of course more important than the layout and design of the classroom space—though the classroom layout and design have to match the physical movement of children needed for the learning happening in that space. Classroom activities that incorporate physical movement have a positive impact on students' energy levels. Incorporating movement into the learning can happen for the following reasons. Sometimes it is necessary to get students moving just to increase blood pressure, heart rate, flow of oxygen to the brain and rest of the muscles. Regular stretch breaks, and opportunities to stand up and move around for a few minutes each hour can achieve this. Movement can be incorporated into the learning by having students move to different stations to complete different tasks, creating physical representations of concepts (all students participating in acting out the steps of DNA replication—each playing a different piece of the DNA molecule for example), or dramatic representations of historic or literary events.

The classroom is a multi-faceted social microcosm. The teacher sets the tone to for this learning community as one built on adversarial, competitive relationships, or one built on self and peer advocacy and collaborative relationships. The culture will develop whether you want to acknowledge this role or not, with or without your leadership, so it is best to accept that role. The students are indeed watching.

# Chapter 5

# The Role of Assessment and Grading in Classroom Culture

Concluding the book section about classroom culture and climate with a chapter about assessment and grading may seem out of place at first. However, no matter how much you try and share the responsibility of creating classroom culture with your students, the reality is that your classroom is not a democracy where all members have equal roles and power. You and your students make up an artificial community brought together primarily by the arbitrary criteria of the students' age, and possibly interest in, or a requirement to study a certain subject. Your job is to make the classroom as inviting, welcoming, and inclusive as possible. Providing students a voice in as much as possible is one effective strategy for accomplishing some aspects of an engaging and inviting classroom culture. However, because there is an imbalance of power, the reality is that your classroom is more likely a benevolent (hopefully!) dictatorship. In the end, you have been given legal authority over your students for the time they are in your classroom. That is a great responsibility. This responsibility manifests itself in large part by how you conduct assessment and evaluate or grade students. No matter what democratic measures you may enact as part of your classroom procedures, and how you invite students into the space and work with families, everyone knows the primary goal of this community is the learning of the subject content and

skills. In the end, this comes down to how you assess students and then report that progress to the students, parents, and administration. That's the job. So, I will close out this section of the book on classroom culture with this topic forming a bridge between classroom climate and culture and the rest of the book in which I will focus on strategies of curriculum development and teaching practices within a classroom exemplifying constructivist learning theory.

## My Turning Point with Assessment and Grading

A few years ago I (finally) learned a valuable lesson that dramatically shifted my teaching. This caused me to turn the corner from traditional teaching, based on essentialism, to progressive teaching based on constructivism. I'm sure my current students could quickly point out when I still slip back down that hill as the constructivism boulder pushes back in my Sisyphean struggle to maintain teaching and learning based on constructivist learning theory. It took the serendipity of three separate events occurring at about the same point in my career for the light bulb to finally illuminate above my head.

I was teaching high school biology. I was one of two biology teachers and the two of us had a strong working relationship. We planned all of our lessons together, used the same assignments, labs, assessments, and grading. One of my students could miss my class and attend my teaching partner's and get the same lesson—though definitely with more laughs and smiles than in my section, as he was definitely more naturally funny, entertaining and engaging than I am with kids.

At the end of a day students had taken a traditional unit test made up of objective questions, some short answer, and maybe a question or two requiring students to write a paragraph or more, I walked into our shared office and dropped the stack of tests on his desk and said, "I'm done. I'm not giving another one of the damn tests."

"So what are you going to do instead?" he asked.

"Well," I stammered. "I don't know." I wasn't expecting right then and there to be challenged to come up with an actual solution. I thought he might agree and also vent off some frustration. Jerk. "These don't tell me what they know." I said, pointing at the offensive pile of papers scattered on his desk. "They only tell me what they don't know, or if they could figure out the question. There are students getting A grades who can't really explain the concepts, make connections or do something with what we're teaching them. And then there are others, that I know from my conversations with them that they get it, but are getting too many questions wrong on the test."

"So, how do we get them to show what we want?" he asked.

"I want them to write about it or explain it and connect the big ideas. I want them to use the information to do something valuable."

"So, how would we grade that?" he asked.

Well, now he was just pissing me off. And like a snowball going down a hill, picking up speed, the further it goes, the more it picks up along the way, so began the final shift in my teaching. Everything began to change after this conversation. Changing how we assessed required changing how we prepared the students for the assessment, which changed how we graded their work, which then changed

the nature of the feedback we gave students. All of this, then greatly affected the classroom culture in positive ways. I learned that curriculum planning begins with assessment.

During that same time period, I attended the National Science Teachers Association conference in Minneapolis. I attended a presentation titled, *The 4-3-2-1 Assessment Grading System* (Osoweicki 2009). A physics teacher presented his method of grading holistically, meaning no individual points were awarded on assignments, just a final grade (4, 3, 2, or 1 in his example). He spoke of how the switch to this holistic grading system changed his conversations with students from being about the points lost and how to get them back to conversations about the content of the assessment and gaps in the student's understanding. That's the conversation all teachers want to have with students! We want to engage our students in deeper conversations about what we are teaching, not why they got five points marked wrong on the test.

Literally, the next day after attending the conference, I was back at school and getting ready to teach my advanced biology class (for juniors and seniors). As I was prepping the day's lesson, a senior girl came into the classroom, and I could tell she was upset. This was a straight-A student. Not just a straight-A student, but a *straight*-A student. Perfection was the goal and anything less was a waste of her time, so get out of her way! She disgustedly dropped her backpack and thumped down an assignment returned to her moments earlier in the literature class she just finished down the hall. I looked at her with a quizzical look, nonverbally asking what was wrong.

"This. This assignment. It's so stupid. It's the first assignment of the unit, and I didn't understand the instructions so I got a five out ten. Now I'm failing the unit. I'll never get those F***ing points back again." This wasn't typical language from this student or typical to what was heard in my classroom, but you have to pick your battles.

"So, what would you do differently?" See, I can play that game too.

"Well I don't know, but it doesn't seem like an assignment that was my first attempt at something should be so important. I can never get 100% no matter how good I do in the end."

Recognizing a teachable moment and an opportunity when it lands in my lap with an f-bomb, I set aside the day's lesson plan and initiated a conversation with the class about grading. I had the good fortune that it was a small class of highly motivated and thoughtful students. They've all had 11 or 12 years of hands-on experience with school and grading. For most individuals those two are inextricably linked—school and grades. I began by telling them about what I had heard the day before. They were intrigued. We spent the class period designing our own system of grading that was holistic and not based on cumulative points earned.

During the rest of the term, the fundamental shift caused by this new grading practice and nomenclature I used to communicate progress to students had a larger impact on student dispositions toward learning than I ever could have imagined. A funny thing happens when you put points on the top of a paper and hand it back to students—say 45/50. The focus shifts from thinking about what he or she did or did not know to how they can get back five points somewhere else. Teachers call this point grubbing.

Even worse than point grubbing is what happens with the small assignments, like ten point reading assignments designed to introduce a new topic. If I mark something wrong, the student loses points and will never get those points back, even if they do exemplary work on the rest of the unit. Cumulative point grading penalizes a student's early struggles, leading to a lack of risk-taking, unwillingness to answer difficult questions on their own, or worse yet—cheating.

Students try to 'steal others' points of view because schools have somehow subordinated the formation of concepts and the building of ideas to high-stakes games of 'right' and 'wrong' answers that produce winners and losers. The system itself gives students the message that it's better to be 'right' than to have interesting ideas . . . Being 'right' often diverts energy away from generation of new ideas (Brooks and Brooks 1993, 8).

Kohn (2011) reports that grades reduce intrinsic motivation and quality of thinking. The grading system that you use as a teacher, assuming you must provide a score of some kind (be it numbers or letters) must match the type of instruction. If your goal is to embrace and encourage discovery, inquiry, and academic risk-taking in order to push students beyond mimetic understanding and learning, then the grading system must reinforce those conditions, not circumvent them.

After designing our plan, I took it to the administration to get permission. This was needed since I would no longer be entering points into the online gradebook the student's parents could see. He gave permission and, with that small group of students we spent the rest of the year piloting and refining the way of evaluating work by designing rubrics, methods of feedback, and means of calculating the final grade, which of course, was still required. This required a great deal of trust between me and my students. I had to trust they would fully participate in the experiment and not try and take advantage of the system to get a better grade, and they had to trust that I would work with them to arrive at a final grade that felt equitable to them. I've been using variations of this method of assessment and grading ever since, the details of which I will share in a bit. Before we get deeper into the weeds with specific examples, I'd like to provide foundational framework of assessment strategies and grading tools and practices aligned to constructivist learning theory.

# Authentic Learning

Authentic learning in the classroom is about the give and take between teacher and student. The teacher provides a framework or scaffold in an "ideal" example for the skill or knowledge. The student begins with the framework or scaffold "ideal" and then enacts that skill or knowledge. Mastery comes when the student can make that skill or knowledge work, or make sense to them, in the context of their prior and lived experience, and then apply that skill or ideal on his or her own without the benefit of the scaffold.

Let me provide you with a tangible example of learners making meaning and incorporating new skills and knowledge into their personal skill set and abilities. When I coached wrestling, I started the season by teaching (or, in most cases, re-teaching) the most basic of wrestling moves—the double-leg takedown. For those unfamiliar with the sport, this is the first takedown most kids learn; it's basically a tackle in which the offensive wrestler dives at his or her opponent from the front, attacking both legs of the defending wrestler and taking him down onto the mat. I started by teaching the "ideal" version of the move, breaking it down into small, carefully choreographed steps the athlete memorized without the presence of an opponent. Then practice partners were added—first one who offered no resistance, then one who put up a little resistance, one who provided still more, until the wrestlers were practicing the move at full speed. For each individual wrestler to master the double-leg takedown, they had to adapt the idealized move to their own particular wrestling style, which in turn depended upon a unique combination of height, agility, and strength. In this way, the generic, ideal move became personalized and fit into the larger arsenal of techniques that make each athlete a well-rounded wrestler.

In their first match, some of my athletes successfully performed the double-leg takedown against opponents who were often trying to perform the same move (or some other takedown) on them. Some of my wrestlers were unable to complete the move

DIG DEEPER into project-based learning on p. 223

successfully. As a result, in the next practice we returned to the "ideal version" of the double-leg takedown. Eventually, each individual wrestler successfully developed his own particular version of the double-leg takedown. However, if needed, he could always return to the "ideal version" and rebuild his own move from that basic starting point. Whether a physical task like a wrestling move, or an intellectual task like solving math problems, constructivism is about the learner making meaning and incorporating new experiences, knowledge and skills, into his or her worldview. Constructivism, then in its purest form is learning that is completely authentic.

Now let's consider the process of authentic learning in school, which, for many students is an oxymoron! As teachers, most of us know and feel that project-based learning, performance assessment, problem-based learning, and so on—anything that fits under the umbrella of authentic learning, is ultimately preferable to a more traditional direct instruction coupled with objective testing approach. The real world isn't about taking a test, it's about completing projects—be they small, like washing the dishes, to immense, like designing a new form of renewable energy. Therefore, if school is to be "real-world" or authentic, then it too should not be about taking tests but instead completing authentic projects.

Yet, often when teachers try and implement project-based learning, things don't go well. The project is often an add-on to the traditional classroom learning. Used this way, learning through projects is not replacing lectures and testing. Students become frustrated when project-based learning is inserted as simply an additional homework assignment. From the student perspective there is little purpose to the project. They know the test grades are what really count. From the students' perspective the teacher must value the tests because that's what he or she spends class time working toward and often not the project. With little scaffolding on how to complete a larger project, students (and/or their frustrated parents) revert to the most basic form of a project—a paper or PowerPoint presentation. In the end, this is really no different than the rote learning aligned to lecture and testing instructional strategies that is happening in the class. A student picks a topic, finds some information and reports it back to the teacher. And if they do it in a group, they end up frustrated with their classmates because the work was not divided up equally—and certainly little meaningful collaboration happened. Therefore, when the teacher introduces the next "project," he or she is met with groans. Sound familiar?

In its ideal, project-based learning should be second nature to children. After all, we as mammals learn by playing, which is really just individualized exploration and inquiry about the world around us—the foundation of project-based learning. If school, from the outset, was built upon these basic skills and followed this model, then project-based learning would be second nature to our students. But, historically, it's not.

Instead, students learn from their first days in school that play is the reward they get to do (call it choice time) after finishing the unpleasant task of practicing a skill or learning something, like reading or math. I think educators, parents, and policy makers have a false notion of what basic skills students need first to become educated. The assumption being we have to first teach children to decode information (reading and math basic skills) before they can then apply those skills to learning about the world around them. So we wait to do any project-based or authentic learning until students have mastered those basic skills. Unfortunately, by the time we get around to allowing students to make learning about exploration and play, school long ago became about completing tasks and grading rather than the act of exploration and learning.

Teachers should capitalize on intrinsic "play" energy and enthusiasm and provide a framework for students' exploration of the world around them so they can use playfulness to create new ideas and ways of understanding. Now this is learning. Of course, decoding information is important too—but done in isolation it has no purpose. In the context of learning about something real and completing a task that is meaningful beyond the graded paper or presentation, basic skills of decoding information have purpose. Learning is really only meaningful when it has purpose.

Like the double-leg takedown, there really isn't an "ideal" project-based learning experience because the one that works for the individual is what should be used. The "ideal" version provides the scaffolding for the exploration—but it isn't until the learners make it their own—adapted for their strengths and overcoming their weaknesses to complete the project that they have become educated, have learned how to learn, and taken a step toward becoming life-long learners. If you were to review many school's mission statement, the notion of life-long learning is often the ultimate goal of many schools, yet most schools do not utilize the necessary practices to teach students the necessary skills to be life-long learners.

Authentic learning, then, can be defined simply as work that matters to students. If it results in a *product* that the student cares about after they have completed the assignment and gotten the grade (assuming it is even graded), then it is authentic. If it addresses a real issue, is relevant, interesting, important, and students want to do it because it is worth doing beyond the extrinsic reward, then it most likely is authentic (Knight 2013). Of course, it would be great if teachers could always provide this experience for students, but give yourself a little grace here. This should be the goal, but the reality is that with a class of students grouped together purely by age, but functioning at different developmental stages of maturity, this is an unattainable goal for each and every student at all times. Students know this and will respect your efforts if they are provided a voice (as much as possible) in at least some of these aspects of the learning activities: what they do, how they do it, how they complete it, or how they present their learning.

While testing usually requires students to demonstrate mimetic knowledge of information, authentic tasks "invite students to exhibit what they have internalized and learned through application" (Brooks and Brooks 1993, 97). This requires students to build on

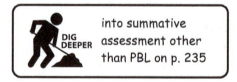

into summative assessment other than PBL on p. 235

prior knowledge and apply new experiences and information to that prior knowledge, and then, to new situations in the future. This allows the teacher to distinguish between the student that is just parroting the teacher's (or someone else's such as a textbook author's) understanding of an idea, from the student who has internalized and made meaning of a concept or idea. Removing the artificial separation between the learning activity and the assessment activity allows teachers to ditch the cumulative test and utilize the data from the learning and formative activities to inform the teacher's assessment of the students' learning, and then assess the students' application of those formative learning experiences to a summative expression of that knowledge, be it formal writing, presentations, conversations, formal projects, and so on.

Additionally, the use of these sorts of authentic tasks also teach and develop in the student the skills we as a society say we want in our graduates, but have done such a poor job of requiring, teaching, and assessing—problem-solving, critical thinking, communication of ideas, creative thinking, and collaboration. The challenge for many teachers is developing classroom practices in which the learning is authentic and the authentic learning and assessment become one in the same—so then the assessment is also authentic and has value to the student.

## Summative Assessment

"But, if I don't give them a test, how will I know they know it?" This question drives the practices of many teachers and policies set by many administrators and legislators. For the sake of this argument, I'm defining a test as mostly objective questions such as multiple choice, matching, true-false, etc., that primarily test memorization of vocabulary and basic concepts. Granted, some objective tests go beyond this and require application of knowledge instead of simple recall, but it is not a stretch to say these are the minority of objective tests. Success on more high-quality objective tests that do assess deeper thinking, however, *still* rely on the test taker's decoding and reading skills in addition to his or her understanding of the content. Teachers of all levels of experience easily fall into this testing trap. This trap is set, in part, by a need for quantifiable scores to enter into a spreadsheet. Anyone who has attended school has been indoctrinated into the notion school is about tests and learning is about answering questions on tests. Experienced teachers, of course, know otherwise. There is, or at least should be, much more to school and, more importantly, learning.

Considerable research now exists illuminating how the brain works and actually constructs knowledge. True knowledge involves incorporating concepts into one's own understandings which is then juxtaposed against prior knowledge. This is how one truly makes meaning and reaches the top of Bloom's Taxonomy. This is what we should strive for as educators—getting as many of our students to the higher-order thinking as described by Bloom's Taxonomy (Figure 5.1). More and more, teachers are correctly implementing rigorous project-based learning, inquiry-based learning, more in-depth writing, and so on, as a part of the teaching tool box. Yet many still follow up that great authentic learning students do with a traditional test as the final measure of learning. Many teachers successfully guide students on a journey pushing that boulder up Bloom's Taxonomy to the higher order thinking skills through carefully sequenced lessons, only to then tumble back down to the bottom of the hill by using an objective test limited to remembering and understanding. The message is clear; all that other stuff was nice but really what matters is memorization of vocabulary and basic concepts.

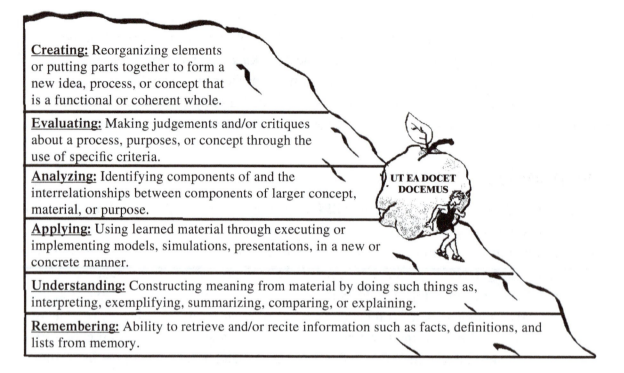

**Creating:** Reorganizing elements or putting parts together to form a new idea, process, or concept that is a functional or coherent whole.

**Evaluating:** Making judgements and/or critiques about a process, purposes, or concept through the use of specific criteria.

**Analyzing:** Identifying components of and the interrelationships between components of larger concept, material, or purpose.

**Applying:** Using learned material through executing or implementing models, simulations, presentations, in a new or concrete manner.

**Understanding:** Constructing meaning from material by doing such things as, interpreting, exemplifying, summarizing, comparing, or explaining.

**Remembering:** Ability to retrieve and/or recite information such as facts, definitions, and lists from memory.

UT EA DOCET DOCEMUS

**FIGURE 5.1**   Bloom's Revised Taxonomy

The time has come for educators to recognize the traditional test, as convenient as it might be, is no longer the right instrument to use as the *primary* summative assessment tool. Deep understanding, not mimetic understanding should be our goal as teachers. There- fore, no matter how enticing that multiple-choice test might be (maybe due to classes of 35 students), it is imperative for teachers to ask themselves what kind of experience will provide data not only about the students' recall of information (as that might be important for your subject), but also how students can apply and use that information in a meaningful context. Then, what type of summative activity(ies) will provide data at the conclusion of a unit of study as to "the cognitive functioning of the student, the disposition of the student, and the status of the teacher/student relationship. Student conceptions, rather than indicat- ing 'rightness' or 'wrongness,' become entry points for the teacher, place to begin the sorts of intervention that lead to the learner's construction of new understandings and the acqui- sition of new skills" (Brooks and Brooks 1993, 88). Put yourself in the shoes of a parent. Which summative data would you rather have? The percentage right, or this deeper under- standing of how your child is making sense of the information being learned. And then ask yourself, as a teacher, by what means can I gather this information? By using the other measures, teachers and parents can measure students' mastery of basic concepts and also so much more. Modern education has outgrown the traditional objective test. Now we educators, parents, and policy-makers just need to recognize that fact.

## Formative Assessment

It is important to shift our assessment discussion from summative assessment used at the conclusion of a unit of study to the majority of activities students complete in school—formative assessments. The word "assessment" may throw you a bit here, thinking that because

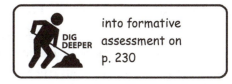

into formative assessment on p. 230

it is an assessment it must be at the end of the lesson, or *after* the teaching. This might indicate slippage back to the old paradigm, and getting pushed back down the hill by the boulder; teachers tell students information and then the students tell it back. Constructivist teachers, however, utilize formative assessment throughout the entire process of learning. "Formative assessments allow for 1, knowing how well students are learning; 2, ensuring students know how well they are learning; and 3, using data to modify teaching" (Knight 2013, 55). Any activity that is providing this feedback, whether at the beginning, middle, or end of the lesson is formative assessment.

Viewed from this paradigm and recognizing that any give and take between the teacher and student provides feedback on progress, is a formative assessment, I find it necessary to further identify two categories I use for formative assessment: formal, and informal. Informal formative assessments are low-stress, usually quickly done tasks, which do not impact a student's course grade. Therefore, students should be less threatened by the assessment, as failure will not affect class grades. Informal formative assessments might be so transient in nature that students are unaware they have been "assessed." Quietly monitoring and tracking student answers during a class discussion is an example of an informal formative assessment. Other examples might include asking students to put a thumb up or down to indicate comfort level with a new topic or skill, having students solve math problems on small white boards and then holding them up for you to see before erasing the answer and moving on to the next problem, individual conversations with individual or groups of students about a new topic or skill, and so on.

This type of assessment is literally conducted informally. While the teacher may track success and struggles with the concept, nothing is recorded in a grade book. Informal formative assessments can be done at any point during a lesson to provide a quick check for understanding to both the teacher and the student. This "data" can then inform the next steps the teacher and student take in learning—proceeding ahead or remediating an area of struggle or confusion.

I define formal formative assessments as anything that is turned in or evaluated in a manner that results in data being recorded by the teacher. This can range from small daily worksheets and reading assignments to paper and pencil quizzes. I like to divide the formal formative assessments into two additional categories. These labels were originally created by my advanced biology students who helped me pilot the first iteration of non-point grading: Introductory Formative Assessments (IFA) and Concept Check Formative Assessments (CCFA). Introductory formative assessments are those tasks that first introduce a topic to a student. Because they are intended to be a student's first look at something, I prefer to evaluate these on effort and thoughtful completion (see rubric in next section) and less on accuracy of the information. The assignment is then used in the next phase of the learning journey to build the students correct understanding of the concepts. Evaluating these tasks on accuracy as well as effort actually renders them useless as initial formative assessment tools for the student and the teacher. Consider this scenario. It's the first day of a unit and I assign students a short reading assignment and to solve a set of problems/questions. If I am evaluating this first look at a new topic for accuracy, and students know this is the culture of the classroom, the students concerned for their grades will often call or text their friend asking them what they got for the answer. In other words, they'll cheat. And why not if they know not doing so will put them in a hole in terms of their grade calculation? Then, the next day I collect the assignments, or we go through them as a class and everyone has everything correct. As a formative assessment, this tells me we can move on. But I might be acting on false data as possibly only one student actually understood the concept and the rest were parroting their peer. Therefore, those assignments need to be evaluated and scored (if recording a score in your gradebook) in conjunction with their purpose: assessing students' initial understanding, exposing misconceptions, and possibly providing data about the students' participation, effort, and progress of their learning journey.

Concept Check Formative Assessments (CCFA) are formalized checkpoints the teacher uses to gauge understanding *at a certain benchmark along the way* to understanding a larger concept or skill. An example of a formal formative assessment taken from the more traditional teaching model is a graded quiz. Even though more "traditional" in feel, a well-designed quiz can be an effective formative assessment in even the most constructivist or inquiry-based classroom. There are times as a teacher, you want recorded data of a student's progress on a concept or skill at a *specific step* in the learning process. Therefore, formal formative assessments often are graded—but they certainly do not have to be. Of course, the ideal might be that nothing is "graded" in the traditional sense, though feedback would still be provided. For most teachers, in most schools, grading is required and formal formative assessments: quizzes, writing assignments, graded homework, labs, activities, presentations, etc., are graded and those grades accumulate to allow the teacher to calculate a final grade for the course. Like informal formative assessments, the goal is the same, even if the stakes are a bit higher. Feedback is provided to the teacher and the student as to his or her progress on developing new skills or understandings toward the bigger goal of unit—which is assessed through one or more summative assessments at the conclusion of the unit.

## Finding a Balance in Grading

The reality is that most teach in a system that requires grading, and all teach in a system that requires assessment and providing feedback—even if not traditional "grades." Therefore, as we begin to explore how to implement grading schemes that have solid foundational roots in constructivist learning theory, we should begin with what should be the purpose of assessment.

At the risk of sounding "jargony," I like to use the term feedforward instead of feedback. It is necessary to shed the old paradigm that teachers teach students something and then give a test, grade it, and return it to the student with a grade on it. If we accept the premise that everything we do with students is formative assessment—even the littlest of assignments, then we as teachers need to constantly provide feedback as to a student's progress so

they can continue toward the ultimate goal of success on the summative (in whatever form students are demonstrating answers/achievement of unit/topic essential question/goal)—hence, why I prefer feedforward.

Feedforward, then should not be just a report back to the learner about the rightness or wrongness of the work, but instead an entry point into the cognitive functioning of the student, which can allow for intervention with struggling learners (Marzano and Pickering 2011) and deepen understanding of exceling learners. Students need the opportunity for guided self-reflection on the learning and the process of learning if they are to become self-regulating and self-aware of their learning progress, strengths, weaknesses, effort vs. accomplishments, etc. Using personal academic goals, and specific guided reflection on progress towards academic content or skill goals is an essential component of feedback that allows students to propel forward in their learning (Marzano and Pickering 2011). The feedback should be the beginning of the next phase of learning. All feedback should be done in a manner that prompts remediation and/or rethinking of a concept along with possibly further discussion, investigation, and inquiry. This can happen in a variety of ways—be it individual conferences and conversations, written questions and prompts provided to students, peer reviewing and evaluation, or individual reflective practices.

Returning to the story of my personal shift to more constructivist practices, the first step I had to make in my transition required that I ditch traditional objective quizzes and tests. To encourage deeper understanding, I shifted away from using tests which assessed what students did *not* know, how well they decoded questions, or had memorized definitions from the textbook glossary, to open-ended essay writing on both quizzes and tests providing students a chance to demonstrate what they *did* know. Open-ended essay writing and project-based learning, allowing for student choice in how to respond to the unit essential question, may increase engagement as it aligns with performance-approach goals, while objective testing often equates to test anxiety and therefore aligns with performance avoidance goals (Pulfrey, Buchs, & Butera 2011). Objective testing becomes, for some students, an exercise in not failing while open-ended essay writing has a better chance to be an exercise in succeeding. This shift in my assessment methods required that students put knowledge in context, apply it to scenarios and examples from class, and use terms naturally instead of supplying definitions. This took more time to grade, but it was worth the time. The act of completing the exam, not just the studying, was a learning process for the students. I have had students say they enjoyed the exam. It felt good to them to write a coherent, substantive response using what they learned during the last month of class. In fact, for many, they didn't fully understand the concept until they wrote about it extensively. While students may initially complain about the amount of writing, more engaging assessment methods such as writing, then followed up with personal interaction with the teacher either through conversation or response to further written prompts and questions from the teacher, can increase engagement, possibly even more so for the struggling students (Carini, Kuh, and Klein 2006). This, of course, depends on you as the teacher providing proper scaffolding and targeted supports for the struggling writer so the act of writing the response does not interfere with his or her ability to express their understanding. Otherwise you have just traded one flawed assessment tool for another.

After shifting to assessments designed to allow students to look at the big picture and answer large, open-ended essential questions about the unit, I realized it was not realistic to parse out individual points when grading it. It was more accurate to establish a standard for each level of work (such as the familiar A, B, C, D, F) and assess their answer holistically. I had the license in my setting to ditch the objective tests and the accumulation of points, but still had to award letter grades.

Clearly communicating the expectations for each achievement level is essential. This allows the grading system to serve as a guide for the students before they begin work on a task, not just what is imposed upon them after completion of the task. The grading system itself becomes something stu-

into grading with rubrics p. 242

dents can interact with in the act of completing the learning instead of just a mechanism to judge them (from the students' perspective). There should be no mystery as far as what is expected when students begin an authentic learning task or summative assessment.

> Students should have a clear idea for the evaluation criteria that will be used on the final product and presentation when they are first starting their work. They will be able to self-assess and revise their own work if they know the criteria for success. When thoughtfully constructed, rubrics provide a clear description of proficient student work and serve as a guide for helping students achieve and exceed performance standards. Rubrics tell students exactly what is expected and should be available at the start of a project. Students can also help create rubrics. Students will try harder to meet the criteria if they have participated in the development of the rubric (NYC Department of ED 2009, 17).

I use an established set of expectations for grading all formative and summative assessments which defines the final mark—be it a letter grade, or other symbolic indicator of proficiency. In the next section I will provide some examples of various rubrics I have used to do this. But, ultimately, each teacher needs to create his or her own which is customized to his or her situation. The commonality of them is that they provide guidance as well as are designed to evaluate the work holistically, and not mete out each and every individual "point." They do however, provide a detailed description of what is expected in content, mechanics of presentation, writing, etc., and style. These templates define the letter grade (or other scoring nomenclature) expectation, but then would be coupled with detailed descriptors of what elements should be included in the final work. In the end, the focus is on the efficacy of the work as a whole in communicating the expected content or skill.

Using a grading rubric of a holistic nature has had the effect in my classrooms of shifting conversations with students from "point-grubbing" to conversations about the content of their answer. This conversation can be enhanced by including the students in on the planning for the grading and the using of the grading tools. Providing students an opportunity to help you set the expectations for an assignment and design the means to assess it does a few important things. First it provides students a voice, which is crucial to demonstrating the "benevolence" of your dictatorship and infusing some democratic functioning into the classroom procedures. Second, it eliminates surprises so students make fewer errors of omission on assessments which might artificially lower their grade below their true understanding of the concept. Third, you can then facilitate the students using the scoring rubrics to peer coach and evaluate assessments before submitted. This provides benefit to both students. The student getting coached and evaluated by the peer produces better work and the student doing the coaching and evaluating has another learning experience with the content. In the end, you as the teacher must provide the final assessment and feedback that results in grades and informs the next steps in instruction, be it remediation or continuing on to the next topic.

Previous to involving students more purposefully in the assessment process, I have watched many students in my classes put aside all their assessments, quizzes, and labs at the end of the unit and rely on a study guide or the textbook to study. Essentially, they discard all that formative work we have completed and try and memorize what's on the study guide and in the text book. I suspect many of those students viewed the assignments as busy work.

To encourage deeper understanding and metacognition about their learning through the formative assessments, I provide different feedback than many teachers. The student's learning is not finished when the work is graded. In fact, it might be just beginning. To construct meaning of new knowledge, one has to work and practice, address misconceptions and errors, and engage in structured reflective learning that guides the learner through rigors of self-inquiry (Kumar, 2006). Therefore, I do not simply mark answers wrong and then give students the right answers in a lecture. Instead, I ask further questions or provide prompts for further exploration on their work and provide additional resources for them to continue to work with the assignment and answer my additional questions and writing prompts. I expect students to make corrections and additions and then use these assignments for further study. Pulfrey et al. (2011) found that grades alone as feedback reduced motivation while formative comments alone increased motivation. This allows learning from errors without penalty. I do not ever "re-grade" these assignments. The grade that was recorded stays as the indicator of what they understood at that particular time and place in their learning journey. With K-12 students, I do check for completion of corrections and additions (the act of "sense-making") on those particular assessments at the end of the unit.

This shift in my assessment practices and grading process required a change in calculating the final grade for a unit, course, or term. Grading could no longer be a mathematical calculation since I did not have points to calculate a percentage "right." I could assign a point value to each formative and summative assessment and then translate the letter grade (or other symbol) into a percentage, but that would mean I really just hid the point value from the students and in the end was still accumulating points. In this new system, I was after their final understanding of the concept *and* their journey to get there. I now had to also consider trends in the grades, effort on assignments, participation in class, and so on, for the final calculation.

I believe it is important to provide feedback on a student's entire learning journey because my role is not just teaching biology facts (or now teaching teachers teaching practices), but also helping students learn *how* to learn and how *they* learn. Therefore, I also collect qualitative data through observation and students complete reflection activities for units or grading periods using a structured grade proposal/reflection. Through this, they have input on their grade—but I, of course, have the final say. If students are not involved with the assigning of their grade this means that students are dependent on the teacher for a resource (the grade). "Dependence on those who distribute value resources is the equivalent of powerlessness, and powerlessness has been associated with a basic inhibition or avoidance motivational orientation" (Pulfrey et al. 2011, 2). Providing students input on their grade provides them with a sense of ownership and control of their learning.

Students review the quantitative data (the grades on summative and formal formative assessments) to first estimate a baseline letter grade for their content understanding. Then they use qualitative data to evaluate their classroom performance and learning skills; this included their completion and effort on the nongraded formative assessments, participation in class, in groups, attendance, organization, sense-making, use of class resources, etc.

With the qualitative and quantitative data in hand, students propose a final grade up to one letter grade above or below his or her baseline grade. After the student completes this proposal, I complete the same rubric using the data and my observations. I look for corrections and additions to previously graded work while reviewing students' portfolios, which I collect from K-12 students. I have witnessed many students actively addressing and changing habits in their learning practices, improving their participation, and content understanding through participating in this form of evaluation and grading.

Utilizing a "nonpoint" or holistic grading process has been well-received by my students of all ages. An overwhelming majority of students have reported in repeated course evaluations and surveys that grading in this manner promoted reflection on their learning, encouraged them, and made it safe to learn from mistakes, while helping them focus more on understanding content and less on the score earned. Shifting away from points and multiple-choice tests, allowed for more holistic assessment and grading practices while also using assessment that challenges students to demonstrate deep understanding of course content. Whatever your school climate, there may be pieces that you could implement without embracing the entire "nonpoint" or holistic grading process. First, use more writing and reflection as assessment tools. Writing about a topic requires organization of thought, application of terms and use of specifics to fully articulate ideas. This gives the teacher a better picture of the student's true understanding. It does require providing

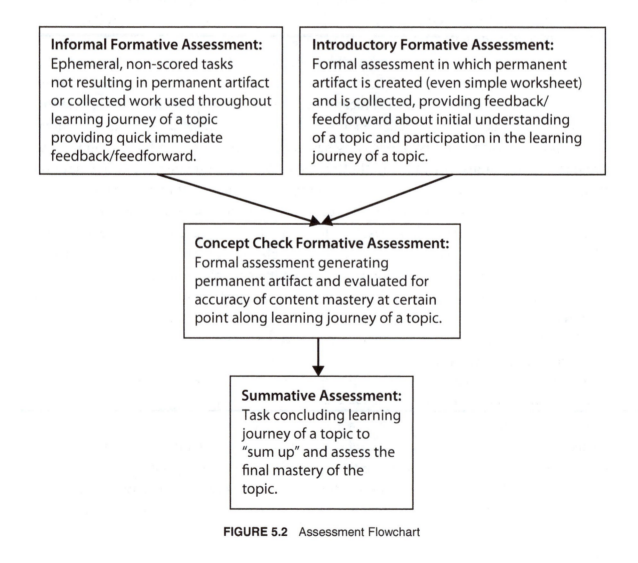

**FIGURE 5.2** Assessment Flowchart

targeted supports for struggling writers so you are not grading their writing skills (unless of course that is the goal of the assessment) and it does take more time to grade, but it is worth the time and effort on the part of both the student and the teacher. Second, require students to make corrections and additions to graded work. Simply telling the students the right answer does not promote construction of new knowledge. In fact, I believe it actually impedes it. Create a system that encourages (and rewards) continued working with and exploration of topics. Lastly, provide students a mechanism to reflect regularly on what they have learned and *how* they have learned. By addressing these three principles, no matter the details of the grading method, students will take more risks in their learning and therefore learn more. See Figure 5.2 for a summary of types of assessments and the functional definitions I use.

## Grading Schemes

I categorize grading methods on a continuum from traditional to progressive (Figure 5.3). Identifying first where on the continuum you feel most comfortable and then customizing what you can realistically implement will allow you to develop your own customized grading scheme to match the age of the students, the subject, and the setting within which you are teaching.

I will first define the terms I will use in describing grading methods.

- *Grading Scheme*: The word scheme when used as a verb often implies nefarious intentions. In this case, as a noun it defines systematic plan or arrangement to achieve a goal—awarding grades to students in the case of education.

- *Holistic Grade*: Final grade on task, unit, grading period/term, or course awarded based on an evaluation of the work as a whole aligning to stated expectations, often on a grading/scoring rubric with number, letter, or symbol nomenclature (A–F; S–U, 1–4, ✓+, etc.) but specifically *not* a mathematical awarding points or percentage calculation.

- *Traditional Grade*: Using a standard letter-grade nomenclature (A–F) based on accumulation of points.

- *Narrative*: Written, individualized feedback in the form of comments, questions, expository explanation and summation.

- *Points*: Score based on awarding of number value aligned to individual parts of an assignment and consequently the assignment as well.

Progressive ▲

| Grading Scheme | Overall Description | Qualities | |
|---|---|---|---|
| | | **Category of assessment** | **Scoring nomenclature/ feedback** |
| Open-ended holistic/ all narrative | No points or grades of any kind. All evaluation and feedback narrative in nature. | Introductory formative | Narrative only |
| | | Concept Check formative | Narrative only |
| | | Summative/Major | Narrative only |
| | | Unit of study | Narrative only |
| | | Term/Mid-Term/Course | Narrative only |
| Course holistic | No points or grades on any assessments or units of study. All feedback and evaluation narrative. Grade awarded at the end of the course, term, or grading period. | Introductory formative | Narrative only |
| | | Concept Check formative | Narrative only |
| | | Summative/Major | Narrative only |
| | | Unit of study | Narrative only |
| | | Term/Mid-Term/Course | Holistic Grade, possibly with narrative |
| Unit holistic | No points or grades on any student work. All feedback and evaluation narrative. Grade awarded at end of each unit and end of course, term, or grading period. | Introductory formative | Narrative only |
| | | Concept Check formative | Narrative only |
| | | Summative/Major | Narrative only |
| | | Unit of study | Holistic Grade, possibly with narrative |
| | | Term/Mid-Term/Course | Holistic Grade, possibly with narrative |
| Summative holistic | No points or grades on formative student work. All feedback and evaluation narrative. Grade awarded for summative assessments, at end of each unit, and end of course, term, or grading period. | Introductory formative | Narrative only |
| | | Concept Check formative | Narrative only |
| | | Summative/Major | Holistic Grade, possibly with narrative |
| | | Unit of study | Holistic Grade, possibly with narrative |
| | | Term/Mid-Term/Course | Holistic Grade, possibly with narrative |
| Formative holistic | No points or grades small assessments student work. All feedback and evaluation narrative. Grade awarded for larger formative and summative assessments, at end of each unit, and end of course, term, or grading period. | Introductory formative | Narrative only |
| | | Concept Check formative | Holistic Grade, possibly with narrative |
| | | Summative/Major | Holistic Grade, possibly with narrative |
| | | Unit of study | Holistic Grade, possibly with narrative |
| | | Term/Mid-Term/Course | Holistic Grade, possibly with narrative |

**FIGURE 5.3**   Grading Scheme Continuum

| Holistic | No points on all assessments with holistic grade feedback and possibly narrative. | Introductory formative | Holistic Grade, possibly with narrative |
| | | Concept Check formative | Holistic Grade, possibly with narrative |
| | | Summative/Major | Holistic Grade, possibly with narrative |
| | | Unit of study | Holistic Grade, possibly with narrative |
| | | Term/Mid-Term/Course | Holistic Grade, possibly with narrative |
| Holistic/points hybrid | No points on some or all assessments with feedback consisting of notation of completion and possibly narrative. Remaining assessments graded using points. Final unit, course, term grade calculation of categorical points, possibly with minimal adjustment of final grade based on qualitative measures | Introductory formative | Holistic Grade, possibly with narrative |
| | | Concept Check formative | Mixture of Holistic Grade, possibly with narrative and points. |
| | | Summative/Major | Points |
| | | Unit of study | Accumulated points with possible adjustment based on qualitative measures |
| | | Term/Mid-Term/Course | Accumulated points with possible adjustment based on qualitative measures |
| Categorical points | All student work worth points. Grade is a calculation of percentage of points earned within weighted categories. | Introductory formative | Points |
| | | Concept Check formative | Points |
| | | Summative/Major | Points |
| | | Unit of study | Accumulated points |
| | | Term/Mid-Term/Course | Average of accumulated points in weighted categories |
| Cumulative points | All student work worth points. Grade is a calculation of percentage of points earned. | Introductory formative | Points |
| | | Concept Check formative | Points |
| | | Summative/Major | Points |
| | | Unit of study | Points |
| | | Term/Mid-Term/Course | Percentage of accumulated points |

Traditional ▼

**FIGURE 5.3**  (Continue)

# Tools and Resources to Design and Implement Grading Scheme

There is debate among progressive educators as to the validity of grading rubrics. Strictly defined, a "rubric" is a grid with descriptors of levels of achievement on one axis (usually horizontally across the top) and descriptors of the elements of the task on the other (usually vertically along the side). For purposes of our discussion, I will use a more liberal definition of a rubric to include any tool that identifies the elements of an assessment, as well as some description of levels of achievement described. Some would argue that using a rubric is just another means of parsing out individual aspects of the work and limiting the authentic learning and inquiry a student completes. The ultimate, for such an educator, might be using the open-ended, all narrative grading scheme in which all work simply results in individualized feedback/feedforward about the achievement of the task without a final "score" of some kind generated. I would agree this would be ideal. I also know that this simply is not practical for nearly all teachers and the system in which they teach. My objective then is to provide examples of resources I have used to allow you as the teacher develop your own grading rubric germane to your students, subject, and situation. I use these to allow for the most holistic and authentic grading systems I can implement within my situation to serve the purpose of providing feedforward for students continued development and also meet the requirements of students, parents, and administrators to "know how the student is doing."

To accomplish this, I have used a variety of rubrics, even if the rubric didn't result in the assignment of a final score or grade. I agree with the critics that a poorly constructed rubric does circumvent the aims of a progressive or constructivist teacher. However, a well-crafted rubric is simply a means of communicating expectations for the student. A well-crafted rubric also provides parameters and guidelines, that otherwise without, many students might be paralyzed by fear of failure to even begin the task. Additionally, a rubric provided as a component of the assignment so that students can utilize it for self-and peer evaluation and coaching aids students metacognition helping them to think not just about the content of the task but also their thinking about their thinking and learning.

# Introductory Formative Assessment Rubrics

It can be argued, that all feedback/feedforward should be only narrative on introductory formative assessments. If truly formative and introductory, then the most comprehensive feedback and also the feedback that will require the students to reflect on the work completed (prompted by the feedback) is narrative feedback without a final "score," be it a certain number of points, a symbol, or a letter grade. The danger of using some sort of final score is the score is shorthand for a larger conceptual evaluation of the work (exemplary, satisfactory, etc.) in the teacher's mind, but the student may just look at the score and set the assignment aside either pleased with the positive feedback, or frustrated by the negative score. Removing the final score, forces students to review the feedback and come to their own conclusion as to the quality of the first attempt at learning that content or skill.

There are some logistical and motivational dangers with eliminating the final score and just providing narrative feedback in the form of prompting questions and evaluative statements. First, it is very time consuming for the teacher. It also requires that the teacher provide adequate positive affirmations of the student's content represented correctly. Imagine this example. A student turns in an assignment at the conclusion of a science lab activity. The teacher reads the assignment, recognizes the student has exemplary understanding of the science process and content, and then writes three prompting questions to challenge the student to dig even deeper into that topic (maybe beyond the teacher's original expectations). In the teacher's mind, this student is achieving at such an exemplary level that he or she can be challenged to go even further, thus the prompting questions asking the student to still dig deeper. Imagine now this high-achieving student getting this lab report returned to her. He or she would most likely interpret it as he or she got nothing correct and three things wrong. Clearly, using only narrative feedback requires the teacher to provide adequate acknowledgement of what was correct to properly communicate to the student where he or she was successful with the assignment. This of course, leads to the logistical difficulty of this form of formative assessment grading. Can you adequately provide this feedback with up to 150 students (or more)? Obviously this is not possible. Therefore, here are a few methods I have used to solve the logistical difficulties of providing students with an assessment of their IFAs that is feedforward.

Figure 5.4 is an IFA rubric using symbols to communicate feedback/feedforward about the student's effort to complete the assignment thoughtfully and thoroughly. I have used

| ✓+ | Entirely completed with complete, thoughtful, full-sentence answers, that though may not be correct at least:<br>• Answer with best guess<br>• Answer what can be answered (such as defining terms in question even if they can't be properly applied to answer the question)<br>• Write a question that needs to be asked to better understand the question<br>• At a minimum, identifies resources used to research the correct answer (page of text, website, notes, etc.) |
|---|---|
| ✓ | Entirely complete but missing one or more element of a "check plus" |
| ✓- | Partially incomplete |

**FIGURE 5.4** IFA Grading Rubric

these in courses, where I have many small assignments a week, such as daily reading assignments, review sheets, small active learning sessions, and so on. The shorthand score aligned to a mutually understood expectation can provide the student quick feedback as well as provide the teacher easy notation in a gradebook to track effort and progress. If the IFA is then used in a class discussion, during which the student can fill in gaps and make corrections to content errors, little narrative may be needed. However, if that is not the case, then the teacher still needs to provide adequate prompts to provide the feedforward necessary for the student to eventually have the correct content information on that task for future reference throughout the unit of study.

More simply than using the above rubric, in some instances for the IFA assignments I simply check the task off as completed and mark in that in the grade book. This works if the nature of the assignment completion is truly binary: either done or not.

When using the IFA rubrics, utilizing a pure narrative evaluation, or simply checking things off as completed, I have also used these two stamps, especially the "Brain On Fire" stamp (Figure 5.5) to adequately mark the aspects of the IFA that are correct without having to write out a full statement acknowledging the correctness of that aspect of the assignment. I can then use the Dig Deeper stamp (Figure 5.6) where necessary with an additional prompting question. I have found that even adult students like stamps!

FIGURE 5.5                    FIGURE 5.6

No matter the nomenclature utilized, the most important factor is to utilize a nomenclature that supports the notion of feedback provided on Introductory Formative Assessments serving the purpose of feeding forward further learning by the student, so it must include an aspect of students continuing to work with the task after it is "graded" through making corrections and additions to deepen their understanding and learn from their experience with that task. This leads to making meaning. Without this step, it is likely the student will not see the value in that experience in developing their final understanding, thus relegating the work to "busy work." No teacher likes to hear that from students.

# Concept Check Formative Assessment Rubrics

Concept Check Formative Assessments are any assignments that are the next phase of the learning journey with a concept or skill beyond the introduction. In a classroom with this level of assignment grading in place of or in addition to narrative feedforward provided by the teacher, I still prefer a holistic grading of the task as opposed to a points-based evaluation and scoring. These tasks are checkpoints along the learning journey where it is reasonable to expect a certain level of mastery with a developing concept, or smaller concept or skill that is part of a larger whole. It *is* of course reasonable to have certain checkpoints along the way where you expect mastery at a certain point in the journey and record that score for posterity and use as a component of the data to arrive at a final grade for the unit, term, or course.

When developing rubrics for tasks of this nature, I like to first begin with a set of descriptors for the level of mastery I can reasonably expect for the students in that situation (see Figure 5.7). That set of descriptors then become the foundation for specific rubrics modified for the situation, be it a specific assignment or specific class (age or subject). These descriptors serve as my starting point and then I can add more levels to include a more precise measuring tool (half letter grades for example). These are still formative assessments mind you and are intended to be checkpoints along the way and provide feedforward guidance for the student, therefore, rubrics for these types of tasks may not need to

| A | Student work *as a whole* shows proficiency at the upper end of expected levels, showing exemplary understanding accurately using terminology and specific content details throughout. |
| B | Work *as a whole* shows proficiency at expected levels showing solid understanding (minor errors or omissions) of the concepts and skills by usually using proper content terminology and specific content details and examples throughout. |
| C | Work *as a whole* is at basic or entry level of expectations showing satisfactory understanding (some errors or omissions) of the concepts and skills but often fails to accurately use proper content terminology and specific details and examples throughout. |
| D | Work *as a whole* is below expectations showing limited beginning understanding (multiple errors or omissions) of the content and skills but very rarely uses proper content terminology and specific details and examples throughout. |
| F | Work *as a whole* shows a lack understanding of the concepts not meeting minimal levels of expected skills and content. Does not accurately use proper content terminology and specific details throughout. |

**FIGURE 5.7**   Holistic Letter Grade Descriptors for Formative Assessments

be as precise in number of levels as one for a summative assessment at the end of the unit. Ideally, a rubric of this nature is provided to students ahead of time so that they understand the holistic expectations on this type of task.

The above rubric can then be combined with specific instructions for a particular type of task in the form of an example, descriptors, of each element, or checklist of required elements of the formative assessment.

Figure 5.8 is another holistic rubric I have used. Notice however that the nomenclature is different than letter grades. While the focus is on understanding, I utilize this rubric for assignments that are indeed checking for content mastery progress, but using a nomenclature that carries less weight and stigma than traditional letter grades. The detail to which narrative prompting questions and comments are needed is dependent on the nature of the follow-up activity allowing the student to make corrections and additions to the work.

| Advanced | Basic | Emerging |
|---|---|---|
| • **Your brain is on fire**<br>• You thought critically<br>• You made clear connections<br>• You provided strong evidence/examples<br>• You used correct concepts and terminology<br><br> | • **It's Ok**<br>• You showed generalized understanding<br>• You sometimes used proper concepts and terminology<br>• You could make more connections<br>• You had some misconceptions<br>• You may have missed some things<br>• You could **dig deeper** | • **Hmmm?**<br>• You needed to use proper concepts and terminology<br>• You had many misconceptions<br>• You needed to provide more evidence/examples<br>• You could **dig a lot deeper**<br>• Suggest you revisit this<br><br> |
| **Comments/Questions to dig deeper:** | | |

**FIGURE 5.8** CCFA Rubric Without Traditional Grades

# Summative Assessment Rubrics

Summative assessment rubrics are required for tasks that are the culminating, final demonstration of students' content and skill development for a particular learning journey. Below (Figures 5.9 and 5.10) are a couple of templates that I have utilized. In both cases, the purpose is to provide a score that communicates holistic evaluation of the task while also providing a logistically manageable means of providing specific feedback regarding certain elements of the task. In both examples, descriptions of each element needs to be added. This description should identify the full expectation of that element. Then each level can be checked off indicating the level of mastery with that component of the task. This still requires narrative explanation for each area scored to adequately communicate what was exemplary, unsatisfactory, or missing, warranting the score for that specific element. The advantage of developing a rubric template of this nature is that it is easily customizable to each summative task and it provides the teacher flexibility in use as each rubric completed for each student has comments specific to that student, but also allows for quick and easily "checking" of level of mastery for each element. It would be certainly possible to assign points to each section, and therefore the final score is a simple mathematical calculation. I still prefer to not assign a point value to each element to avoid point-grubbing conversations, and to allow me as the instructor to still assign a grade based on the "whole" of the work.

A true "rubric" is one in which each level and each element has full description in each box. This has some clear benefits and some clear downsides. First, it requires more up front work by the teacher to fully anticipate what the student will do, say, or present to qualify as, say, "satisfactory" for element 2 of the task. If this can be arrived at accurately by the teacher, then the rubric properly used can be used by the teacher to efficiently provide detailed feedback about each element to the student. Another upside of this level of detail on the rubric is the rubric itself can serve as a guide for the student for successful completion of the assignment. A downside is that as the teacher you may find yourself having to choose elements of multiple levels for one element. If you have assigned each level and element a point value this becomes cumbersome. If no points are assigned, and the end evaluation is holistic, this is less of an issue. In both cases it does require that the student must fully read the rubric and understand the teacher language used in each box for the feedback to have any value as feedforward guidance. My observation is that unless I provide specific time and guidance for how to read the rubric and address gaps or errors, most students simply just skip over the details and look at the final score.

| Element:<br><br>Each topic below is scored holistically based on the content of the written answer(s) to questions or the project being completed.<br><br>Comments and/or questions for further review and exploration are provided on the document with items circled which require further attention and/or correction. | Advanced Proficiency | | Basic Proficiency | Emerging Proficiency | |
|---|---|---|---|---|---|
| | Expert | Strong | Satisfactory | Needs Improvement | Not Yet / Absent |
| *Insert topic/term here* | | | | | |
| *Insert topic/term here* | | | | | |
| *Insert topic/term here* | | | | | |
| *Insert topic/term here* | | | | | |
| *Insert topic/term here* | | | | | |
| *Insert topic/term here* | | | | | |
| *Insert topic/term here* | | | | | |
| *(for quizzes, exams, projects that are long free-response to topic or theme question include this descriptor):* Application of content terms and concepts to coherency of answer to topic question | | | | | |

**Final Grade**: Holistic letter grade assigned based on the totality of the work as described by the criteria below. This is graded holistically, with the checklist above as a guide to the grader to assign the final letter grade. Read the letter grade descriptors carefully.

| | |
|---|---|
| A | Student work *as a whole* shows advanced proficiency, demonstrating strong to expert levels of understanding by accurately using terminology and specific content details throughout. |
| B | Work *as a whole* shows advanced proficiency, demonstrating strong understanding of the concepts and skills by <u>usually</u> using proper content terminology and specific content details and examples throughout with <u>minor errors or omissions.</u> |
| C | Work *as a whole* shows basic proficiency, demonstrating generalized, satisfactory understanding of the concepts and skills by <u>sometimes</u> using proper content terminology and specific content details and examples throughout with <u>some errors or omissions.</u> |
| D | Work *as a whole* demonstrates emerging proficiency with the generalized concepts and skills but fails to use proper content terminology and specific content details and examples throughout with <u>multiple errors or omissions.</u> |
| F | Work *as a whole* is lacking demonstration of proficiency in concepts and skills, proper content terminology, specific content details, and examples throughout with <u>significant errors or omissions.</u> |

**FIGURE 5.9**   Summative Assessment Rubric

| | Advanced | | Basic | Emerging | |
| --- | --- | --- | --- | --- | --- |
| | **A** | **B** | **C** | **D** | **F** |
| **Final Grade**: Holistic letter grade based on the totality of the work as described in the elements below and evaluated based on the letter grade criteria to the right. | • **Your brain is on fire**<br>• You thought critically<br>• You made consistently clear connections<br>• You provided strong evidence/examples<br>• You consistently used correct concepts and terminology<br><br>BRAIN ON FIRE! | • **Bravo!**<br>• You provided strong evidence/examples<br>• You made clear connections<br>• You mostly used correct concepts and terminology | • **It's Ok**<br>• You showed generalized understanding<br>• You sometimes used proper concepts and terminology<br>• You could make more connections<br>• You had some misconceptions<br>• You may have missed some things<br>• You could dig deeper | • **Hmmm?**<br>• You needed to use proper concepts and terminology<br>• You had many misconceptions<br>• You needed to provide more evidence/examples<br>• You could dig a lot deeper<br>• Suggest you revisit this | • **What Happened?**<br>• Too many things are missing to consider this work complete<br>• You need to revisit this<br><br>DIG DEEPER |
| **Assignment Elements:** The boxes below describe the specific elements of the assignment being assessed with this rubric. | | | | | |
| | Evaluator: Check the appropriate box and provide comments as needed | | | | |
| | **Comments/Questions to dig deeper** | | | | |
| | **Comments/Questions to dig deeper** | | | | |
| | **Comments/Questions to dig deeper** | | | | |
| | **Comments/Questions to dig deeper** | | | | |

**FIGURE 5.10**　Summative Assessment Rubric

The argument for purely narrative feedback can be made for these assessments same as with the IFAs and CCs. Removing that final score requires the student to engage in understanding the teacher's comments and questions and therefore participate in valuable metacognition about their mastery of the content and/or skills and their learning process.

# Term/Grading Period/Course Rubrics

Utilizing any grading scheme that involves any level of narrative or holistic evaluation in place of strict accumulation of points presents a problem. In most scenarios, the teacher is required to provide a letter-grade score at the end of the course, term, or grading period. If some or all of your data is qualitative or "holistic" grades, short of assigning a final point value to each item, you must have another means to adequately decide on a grade and communicate the validity of that decision to the students, parents, and administrators.

To do that, I have utilized methods that do two things. First it provides feedback/feedforward to the student on not just the content mastery, but also on dispositional qualities of classroom performance and development of learning skills. If the goal is to produce life-long learners, then these "soft" skills and dispositions should not be ignored. The second thing is that it should involve the student having a voice in the evaluation process. Figure 5.11 shows descriptive language I have used for each level of the three aspects of a final grade. Figure 5.12 is an example of a self-evaluation tool I have utilized providing students to complete a self-evaluation and then propose the grade they feel they have earned in the unit, grading period, term, or course.

| Rating | Understanding | Classroom Performance | Learning Skills |
|---|---|---|---|
| A | The collective of the summative and formative assessments shows exemplary understanding of the concepts by almost always accurately using proper content terminology and specific content details throughout. | Exemplary at:<br>–Use of class time; preparation for class; quality of assignments; class participation; group participation | Exemplary at:<br>–Organization; Sense making; Use of Tools |
| B | The collective of the summative and formative assessments shows solid understanding of the concepts by usually using proper content terminology and specific content details throughout. | Strong at:<br>–Use of class time; preparation for class; quality of assignments; class participation; group participation | Strong at:<br>–Organization; Sense making; Use of Tools |
| C | The collective of the summative and formative assessments shows satisfactory understanding of the concepts but often fails to accurately using proper content terminology and specific content details throughout. | Satisfactory at:<br>–Use of class time; preparation for class; quality of assignments; class participation; group participation | Satisfactory at:<br>–Organization; Sense making; Use of Tools |

**FIGURE 5.11**   Term/Course Rubric

| Rating | Understanding | Classroom Performance | Learning Skills |
|---|---|---|---|
| D | The collective of the summative and formative assessments shows beginning understanding of the concepts but very rarely uses proper content terminology and specific content details throughout. | Poor at:<br>–Use of class time; preparation for class; quality of assignments; class participation; group participation | Poor at:<br>–Organization; Sense making; Use of Tools |
| F | The collective of the summative and formative assessments shows a lack understanding of the concepts by never accurately using proper content terminology and specific content details throughout. | Did not:<br>–Use of class time; preparation for class; quality of assignments; class participation; group participation | Did not use<br>–Organization; Sense making; Use of Tools |

**FIGURE 5.11**   (Continue)

| Name: | | Period: | Date: |
|---|---|---|---|

**Directions**

- Complete the rubric by circling the parts of each description that best applies to your performance so far this term
- Use narrative to explain your evaluation of that section
- Based on your narrative and the trends not just an average of how you rated yourself propose a letter grade.

**Understanding Course Content**

| A Extensive understanding | B Solid understanding | C some understanding with gaps | D Limited understanding |
|---|---|---|---|
| Ratings of mostly As on summative assessments, with a mixture of Bs and As on formative assessments | Ratings of mostly B's on summative assessments, with a mixture of Bs and As on formative assessments | Ratings of mostly C's on summative assessments, with a mixture of As - Cs on formative assessments | Ratings of mostly D's on summative assessments, with a low scores on formative assessments |

Explanation of rating:

**Classroom Performance**

| | A Exceptional | B Strong use of class time | C Should improve use of time | D Does not use class time well |
|---|---|---|---|---|
| Use of Class Time | • Always on time<br>• prepared when class starts<br>• on task during class<br>• Follows directions well | • Almost always on time<br>• prepared when class starts<br>• on task during class<br>• Usually follows directions | • Sometimes late and/or<br>• prepared when class starts, and<br>• usually on task during class<br>• Struggles to follow directions | • Often late and/or Unprepared when class starts, and<br>• Often off task<br>• Fails to follow directions |
| | Explanation of rating: | | | |

**FIGURE 5.12**   Grade Proposal

| | **A** Timely and professional | **B** Professional | **C** Semi-professional | **D** Unprofessional |
|---|---|---|---|---|
| **Brings all materials to class** | Always has <br> • text, <br> • binder, <br> • lab notebook, <br> • assignments | Usually has <br> • text, <br> • binder, <br> • lab notebook, <br> • assignments | Sometimes forgets <br> • text, <br> • binder, <br> • lab notebook, <br> • assignments | Often does not have <br> • text, <br> • binder, <br> • lab notebook, <br> • assignments |
| | Explanation of rating: | | | |
| **Quality of Formative Assignments** | **A** Exceptional | **B** Solid | **C** Satisfactory | **D** Limited |
| | Almost all IFA's are scored check plus | Almost all IFA's scored check plus or check | Some IFA's scored check or below | Many IFA's scored check minus or below or "0" |
| | Explanation of rating: | | | |
| **In Class Participation** | **A** Exceptional | **B** Solid | **C** Satisfactory | **D** Limited |
| | Actively engaged in class: <br> • Shares thoughts and ideas that add to the class's overall understanding of content <br> • asks relevant questions <br> • Often enriches learning environment by adding to discussion and helping others. | Actively engaged in class: <br> • Some participation in class discussions <br> • Always active listening <br> • asks relevant questions; <br> • Sometimes enriches learning environment | Sometimes actively engaged, usually passively engaged: <br> • Sporadic participation in class; <br> • Sometimes actively listening <br> • Sometimes off task and distracting others or distracted by others <br> • Sometimes enriching learning environment | Unengaged much of the time: <br> • Poor use of class time <br> • Behavior disrupts the learning environment <br> • Body language suggests disengagement such as not sitting up, head on desk, lack of eye contact etc |
| | Explanation of rating: | | | |

**FIGURE 5.12**    (Continue)

| | **A** Exceptional | **B** Solid | **C** Satisfactory | **D** Limited |
|---|---|---|---|---|
| **Group Participation** | Active engagement:<br>• Provides leadership, insight, creativity to help the group complete its task meaningfully<br>• Knows when to "follow."<br>• Responsible for own work | Active engagement:<br>• An active participant in the group<br>• Adds to meaningfulness of group work<br>• Responsible for own work | Sometimes actively engaged, usually passively engaged:<br>• Has to be told what to do some of the time by group members<br>• Sometimes "along for the ride" in group<br>• Requires group members to prod completion of work | Unengaged much of the time"<br>• Not always willing to participate<br>• Sometimes a distraction<br>• Not responsible for own work, relies on copying some portions of the lab from others |
| | Explanation of rating: | | | |

**Learning Skills**

| | **A** Exceptional | **B** Solid | **C** Satisfactory | **D** Limited |
|---|---|---|---|---|
| **Organization** | • Table of contents completed<br>• Binders organized by topics on unit outline with papers secured in proper sections<br>• notes and all written work is neat, clearly written, easy to follow | • Table of contents completed<br>• Binders organized by topics on unit outline with papers secured in proper sections, notes and<br>• most written work is neat, clearly written, easy to follow | • Table of contents present but not completed, <u>or</u><br>• Binders not organized by topics on unit outline papers secured in proper sections, notes and but <u>most</u> work is present, <u>or</u> most written work is not neat, clearly written, or easy to follow | Binder is unorganized, lacking multiple required items such as<br>• Table of contents<br>• Required papers present<br>• Not Organized into sections<br>• "A complete mess" |
| | Explanation of rating: | | | |

**FIGURE 5.12**   (Continue)

| | **A** Exceptional | **B** Solid | **C** Satisfactory | **D** Limited |
|---|---|---|---|---|
| **Sense Making** | • Narrative notes and corrections to all work show thought process<br>• Errors are corrected and clarified<br>• Evidence of further work on all of the assignments & labs<br>• Evidence of studying from assignments | • Narrative notes and corrections to most work shows thought process<br>• Most errors are corrected and clarified<br>• Evidence of further work on most of the assignments and labs<br>• Some Evidence of studying from assignments | • Narrative notes and corrections to some work shows thought process<br>• Some errors are corrected and clarified<br>• Evidence of further work on Some of the assignments and labs<br>• Little Evidence of studying from assignments | • Few if any narrative notes and corrections work<br>• Few if any errors are corrected and clarified<br>• Little or no evidence of further work on Some of the assignments and labs<br>• Little if any evidence of studying from assignments |
| | Explanation of rating: | | | |
| | **A** Exceptional | **B** Solid | **C** Satisfactory | **D** Limited |
| **Use of Tools** | • Regular visits to Moodle to keep up on daily postings,<br>• Evidence of using extra tools such as<br>  • extra help when needed<br>  • making of study guides, extra notes, etc | • Regular visits to Moodle to keep up on daily postings,<br>• Some evidence of using extra tools such as<br>  • extra help when needed<br>  • making of study guides, extra notes, etc | • Some visits to Moodle to keep up on daily postings,<br>• Little evidence of using extra tools such as<br>  • extra help when needed<br>  • making of study guides, extra notes, etc | • limited visits to Moodle to keep up on daily postings,<br>• no evidence of using extra tools such as<br>  • extra help when needed<br>  • making of study guides, extra notes, etc |
| | Explanation of rating: | | | |

| **Student Proposed Grade:** | | **Teacher-Assigned Grade:** | |
|---|---|---|---|
| Teacher Comments: | | | |

**FIGURE 5.12**　(Continue)

These are just a few examples of evaluation tools that can be used. It is crucial that you as the teacher develop your own evaluation tools that match the culture of the classroom, your expectations for your students, the subject you are teaching, the age of your students, the expectations of parents and administration. Ultimately, our goal as constructivist teachers is to provide students experiences to build upon previous experience and perceptions to become life-long learners and creative problem solvers. This goal requires significantly more nuanced and purposeful evaluation than a simple accumulation of points.

# Student-Centered Curriculum Design

In Part 3 we shift from the philosophical foundation of Part 1, and the climate and culture foundation necessary for an engaging classroom to curriculum design topics of Part 2. The purpose of this section is to provide for you a method of curriculum design that follows the Consider, Construct, Confirm (CCC) learning cycle. I will lead you through the process of creating a unit of study that follows the CCC cycle that also utilize backward design principles. Of course, organizing lesson plans into units is not new. However, I am advocating for a method of building units of study around conceptual themes (as opposed to single topics, ideas, or things), and then utilizing essential questions to organize and frame the unit, which will then lead us into Part 5, in which we will explore inquiry-based instruction.

# Chapter 6

# Thematic, Inquiry-Based Curriculum Design

In this section of the book I provide foundational pieces necessary for designing thematic, inquiry-based curricular units of study aligned to constructivist learning theory. As we explore those fundamental pieces, it is important to identify where they fit in the Consider, Construct, Confirm (CCC) learning cycle. This will help you frame each process as a part of a constructivist classroom. Therefore, with each described step that follows, keep in mind how that component of the curriculum provides the means for students to complete the following metacognitive functions: consider what they already know about a topic and build interest in that topic; have lived experiences to build new understanding and make meaning with and around that topic; and finally, resolve any cognitive dissonance or disequilibrium between the new lived experience and prior knowledge and experiences to make meaning and *own* that new knowledge and/or skill.

## Providing Meaningful Context

Curriculum planning is traditionally often approached in a very linear fashion. First, write objectives or guiding questions. Next, find activities for those objectives or questions. Then, figure out how to assess what students learned through those activities. This is assuming that you as the teacher are even planning the curriculum. Many times a teacher isn't even thoughtfully designing curriculum as much as he or she is simply following a curriculum.

Let me provide an example that is frankly, a bit embarrassing. A number of years ago I changed jobs and began teaching at a different school. I, and another teacher new to the school (but both of us veteran teachers), were teaching biology. We began our planning in August by doing what many high school teachers do, previewing the textbook provided by the school and the corresponding curriculum materials. Like most high school biology textbooks, the publisher provided different outlines of how to proceed through the chapters depending on the focus the teacher wants to emphasize. From that, we mapped out the scope and sequence of the chapters and topics, emphasizing some more than others, and then planned the activities for the first unit. As we proceeded through the units, we utilized a combination of activities from the publisher and activities we designed, modified, or pulled from other resources. When we reached the end of a unit in the text, we developed the exam utilizing the test bank from the publisher and from other texts. In this manner we proceeded through the units and chapters in the text. The amount of time spent on a unit was determined by how long it took to do all of the lab activities, discussions, lectures, and quizzes and tests, for the unit. We taught until we ran out of materials and then wrote a test that matched the lessons the students had just completed.

About three fourths of the way through the school year we had a moment of panic. We weren't going to make it through the curriculum. We had only completed about half of what we had mapped out. What went wrong? How could two veteran teachers so poorly map out the curriculum for the year? We went back and started counting up the number of days we spent on all the previous units. The amount of time spent on the units seemed to be appropriate for what the textbook curriculum rec-ommended and matched our previous experience. Then, we actually counted the number of class periods we had with the students. We had assumed a school year was essentially the same at this school as any other we'd taught in: somewhere between 170 and 180 days. This wasn't the case. As it was a boarding school, the breaks were lon-ger and there were other special events that inter-rupted the normal school days and further reduced the number of actual class periods. We simply had considerably fewer school days than the textbook and curriculum writers intended and also than we had in our previous experiences. We felt a bit fool-ish. Okay, a lot foolish. In the end, however, this was an important lesson for me as a teacher. Don't just follow a curriculum, *own* the curriculum.

We found ourselves stuck in what I call "the activity trap." Think of this as a pitfall trap. I don't think we were doing anything different in curriculum planning than what many teachers do. Curriculum planning was driven by a provided sequence of topics, lessons were largely determined by a curriculum provided, and what we had previously used in a biology class, and the assessment was designed at the end of the unit when we reached the conclusion of our class activities. It wasn't until we saw the end of the year looming that we realized we were in the trap and had to climb our way out of it. We had developed a curriculum that was a collection of activities, while on topic, did not readily connect to the big picture of our curriculum planning because there wasn't one beyond the broad

umbrella of an entire discipline: biology in this case. Because of this, we made no attempt to prioritize what we thought was important (because it all was) and then map out learning activities specifically focused on preparing students for what was most important and going to be assessed at the end of the unit. It was all important, so all might be assessed. It also meant that the summative assessment at the end might not account for all we had taught. We've all been in the class where we had to guess what might be on the test, because so much was taught, to test it all would require an hours-long exam. Out of that mistake, however, came the process of developing purposefully designed thematic, inquiry-based units that I will present to you in this section.

Before any lessons are developed, you as the teacher, must first identify the goals of the unit and the purpose for what you are going to teach. Goals are broader than specific learning objectives tied to specific lessons. For your students to be engaged, they must be able to find the purpose for what you are about to teach them—beyond getting a good grade. If we want our teaching to be grounded in constructivist learning theory, then we have to develop curriculum that is not simply a sequence of unconnected lessons. Even if the lessons are masterfully designed to be fun and exciting to kids, those ideas must be placed in a meaningful context. Constructivist learning theory does not support the dismantling of concepts into discrete entities to be taught out of context. For learning to be meaningful, students must be able to utilize lived experiences to look for patterns in what they are learning while using their own models, concepts, and strategies of inquiry to answer relevant questions (Fosnot 1996).

To address these issues and provide a practical means for developing curriculum that is rooted in constructivist learning theory, I promote developing curriculum that is structured around "thematic, inquiry-based units." I use the term thematic instead of the more commonly used terms that I would consider subsets of thematic: multidisciplinary, interdisciplinary (or integrated), and transdisciplinary (Moyer 2016).

See Figure 6.1 for a continuum of curriculum design. The more to the right on the X-axis, the more the lines between subjects are blurred, from traditional subjects on the left, to parallel (two disciplines studying same theme or resource like a novel at the same time), to multidisciplinary (multiple disciplines studying same theme or topic, to interdisciplinary (where specific connections are made between the subjects) to ephemeral integrated units (a day/week unit where individual subjects melded together) to transdisciplinary (where the lines between subjects disappear). The Y-axis is the continuum of the content of the curriculum, from randomcrap-tastic (you can probably guess!) at the bottom all the way to a conceptually abstract theme that will require considerable evaluative, critical-thinking application of content to arrive at a final conclusion for the unit essential question. Certainly, I would advocate that the higher up on the Y-axis the better, and the more to the right on the X-axis the better, though that is highly dependent on the age you are teaching, the school setting, and the subject.

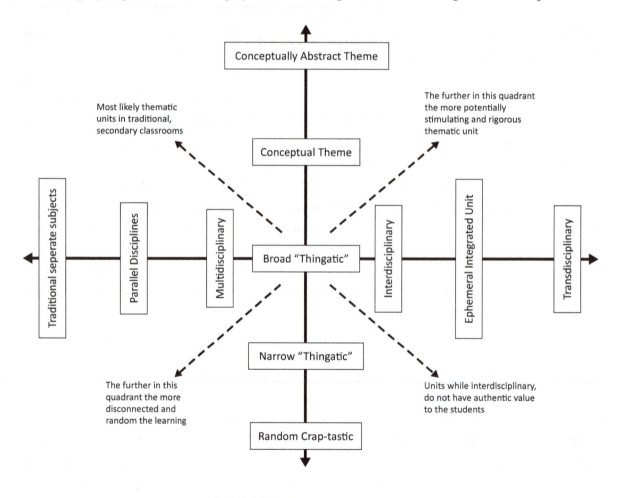

**FIGURE 6.1**    Curriculum Continuum

All of these terms require breaking the barriers between the individual silos of subjects pervading too much of students' school experience. At the elementary grades it is easy to visualize units and lessons that are interdisciplinary as one teacher may have the students for a majority of the day and be responsible for guiding those students through the various subjects of the traditional core curriculum. Too often, however, even as early as kindergarten, teachers are already breaking the day into discrete subject-matter blocks. This is simply counter to how humans experience the world and just plain unacceptable.

I prefer to use the term thematic as it is broader and can be applied by teachers truly integrating the cores subjects together, yet can also be used by secondary teachers teaching a course that by nature is a silo of one subject. Thematic is then more than just identifying the connection between disparate subjects, such as teaching writing skills while learning science, or using historical fiction as a means to understanding history while learning about the craft of literature and writing. Thematic curriculum planning requires that the learning is organized around a central conceptual theme with an essential question to explore. This theme can be explored in a transdisciplinary manner, as might happen in an elementary school where one teacher teaches all core subjects, or in a nontraditional secondary setting that is not separated into subject-matter silos. This theme can also be explored through the lens of a single subject, providing a new lens through which to understand that subject, as well as possibly then making connections to other subjects. Instead of presenting a discipline in a secondary classroom as a collection of topics in a subject (and the subject being the only organizing concept: biology, U.S. history, early American literature, etc.), thematic curriculum is built around conceptual themes endemic to that subject area. Using those concepts can provide a richer, more meaningful organization of the specific topics of study for a subject that will (hopefully) have a meaningful context for the students. Without a thematic core to build around, then, curriculum is often developed from a reductionist paradigm. All of the little bits are provided for the student, beginning with the smallest and building to an expected grand awakening or a-ha by the learner. That's what the teacher is hoping for. The teacher, because he or she has already explored this topic in a conceptual manner through years of studying and teaching it, now understands how all of the little bits fit together to tell a whole "story" of that subject, but the students do not even have the chance to see the big picture until the end of the course—which means most of them never do. It was really just random crap to memorize for a test that didn't mean anything beyond that. There was no "story" to discover for them. And so the teacher is frustrated because the students "just don't care" or "just don't get it." In fact, the students got it perfectly. They memorized and repeated exactly what was asked. We often just don't ask rich enough questions!

Using themes to structure instruction has been popular since John Dewey first proposed a curriculum related to real-life experiences of the children. Thematic organization of a unit of study can provide a framework for students to understand otherwise fragmented knowledge (Moyer 2016). In fact, as humans, providing themes is what we do to make sense of our learning. As discussed previously, if you have truly learned something, you have experienced constructivism—the act of taking knowledge and making it your own, making it fit your worldview, and owning it so you can later use, understand, modify, and manipulate that understanding. Our strongest students have always done this in the areas that they might self-describe as those areas they were "good at." Providing themes up front for students to organize the units of study around provides an opportunity for students to synthesize the otherwise random bits of knowledge and make personal connections fostering excitement because there exists a "unifying or dominant idea that can link concepts to prior knowledge and grow new knowledge" (Moyer 2016, 9).

The human brain seeks patterns and naturally connects facts and ideas in order to make sense of new experiences. Utilizing themes organizes the learning around a larger whole or big idea (Davies and Shanker-Brown 2011). The human brain will always put learning in context (if it is actually learned) otherwise the new information and skills separated from prior knowledge, experience, and a proper context will result in learning that is limited to the abilities of mimetic learning and memorization (Moyer 2016). Using a theme also has the practical advantage of boosting student motivation and improving academic achievement simply because students can begin to uncouple the profit motive (grade) from the task and link it to the purpose motive.

We know that many students struggle to learn concepts in isolation. I cannot think of another subject where this is as evident as biology. Learning biology can be a drudgery of memorizing metabolic pathways and cellular processes such as photosynthesis and cell respiration. To the biologist teaching it, these processes connect the living cell to the other living cells and to the larger ecosystems in which that organism lives. Those connections are fascinating, creating an awesome, elegant dance of interconnected living systems. I'm not overstating this. This is why many of the biology teachers you know are so annoyingly passionate about the natural world and don't hesitate to tell you about it! Without a context, however, most students memorize the equations long enough for a test, but never really understand the impact of those processes on their very own existence in the same way as the teacher does, therefore most students never experience that same sense of awe when learning biology. This is of course my frame of reference, but the same can be said for teachers of any subject area. It means what it does because it is relevant to the teacher in understanding their place in the world. The relevance does not have to pre-exist for students, however. Your role as teacher is often to provide that relevance, which can be done through a meaningful central theme or big idea (Brooks and Brooks 1993).

When subjects are separated, students lose sight of the original aim of the learning (if they ever saw it), but learning organized around a theme or big idea creates an opportunity for students to think differently about the topic at hand, allowing that topic to become more relevant when connected to the larger theme or big idea. Learners of all ages are more engaged by concepts introduced by the teacher and constructed by the learner from whole-to-part, rather than part-to-whole.

Providing a thematic framework for learning is supported by the most current research about the brain but is hardly a new idea. According to Noddings (2007) "Dewey wanted students to experience a personally unified curriculum—one that makes sense to them in terms of human experience and, particularly, in terms of their own experience" (p. 40). The challenge for the teacher is developing truly intriguing themes around which to build the curriculum.

## Thematic versus Thingatic

In my work with teachers (from pre-service to *well-aged* veterans—like fine, gray-haired, wine!) the most common error I see in developing thematic units is to actually develop "thingatic" units. A theme is an overarching concept that incorporates discipline-specific content/skills, but the specific content is provided context by the thematic concept. The theme provides a purpose for learning the discipline-specific content/skills. A thingatic unit is an interdisciplinary unit built around a thing. Recently I found a book on a shelf that, according to the title, was all about teaching using thematic units. Oh no, I thought, some-one has already written the book I'm writing! A quick review reassured me that no, my book had not been published 10 years ago and just waiting for me to discover and use in my teaching of teachers. I found the same thing that I have found in many other books written for teachers or through internet searches about so-called thematic units; what I usu-ally find in these searches are examples of ideas for thingatic units. This is especially true for elementary grades. A unit built around "the apple" during October is an example. While you could teach about plants, have students read write stories, learn about food, etc., in the context of an apple, this is not a thematic unit. There is no overarching essential concept tying these lessons together. The apple is really just serving as the excuse or entry-point to content/skills aligned to this thing by the teacher. Granted, this may be more engaging for students than practicing literacy, art, and math skills, and learning science and social stud-ies content simply for the sake of learning it, but a thingatic unit still is unlikely to feel essential enough to students to have a chance to tap into the students' purpose motive and move beyond the profit motive—unless they love apples. Thingatic is certainly better than random lessons sequenced the way they are because that matches the required standards, so it is a step in the right direction, but I think we can do better.

Recently, I was working with elementary teachers learning to develop thematic units. One team of teachers decided to build a unit around the topic of measuring angles and area. They then dove headfirst into the activity trap and started thinking about the assignments the students would complete to measure angles and area of their bedroom (and smaller objects in the room). While the activities might be engaging for students as they used their content knowledge of angles and area to explore their own bedroom, this truly was a "thingatic" unit. There could also be lots of reasons a student would not care to bother completing the task, except because it was assigned and presumably for the extrinsic motivation to complete the task and get a grade. Beyond using the two pieces of math content/skills to measure their room, there was no purpose for exploring one's bedroom angles and area. Granted, this is way better than random worksheets and problems measuring angles and area. As we brainstormed, a much more conceptual theme emerged. Instead of building around the math content and finding a thing to explore and do to justify learning the content, the students could explore the theme of how much space they need to live. This theme of how much space they need to live has multiple possible right answers. It could serve as a means to learn many different discipline-specific content/skills such as, yes measuring angles and area, but also topics of ecology and environmental science, social studies and human behavior, animal behavior and adaptations, even the space and design of the students' classroom to allow for adequate learning. Now, that's a theme worth conducting inquiry about. And it could be done at any age. In fact, it could be done over and over, spiraling larger and larger as students mature.

Let me provide another example that initially, might seem less "thingatic" and more thematic on first glance. Two teachers were designing a solar system unit intended for a fourth grade class. They envisioned students learning about where they live, beginning with their town, then county, state, country, continent, and culminating with learning about the solar system. Within this context they were already spinning out ideas for science, geography, writing, and math lessons. As I tried to pull them back from the edge of the pitfall of the activity trap and got them to consider what would motivate students to learn this and what question they might ask students, we realized that, while this initially looked promising (and it was to a point) it still was a bit too thingatic and not thematic enough to feel essential. For the students, even though it was centered around them, which is always good for motivating children, it really was still just learning about the solar system. There was only one discovery that students could arrive at through the unit—the solar system is really big, mostly empty space, except for the sun, planets, moons, asteroid belt, and whatever Pluto is now.

The next day, these two teachers came back to share their idea with the group. This time the theme was built around students exploring an essential question of who they are and how where they live impacts who they are. Within this concept the students would explore three smaller concepts: heritage, culture, and tradition. This has the opportunity to be essential for the students, unique to each one of them, but arrive at those unique discoveries utilizing discipline-specific content/skills that could be aligned to standards. The end goal wasn't to discover the right answer to a "thing." The end goal was to explore a theme and in the process of exploring that theme (with no one right answer) use and build discipline-specific content/skills under the direction of the teacher. This has much more *potential* to tap into the purpose motive of the students.

In both of these cases, the teachers found that they actually had to reign in their ideas for the discipline-specific content/skills that could/should be used for students to explore the theme. The ideas began to spin out of control and the theme got larger and larger until pretty soon in both cases they had a topic that was so thematic it could become existential. This is the mark of a good theme! If, in the design process you have to wrestle a bit with it to contain it, then it is fertile for meaningful exploration of discipline-specific content/skills. The task of the teacher is then to put age-appropriate boundaries around the theme to properly scaffold the students' inquiry to keep the scope of the theme manageable while still meaningful and potentially purposeful for the students, and also ensure covering the content you as the teacher have an obligation to "teach."

In some regards, this process is easier for elementary teachers than it might be for secondary teachers. This is quite simply because most elementary teachers are in a setting where they teach the core subjects to the same group of students for a majority of the day. The structure is already in place to have a small learning community for extended periods of time. That is fertile soil to grow thematic, inquiry-based units. But what to plant?

Think of it this way. We humans primarily use two disciplines to organize all we know about the world. We organize phenomena we experience in the physical systems of world around us in the natural sciences. We organize phenomena we experience in the social systems within which we live and interact through the social sciences. Literacy with written language (reading) and math are the decoding methods we use to investigate and gather "data" about those phenomena. The arts (including literature, not to be confused with literacy) are used to make sense of and express what we learned about those phenomena. For this reason, it is often easiest for elementary teachers to start brainstorming topics for themes by making observations about the physical and social systems in which we live. Therefore, beginning with a social studies topic or science topics can be fertile ground to grow a thematic unit. As you develop the theme and dig into the aspects of the topic that are essential to that theme, you will find that the opportunities to use and apply the language arts, math, and visual or performing arts naturally emerge as you figure out what the students are going to do with this topic.

At the secondary level, the opportunity is far more limited for true *interdisciplinary* thematic units. In some cases, you may have a setting that allows you to plan and work with a teacher in another department who also has the same group of students, but this is rare in most secondary schools. Therefore, we'll proceed under the assumption for secondary teaching that the theme will be contained to your class and subject and therefore you will really be designing *intra*disciplinary thematic units—units of study that identify themes and connections within the discipline to reveal larger ideas and concepts. These themes might also be able to be explained through the lens of another subject, but in your setting would be explained through the lens of your class. You will also find that the process of developing a thematic unit so naturally lends itself to interdisciplinary curriculum design that if presented with the opportunity, you can easily expand on the theme to take advantage of the opportunity for interdisciplinary learning if one were to present itself in your school setting.

When choosing a theme within a discipline it is more fertile for critical thinking, authentic assessment, and student inquiry if the theme is a central concept as opposed to a "thing" that is a traditional topic within that discipline, unless it naturally fits into a broader theme for the course. For example, when teaching biology I did not do a typical unit at the beginning of the year on cells (which is common). Instead I taught different aspects of cells in the context of concepts that helped students define their role in an ecosystem. Therefore, I taught how the cell burns energy in the context of humans' role in matter and energy in an ecosystem. As a new teacher, you do have to be realistic about your creativity and accept that sometimes the best theme you can develop might be based around a historical event, scientific discovery, influential person, etc. The danger of the latter is that you haven't really provided the students (beyond those already intrinsically motivated about that subject) any purpose or reason to care to learn it, since it may not connect to a broader aspect of their daily lives. To engage more of your students so they invest in learning it to the point of *owning* it, using a broader theme that can encompass that topic and connect it to other aspects of the discipline, or to aspects of questions that affect *their* understanding of how *they* live in the world, the more likely students will engage and invest in the inquiry process. Consider this question, "What universal questions are all children trying to figure as they grow up?" They are trying to answer for themselves, who they are, where they fit in, and who they want to be. That's what growing up is about. The curriculum you design has to make what content you want to teach somehow help students develop answers to those questions right now, not abstractly in the future. If it doesn't, then their only motivation will be extrinsic motivators. It is the rare student who can recognize that what you are teaching might someday help them answer those questions, so they will be intrinsically motivated to learn it. But for most children, especially younger children this is not the case. When kids don't have a sense that they are able to answer those questions, or worse yet, see no future for themselves, then, what you are teaching will most likely not tap into a student's purpose-motive. Then in that instance, the best you can hope for in terms of engagement is level 3 on the engagement ladder—basic compliance. Therefore, the themes you choose and how you present those to students must help them answer those fundamental questions children are seeking as they mature.

As you develop your theme, it is always important to focus on depth versus breadth. Don't be tempted to include every possible facet of the theme and connection to other disciplines at the risk of overwhelming the students with information so they cannot keep up with how that information helps them understand the main theme and answer the essential question of the theme. At that point, the lessons slip back into being perceived as busy work or as pointless by the student (Horton and Barnett 2008) which will certainly undermine their climb up the engagement ladder.

## The Importance of Inquiry

The next logical course of action for students when presented with a theme is to investigate the nature of that theme. To remain true to constructivist learning theory, your role as the teacher is to provide students means to conduct that investigation, not to tell your students all they need to know to understand the theme. To do so would provide them with your understanding and meaning of that theme. Your job, remember, is to resist this. It may *feel* like the natural thing to do (that metaphorical *natural* golf swing), but that is only because that is the education that most of us have experienced. Your job is to help them investigate and discover. Sounds like a detective or scientist. Well, in many ways it is.

Inquiry-based education very much mirrors the scientific process. While there is value to the dogmatic *scientific method* taught in science class: make observations, ask questions, write a hypothesis, test hypothesis, answer question and refute or support hypothesis with data, and then start the process over again, in reality, scientists don't necessarily follow such a rigid, methodical process. All of these things do occur, but the process might often be more fluid, creative, and even accidental at times as well. But we teachers can take from this the process of asking questions and seeking answers based on experience and "data." I put quotes around data because it is important to realize that data is and should be much more than limited to quantifiable measurements. When we take these lessons from the scientific method, we find this process can apply to any subject—and in fact does in graduate school. No matter the discipline, graduate students studying everything from photosynthesis to the works of Shakespeare all utilize the ideals of the scientific process and conduct inquiry. No matter the topic or the age of the student, they can be coached to ask questions and seek answers to those questions, possibly for example, by analyzing then the works of Shakespeare to find the data to answer their investigative question.

Yet, in K-12 schooling this is often seemingly forgotten by teachers, and we slip into simply telling the students everything they need to know, forgetting we ourselves developed expertise invariably by conducting inquiry about aspects of the subject that we found alluring and fascinating. Your enthusiasm for the subject should be infectious and spark their enthusiasm in the subject as well, but ultimately, they have to build enthusiasm of their own to truly and deeply engage with the content. The students in your classroom are not scientists or even true scholars. As a teacher, you do have parameters and limitations provided in resources, a diversified group of students, and mandated curriculum goals or standards to address. Additionally, your students are still not only students of the subjects you are charged with teaching, but also students in the act of learning and learning how to learn (Kerlin, McDonald, and Kelly 2008). By utilizing an inquiry approach, no matter the subject, you will be helping students learn how to engage in scientifically oriented questions, even if about topics not traditionally thought of as science, formulate explanations based on evidence, and then evaluate those explanations based on those findings. To put it in the language we've been using in this book, students will consider what they already know about the topic, construct explanations about the topic through new experiences, and then confirm that learning by juxtaposing new experiences with prior knowledge, and formulate their own understandings triangulated by prior knowledge, new experiences, and accepted understanding of that topic (Figure 6.2). Piaget and Inhelder (1971) wrote, "The current state of knowledge is a moment in history, changing just as rapidly as knowledge in the past has changed, and, in many instances, more rapidly. Scientific thought, then is not momentary; it is not a static instance; it is a process. More specifically, it is a process of continual construction and reorganization" (pp. 1–2). You may not be a *science* teacher, but you should be a teacher of inquiry, no matter the subject.

By conducting inquiry, students dig deeper into the subject, learning the content but also the process of learning along the way (Wilhelm 2012). As their skill and knowledge

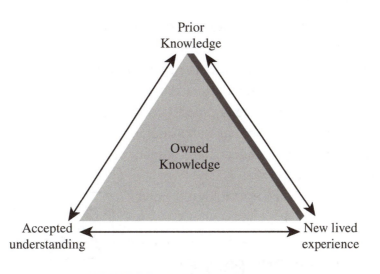

**FIGURE 6.2** Triangulating Learning

base progresses, students can then apply that knowledge and skill to still further inquiry, or in other words, begin to become life-long learners. MicTighe and Wiggens (2013) write, "Successful inquiry leads us to 'see' and 'grasp' and 'make sense' of things that were initially puzzling, murky, or fragmented; thus questioning is meant to culminate in new and more revealing meaning" (p. 17). In making sense from their own inquiry (even if designed and guided by the teacher) the student not only will develop deeper understanding, but also possibly an intrinsic enthusiasm for learning.

Conducting inquiry just for the sake of inquiry, however, will not be engaging for most of your students. The same students that would have made meaning from a didactic approach to the subject will embrace an inquiry approach to learning about the subject, but those not already intrinsically motivated to learn about what you are teaching won't engage, except for extrinsic motivators. In fact, those students might be less inclined to engage as inquiry is harder work than passively listening to a lecture and memorizing enough to get by the test. In other words, they aren't buying what you are selling.

This is why I couple inquiry with thematic. Your job is not just to cover content. It is to "uncover the important ideas and processes of the content so that students are able to make helpful connections and are equipped to transfer their learning in meaningful ways" (McTighe and Wiggins 2013, 26). When uncoupled from the theme, the learning is unmoored from the purpose motive. Providing the theme provides opportunity for more of your students to embrace the topic and inquiry process simply because they can see the value of it now. "Therefore, the classroom needs to be a place that equips students with the skills and interest necessary to delve into their own deep inquiry so they can identify problems and find answers relating to the subject outside of the classroom setting" (Virgin 2014, 202). With this in mind, your role is to provide a theme with potential for promoting student-generated questions and genuine interest in discovery. Then, you must provide a classroom setting that affords students time to conduct inquiry and even leave space for students to let their inquiry take them into areas of the subject you had not planned for. One way for this to occur is to utilize independent student projects and inquiry as a component of the assessment for a unit.

When I last taught high school biology, I developed a thematic curriculum that consisted of six units for the entire school year. At the conclusion of each unit, students took an essay exam assessing the content *I* deemed crucial to understanding that theme. However, that was only half of the unit assessment. The other half was for students to complete an independent project to delve deeper into one aspect of the unit of their choosing. In the first unit, I provided a list of potential projects with fairly descriptive instructions—though students could also choose to design their own inquiry project as one of the project choices. With each successive unit, I removed more and more of the scaffolding for what to investigate and how to investigate it, so that by the end of the last unit, there was no scaffolding as to topic choice or method of inquiry and presentation of learning. Though this was a science class, not all of the questions students asked and answered required science experiments. There is no reason why independent inquiry involving students asking questions, seeking information/data to answer the question and presenting their findings cannot happen in any classroom, at any age level, about any subject area.

DIG DEEPER into student-designed PBL as content assessment p. 225

If you can find a way to frame units of study that provide a means for students to conduct inquiry into fundamental themes of a discipline, you have the greatest chance of engaging the majority of your students in active, student-centered learning. When engaged in this active learning that has true purpose for the student in learning about something that affects their daily lives (right now), then you also have the greatest chance of guiding your students to the top of the engagement ladder. The first step up that ladder through inquiry requires the use of meaningful essential questions to frame the thematic, inquiry-based experiences for the student. This is the topic of the next chapter.

# Chapter 7

# Teaching From Questions

All children have questions. Some may not vocalize those questions much, and others may vocalize them with exhausting and mind-numbing persistence. "Daddy, why is the sky blue? Daddy where are we going?" "Daddy, why did that car honk its horn?" "Daddy, what does f**k mean?" Okay, this may not have been one of my finer parenting moments. Inquiry-based thematic instruction is rooted in the use of questions. If our intention is to use curriculum built around student inquiry into meaningful themes, then we must build it around questions.

## Essential Questions

Most teachers are taught to write objectives for units and/or lessons. Most textbooks (which drive most teacher's lesson planning) have objectives written at the beginning of each chapter. Let's look at an example:

> Students will demonstrate understanding of the Linnaean taxonomic system by explaining the phylogenetic relationship among organisms.

Technically, this is a good objective. It clearly states what the students will know and do. However, if I was sixteen and provided this at the beginning of a unit or lesson, my answer would probably be, "Huh?" More likely I would ignore it, recognizing such statements as "teacher-speak" and not really relevant to me as the student. The objective has great value for you as the teacher in providing a purpose for the lesson and providing guidance on the content and form of assessment used. This is emblematic of the problem with much of the teaching that occurs. Listen

DIG DEEPER into writing learning objectives p. 196

up teachers. It isn't about you! You already know the content. It is about the students. Everything you do is to make it possible for students to learn as much as possible, as efficiently as possible. The first step of that task is to engage the students in the consider phase of the learning cycle. Objectives may frame the lesson for you but they do not effectively address the goals of the consider phase of a lesson or unit. Because of this, I prefer to use guiding questions to communicate the objective of a lesson than the traditional learning objective.

Instead of the previously stated objective, what if the teacher started with guiding question such as:

"How are living things organized into groups and what might that tell scientists about the relationship between species?"

Why waste the first day of instruction explaining the meaning of the objective? Why not ask students questions they can begin to answer right away, instead of only at the end of the unit? Admittedly, they would not be able to answer the questions using the correct terminology, but they could begin to form an answer to the question within the first five minutes of the unit of study or lesson for the day. Beginning with a lesson objective loaded with new terminology can initially marginalize students struggling with the course, whereas, beginning with an

 into facilitating accessing prior knowledge p. 215

answerable question doesn't exclude any learners. Anyone can fashion an answer that is their best guess. Your job as the teacher then becomes to not accept "I don't know," as an answer from the student. Instead you will need to prod them take an educated guess—an hypothesis. Everyone knows something, because all have experienced life. The journey into a new topic should always begin with what they already know. They might be surprised by how much they have observed and already know about a topic. As the unit or lesson progresses, you will guide students to juxtapose what they knew at the beginning of the unit or lesson to what they know now at the end. Your job is to help them refine that knowledge by allowing time for cognitive dissonance between what they have already observed and knew, and their new experiences and discoveries about the topic.

More pragmatically, using essential questions to frame units and lessons provides students with practice exam questions. When students study and review for an exam using learning objectives they are often engaging in a passive and binary activity and response. It's either, "Yep, I can do that." or "Nope. Don't get it." Using essential questions, however, elicit active work as they actually respond to the question, hopefully, now for a second or third time, and in much more detail (hopefully) than at the beginning of the unit. It also allows the student to see how much he or she has actually learned and, therefore, feel a sense of accomplishment. Everybody likes to know stuff, right?

Maybe most importantly, beginning with a question creates a culture of mutual discovery and exploration. I believe this creates a more inviting learning environment than a statement communicating an intellectual separation between the teacher and students. Yes, you are the expert on the topic, but you should be the expert at facilitating a culture of mutual discovery in which the student is empowered to learn. In the other setting, the student is the compliant receptacle of information from the teacher. This might make for a quieter, more orderly classroom, but also makes for shallower learning and less meaningful construction of knowledge on the part of the student.

Ted Sizer first published the phrase "essential questions" in *Horace's Compromise: The Dilemma of the American High School* (1985). Grant Wiggins is responsible for making that phrase a regular part of teacher training and thinking. Using questions as a means to engage learners aligns with constructivist learning theory and the progressive educational philosophy of John Dewey. He believed students will be more engaged in learning when exploring questions instead of being told the answers. He advocated for schools to involve students in active researching, experiencing, discovering, and ultimately connecting subjects to their own lives (Dewey 1916) instead of as lists of terms to be memorized. Essential questions promote a more student-centered classroom environment (Virgin 2014) which is necessary for teaching methods based on constructivist learning theory. Essential questions help "learners construct meaning out of otherwise abstract notions and disconnected facts" (McTighe and Wiggins 2013, 31).

Essential questions are questions that have the following characteristics (Markham 2003; McTighe and Wiggins 2013; Wilhelm 2012):

- Open-ended, not answered through recall or with a single sentence
- Thought provoking and able to spark discussion and debate
- Requiring of analysis, inference, inquiry, prediction, etc. by learner
- Inviting and intriguing so as to sustain student interest
- Important and relevant to the student now (not for future needs or goals)
- Require knowing and doing same types of inquiry as real experts in the field
- Concise and clearly stated

For our purposes of using the CCC learning cycle model for curriculum development, I define an essential question as any question that is useful to both the student and the teacher in framing the topic of the unit or lesson, facilitating accessing of prior knowledge, inquiry, and assessing culminating knowledge and/or skills. There are a variety of essential questions that I will use as we explore curriculum design and instruction processes throughout the remainder of this book. The table below (Figure 7.1) provides a short description of each type of essential question I will use as well as comparisons to traditional curricular resources/models to help you comprehend the size or scope of each specific type of question.

The big idea, thematic, and sub-theme questions are questions that McTighe and Wiggins (2013) would clearly define as "essential" and would fit their list of essential question characteristics. McTighe and Wiggins would not define guiding, leading, or questions that hook as essential, though for them that does not denigrate the importance of those types of questions as teaching tools. I prefer to include all of these types of questions as essential questions, as the smaller questions should align to, built on the expanding foundation of each below it questions (see Figure 7.1). If they aren't, then, I would not consider them *essential* questions. I also choose to define all as essential simply so we do not get mired down in semantics.

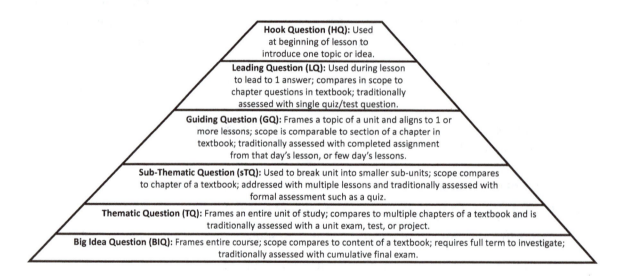

**FIGURE 7.1**    Essential Question Types

Essential questions are a crucial part of pedagogical methods based on constructivist learning theory from both the perspective of the student as a learner, and the teacher as a facilitator of learning and curriculum designer. A constructivist teacher asks students fewer, but broad-in-scope questions requiring time to think about and use of multiple resources to answer. This is quite different from asking many specific questions with simple answers, and when not immediately answered, then asked *and* answered by the teacher (Brooks and Brooks 1993). For me this brings up the image of the teacher in the 1986 John Hughes film *Ferris Bueller's Day Off* star-

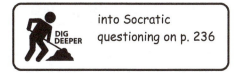

into Socratic questioning on p. 236

ing Mathew Broderick as the (much smarter than all the adults) teenager concocting an elaborate scheme to skip school. At one point in the movie we see the economics teacher played by Ben Stein droning on and on about a subject, pausing to ask a question, then in the same monotone, asking, "Anyone? Anyone? Bueller? Bueller?" and then immediately giving the answer. It is of course a hyperbolic demonstration of the classroom, but might provide a view of traditional teaching through the eyes of children who quickly learn it is easier to say nothing and sit quietly than to engage in the questioning which just prolongs the lesson (and agony).

Essential questions should set the class off on an inquiry and learning journey instead of just requiring the repeating back previously delivered information. Essential questions should require student inquiry and investigation. While the response may be provided through traditional forms of writing, it might, instead, require more authentic means of expressing the information—more performance-based assessment such as plays, museum exhibits, presentations, citizen action, etc. When seeking answers to such questions, students are then engaged in constructing meaning for themselves (McTighe and Wiggins 2013). "The point of essential questions . . . is not merely to engender student curiosity, but also to help students inquire into important ideas of disciplines at the core of a good education. Both goals have to be attained: academic understanding and personal meaning via questions and the disciplined pursuit of them" (McTighe and Wiggins 2013, 59).

Participating in courses, units, and lessons framed by essential questions, in addition to being more engaging and inviting to the student, also allows the student to make connections between otherwise disparate topics within a course. Additionally, using essential questions and corresponding open-ended writing and performance application of content and skills, can more easily be modified to the learners' needs, be that preferences in modes of learning or modifications for learning disabilities (Virgin 2014).

To do this, essential questions should frame a problem to be solved that connect to the students' lived experiences and connect to the real world as much as possible (Jorgensen 1994; Wilhelm 2012). This requires that exploration of the essential questions involves students moving between answering the question, to exploring new resources, having new experiences, and then returning back to the question and revising, changing, or confirming their initial understandings around that question (McTighe and Wiggins 2013).

The ideal essential question is one that can be used at the beginning of the unit (TQ) or lesson (GQ) and also then at the end of the unit or lesson to achieve the above goals and characteristics. That is no small task! Allow yourself some grace as you begin to utilize essential questions in planning and instruction. The questions should serve as doorways to the important, timeless, and enduring or foundational aspects of a topic (McTighe and Wiggins 2013). Writing such questions requires you to have a solid understanding of the topic you are teaching. Teachers wanting to write good essential questions must recognize any limitations they have in the subject and seek resources to bolster content knowledge and expected components of subject matter through the use of primary source documents, existing curricular resources, and content standards. By "unpacking" the standards and other resources, you can begin to envision the questions that the experts who wrote these resources must have been asking themselves. This can provide a starting point for identifying essential questions (McTighe and Wiggins 2013).

As you proceed in writing, revising, and rewriting essential questions, the act of doing so will allow you to accomplish two important aspects of pre-planning before hammering out the details of specific daily les-

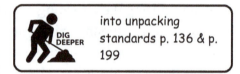

into unpacking standards p. 136 & p. 199

son plans. First, you will be required to prioritize and identify the most crucial aspects of the topic, and second, it will help you, as the teacher, identify your strengths and weaknesses with your own comprehension of the topic (McTighe and Wiggins 2013; Knight 2013). This process will then inform, not only the scope of the unit or lesson, but also the scope of study required before you can teach it! McTighe and Wiggins provide an eight-phase process for implementing essential questions (2013, 49).

1. Pre-instructional planning and design,
2. initial posing of the questions,
3. eliciting of varied student responses,
4. probing of those responses (and of the question itself),
5. introduction of new information and perspectives on the question,
6. in-depth and sustained inquiry culminating in products or performance,
7. tentative closure, and
8. assessment of individual student inquiry and answers.

More specific aspects of the process of creating and implementing all types of essential questions will be explored throughout the remainder of the book in exploring the process of designing units, lessons, and formative and summative assessment techniques.

Ultimately, the purpose for becoming proficient with utilizing essential questions in your teaching is to not only teach students the content of the curriculum, but also to train students to be critically literate with the ability to analyze individual and collective problems. This is necessary for a properly functioning democratic society. "Without the power to criticize, literate people may simply accept the messages given by the dominant culture. They become accomplices in their own exploitation. Critical literacy requires a mode of critical thinking. People need to know not only how to read but also how to question, analyze, and solve problems" (Noddings 2007, 74). I cannot think of a better purpose for education.

# Chapter 8

# Designing Thematic, Inquiry-Based Units

Though my training is in biology and education, I believe I have always been an artist at heart. No matter the job, I'm happiest when there is an opportunity for me to create something new. One of the most rewarding aspects of teaching is, (yes, yes, of course seeing the kids light up with new knowledge, blah, blah, blah…) I have to selfishly admit, creating new ways for students learn something. I'm most satisfied when I'm teaching curriculum I designed AND the students light up with new knowledge. I think it was Michelangelo that said sculpting was just chipping away the extra material to reveal the sculpture trapped in the marble. So too is curriculum designing—chipping away the distractions, the extraneous information, and revealing the most essential aspects of a topic, theme, idea, or discipline.

## Hamburger Model of Curriculum Design

I'd like to provide for you a model for the components of a thematic unit. I call it the hamburger model of curriculum and instruction (Figure 8.1). I provide this model to help you avoid falling into the activity trap. Keeping this model in mind and the subsequent design steps to create curriculum with these components described next will help you avoid the situation of only using an activity because you really like it, have always done it, or students love it. If the activity doesn't fit the theme and purpose of the unit, and then help students respond to the essential questions, then it must go!

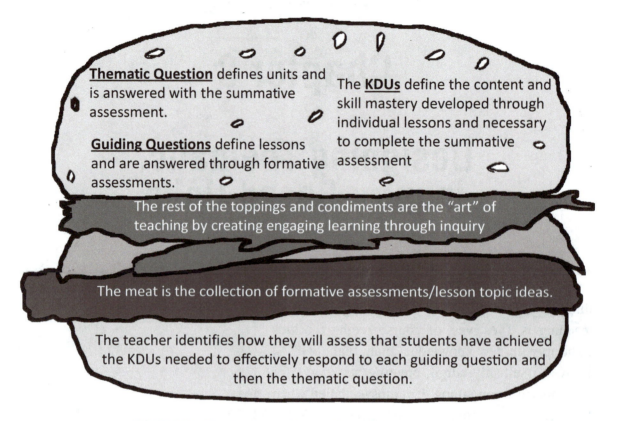

**Thematic Question** defines units and is answered with the summative assessment.

**Guiding Questions** define lessons and are answered through formative assessments.

The **KDUs** define the content and skill mastery developed through individual lessons and necessary to complete the summative assessment

The rest of the toppings and condiments are the "art" of teaching by creating engaging learning through inquiry

The meat is the collection of formative assessments/lesson topic ideas.

The teacher identifies how they will assess that students have achieved the KDUs needed to effectively respond to each guiding question and then the thematic question.

**FIGURE 8.1** The Hamburger Model of Curriculum and Instruction

The specific details of the components of this model (essential questions, KDUs, formative assessment/learning activities, summative and authentic assessment) will be covered next, followed by a step-by-step process of how to build a unit of study from this model. But first, we'll look at how those components fit together before digging further into each component and the specific thematic, inquiry-based unit design process.

The top bun of the hamburger defines the content of the unit. The content is outlined by the essential questions and then the specifics that students will need to Know, Do, and Understand (KDUs). Students will use this content (the top bun) to complete the summative assessment which is represented by the bottom bun. The top bun tells you where you are going and the bottom bun provides the benchmark to know when students have completed the journey. The buns provide the necessary framework of the hamburger so you can pick it up with your hands and dig in. Without the buns, your hamburger would be a pile of meat and toppings, but lacking the coherency of a hamburger. Without the framing of the essential questions and summative assessment, your unit of study runs the risk of being a sequence of random lessons and activities for students to complete without really understanding why.

The middle of the hamburger—the meat (or veggie patty if you prefer) and all the additional ingredients gives the hamburger its flavor—represents the actual "act" of teaching through carefully designed lessons. It is between the two buns where we have the meat, the cheese, tomato, lettuce, condiments, and whatever else you put on a hamburger. It is the extra ingredients that spice up the boring hamburger to make it something special. So it is with your curriculum planning and instruction.

"HOW AM I SUPPOSED TO EAT THIS THING?"

Before we can get to spicing up your delivery of lessons it is crucial to carefully and purposefully frame the unit and all that students will learn. When you know what understandings you are aiming for as the teacher and how students will demonstrate those KDUs, that you can begin planning the activities students will do. And this is key—you don't want to be thinking about what *you* will do with this theme, but instead what *students* will do with the theme. How will *they* engage in inquiry to answer the essential questions to have meaningful experiences that allow *them* to make sense of this information in the context of the broader theme? It is at this point you will begin mapping out the activities which will facilitate student knowledge construction. A list of activities alone are not lesson plans. Let's repeat that sentiment: *an activity by itself does not a lesson plan make!* Lesson planning will come in the next section of the book. In that section we will explore the details of how to take the outline of formative assessment/learning activity ideas making up the meat of the hamburger and create coherent lessons following the Consider, Construct, Confirm (CCC) learning cycle.

We aren't ready for lesson planning yet. Step away from the activity trap! First we need to build the unit plan within the context of the CCC learning cycle (Figure 8.2) Within the completion of the unit, students will first complete activities to *C*onsider any prior knowledge about the topic, complete lessons to *C*onstruct new knowledge, and complete the learning cycle by *C*onfirming their new knowledge juxtaposed to their prior knowledge all within a meaningful context for them as individuals.

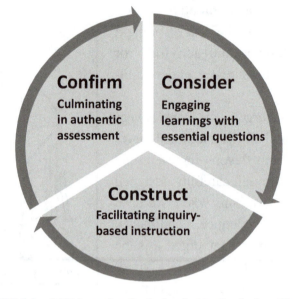

**FIGURE 8.2**   CCC Learning Cycle Applied to Curriculum Planning

# Building Thematic, Inquiry-Based Curriculum

Okay, well now all that's left to do is to actually build a thematic unit! By looking at this process in a more step-by-step manner using this flowchart (Figure 8.3). It is important to recognize that this is an iterative process. Each step along the path to creating a thematic, inquiry-based unit of study might impact something you have already created (theme, questions, assessment choices, etc.) and require you to circle back and revisit or revise previously designed aspects of the unit.

When designing curriculum for a subject-based course (modern American literature, biology, one of the visual arts, geography, etc.) I like to start with a course Big Idea Question (BIQ). This is the question that frames the entire course of study. No small task I realize. Teaching high school biology, I could began the class with this BIQ: What is your role as an individual, and member of the human species, in the biological world? I would pose this question to the students on day one of the class and have them answer it to the best of their ability. As we would proceed through the course, this question would stay posted in a prominent place for them to see and continue to think about. The course final exam would then give the students a chance to respond to this prompt:

> Based on what we have learned in all the units this year, write an essay about your ecological identity by answering this question: Then, how ought you to live within your role as a member of a biodiversity? This is your chance to apply the biology you have learned throughout the entire year to your own life.

# Thematic, Inquiry-Based Curriculim Scope and Sequence Design Flowchart

1. Big Idea Question (BIQ) / Question for whole course

2. <u>Thematic Unit Scope:</u> Break BIQ into units identified by Thematic Questions (TQ) and create outline of Summative Assessment/Project that will allow students to demonstrate the Know, Do, and Understand (KDUs) for the unit.

3. <u>Theme Chunking:</u> Based on the KDUs for the unit develop draft of further questions (GQ & sTQ) that break theme into small enough chunks for students to manage the breadth of content and skills for that unit.

4. <u>Final Draft GQs and KDUs:</u> Revise TQ and summative assessment, write final draft of GQs (and sTQs if necessary) and align/revise/ KDUs to each GQ.

5. <u>Final Thematic Unit Scope and Sequence:</u> Identify of potential /formative assessment(s)/learning activit(ies), and content standards for each guiding question and corresponding KDUs.

6. Write lesson plans in which the teacher facilitates students' exploration of essential questions (TQ and specific GQs) through the completion inquiry-based learning tasks.

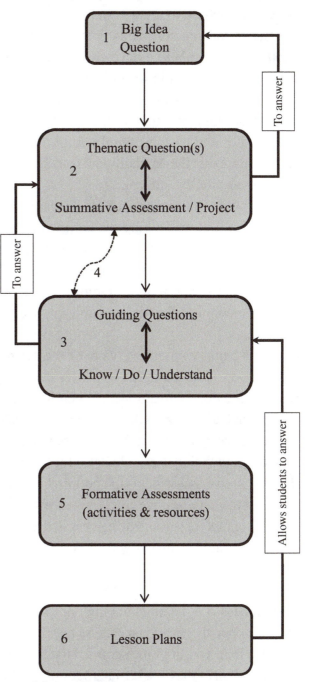

*This is an iterative process, as adjusting one aspect might prompt the teacher to make adjustments to other aspects of the unit

**FIGURE 8.3** Thematic, Inquiry-Based Curriculum Scope and Sequence Flow Chart

They would have access to an outline of all the units we've studied and all of the vocabulary/ concept terms used throughout the year to help them organize their thoughts and provide a coherent response to the question. I could use slightly different wording to ask the BIQ at the end of the course, as this time I could expect them to know terms such as *ecological identity* and *biosphere*. I have always been amazed at the veracity and tenacity with which most students go about responding to the question. At the beginning of the year, they may write a couple of paragraphs about their *role*. By the end of the course, they might write pages describing how they view their place as a biological being, as a citizen, as a consumer, that is informed by their family, faith, friends, and media. It provides for a much richer summative exam than a traditional test. The act of writing the exam might itself be a process of discovery for the student.

Working with teachers of all levels of experience, I have often found that planning curriculum by first framing the entire year with a BIQ is too overwhelming. Conversely, beginning with lessons and assessment ideas is too specific for developing meaningful, rich themes. Therefore, we will begin where Knight (2013) has also found to be the most effective starting point in designing curriculum—at the unit level (a coherent sequence of lessons spanning a few days to multiple weeks depending on the topic and the age of the student).

Let's begin with an overview of the entire process, and then I'll provide step-by-step instructions as well as an example for each step outlining the first unit of the biology curriculum previously mentioned. When looking deeply at how to design thematic, inquiry-based curriculum, we will focus on the development of a unit of study around a central theme. Once a theme has been chosen (refer to Chapter 6 to review difference between thematic and "thingatic) and KDUs for the broad theme identified, you can begin to outline the summative assessment (the bottom bun). Once you know where you are going, even if only in a vague, big picture sense, you can begin the process of refining and narrowing your focus. This begins with "theme-chunking." This is the process of outlining the smaller topics with this larger theme. The process of "theme-chunking" not only helps you discover the many aspects of the theme, but can also help you limit the scope of the theme and retain control of the breadth and focus of the theme to be explored in accordance to the subject or age of the students. Once you have a rough outline of

"WAIT...DID YOU SAY PUNKIN' CHUNKIN'?"

the theme, then, you can begin organizing the thematic unit around guiding questions, the KDUs for those questions, and *then* generate the ideas for the formative assessments/learning activities. That's a lot, so let's take the creation of the unit scope and sequence one step at a time. Remember that we are skipping the course big idea question and starting with a unit or theme.

## Thematic Unit Scope and Sequence—The Scope

The first step is to identify the scope of the unit. This is defined by the thematic question (TQ), the summative assessment, and the KDUs. Recall that this is an iterative process and you will likely come back to these throughout the design process to tweak and refine the question, summative assessment, and even the KDUs as the unit plan evolves.

The step-by-step process of identifying the scope of the unit can be done using Appendix 1: Thematic Unit Scope and Sequence—The Scope. Most teachers find it easiest to begin with what students will need to <u>K</u>now in order to fully respond to the question. Creating a list of vocabulary terms, concepts, and other "information" related to this topic is easily done by reviewing content standards, subject-specific texts, as well as probing one's own expertise about topics related to the theme. Next, most teachers usually define what students will need to <u>D</u>o to demonstrate proficiency with the theme. This is not a list of activities students will do in class to learn the content. Instead, this lists the skills and procedures students will be able to do once proficient with the content/skills related to the theme. These might be hands-on or kinesthetic skills, such as properly using lab equipment, performing a physical task in physical education, or properly solving a math problem in a step-by-step procedure. Lastly (for this first iteration anyway of the KDUs), is to identify what students need to <u>U</u>nderstand. Through identifying the "understand" you can get your first sense as to the richness of your theme. The understand most likely will be an extension of the Ks and Ds as you brainstorm what the students will do with the information and skills that are meaningful and potentially important to them to demonstrate understanding of the conceptual aspects of the theme. To think of it in the form of a question to answer as the teacher: How will the students use the vocabulary to explain complex processes, relationships between phenomena, apply the information to solving a problem, ask another question or create a new idea? It is the understandings that align to the higher-order thinking identified at the top of Bloom's taxonomy, which should be our ultimate goal for student learning.

With the first draft of the KDUs for the unit completed, the next step is to identify how the students will demonstrate their final or cumulative knowledge and application of knowledge and skills to answering the thematic question. Depending on the nature of the KDUs, you can decide if students should be presenting memorized information, applying concepts to making a controversial decision, taking action steps as concerned citizens, and also how they should be demonstrating their new-found knowledge and skills. This could range from traditional testing, performance assessments, in-depth projects, writing, or even a combination of multiples of these presented as a portfolio of work. Most find, in this model of curriculum design that traditional testing of required memorization usually happens not at the end as part of a summative assessment, but as formative assessment leading up to a more authentic and meaningful application of those facts to larger concepts related to the theme's final summative assessment. Because of this, project-based and authentic assessments rather than an objective tests, are often better choices for summative assessments at the conclusion of a truly thematic, inquiry-based unit of study. It's one thing to have memorized something. But, if the theme is rich and conceptual, you will want to see students apply that knowledge to something higher on Bloom's taxonomy than recalling information. If not, then I'd argue you have not developed a theme worthy of student inquiry.

In the early stages of the development of a thematic unit, the idea for the summative assessment is often a pretty straight-forward task of recalling and using the unit content. As you dig deeper yourself, become better versed in the topic and work with it, allow yourself to consider more authentic means for the students to use the content while applying the content to solving, or at least understanding, a real-world problem. This requires in-depth understanding of the topic on your part as the teacher. Consulting content standards, textbooks, primary sources, etc., is very helpful for creating a rich thematic question that is "essential" as described previously. Figure 8.4: Biology Unit I Scope is an example of a completed "scope" for the previously mentioned high school biology unit. Notice that it is an exhaustive list of the KDUs. The amount of KDUs are your guide to the length of the unit. There's a lot of KDUs in this example, justifying a 6 week unit. Also notice that the summative assessment is two tasks. The first requires understanding and application of content I, as the teacher, feel is most important to meet my agenda (the required content standards and what I feel is important for students to know about biology). While it is an essay exam answering the thematic question (in some variation if not directly), the use of a more open-ended question(s) allows the student to explain the concepts in their own way, therefore limiting the presence of mimetic regurgitation of memorized definitions as much as possible with this kind of exam. The second component of the summative assessment provides an opportunity for students to dig deep into one aspect of the unit. This becomes an opportunity for students to complete an investigation of their own choosing while also developing inquiry skills. As this is the first unit of the year, students would be provided a menu of defined project choices as well as

# Thematic Unit Scope and Sequence – The Scope

Step1 - Briefly describe the topic or theme to be explored by students in this unit of study:
This unit is the first unit of the course and is about the way in which the Earth captures the
sun's energy through plants and then how that energy and matter made from the energy is
cycled and recycled through the living and non-living components of an ecosystem.

Step 2 - Identify the grade level of study and potential length of unit:
Grade Level: 9 - 10        Length of Unit: 6 weeks

Step 3 - First draft of thematic question:
How do you participate in an ecosystem's flow of energy and matter?

Step 4 - Means by which the student will demonstrate/put into use culminating understandings
for the unit theme:
Students will complete an exam responding to the thematic question properly using specific
terms and examples & also complete a student-designed project investigating and applying
further one concept from the unit

Step 5 - Identify that which students will have to Know, Do, and Understand to complete the
summative task and demonstrate understanding:

<u>Know</u> (vocabulary terms; single concepts; observable facts; rote-learned information; names and
dates; formulas; etc.):
Homeostasis, emergent properties, biome, biosphere, community, ecosystem, biotic, abiotic,
Gaia Hypothesis, consumer, fusion, spectrum, carbohydrate, atom, thermodynamics ($1^{st}$ &
$2^{nd}$), bonds, glucose, $CO_2$, $H_2O$, light energy, photons, chlorophyll, chloroplasts,
photosynthesis, light reaction, Calvin cycle, ATP, NADPH, starch, polysaccharide,
monosaccharide, disaccharide, respiration, aerobic respiration, anaerobic respiration,
fermentation, glycolysis, mitochondria, Citric Acid cycle, chemical energy, matter, biomass,
stoma, decomposers, bacteria, fungi, hyphae, mycelium, sac fungi (ascomycota), club fungi
(basidiomycota), imperfect fungi, penicillin, nitrogen ($N_2$), potassium, phosphorous
<u>Do</u> (skills, procedural steps, application of rules, etc.):
Use microscope; design and conduct experiment using scientific method; Follow energy flow
from sun through organisms and out of system as heat; Follow path of carbon and nitrogen
as it cycles through ecosystem; describe interaction of organisms (humans/animals, plants,
fungi, bacteria) to maintain ecosystem homeostasis
<u>Understand</u> (Application of concepts; connection between "know" items; cause and effect, etc.):
Relationship between photosynthesis and respiration; how ATP is produced and leads to
"action" in a cell; basic thermodynamics applied to living systems; difference between matter
and energy; the role living organisms play in cycle matter through ecosystem

**FIGURE 8.4**   Biology Unit I Scope

allowed to design their own investigation. This allows students to choose among projects with different levels of specificity in the instructions depending on their experience with project-based learning. With each unit, the teacher-designed choices would be reduced until the final unit when students must design their final project from question to final product in its entirety.

# Thematic Unit Scope and Sequence—Unpacking Standards

With the scope of the unit in at least a draft form, the next step (if necessary) is unpacking the standards. This step really is just to get to the more important task of refining the theme by doing a process I call

DUG DEEPER ↘ into unpacking standards from p. 124

theme-chunking. Unpacking the standards can possibly be helpful in producing a better chunking of themes and richer guiding questions. I say "possibly" because while this step can be helpful (especially to new teachers) in developing rich questions to flesh out the theme idea, the standards can also limit your thinking about the theme because, by their nature, standards separate subjects into individual silos. If one goal of thematic curricula is creating a curriculum that is interdisciplinary, then it is crucial to unpack standards from all the disciplines that might fit into the thematic unit you are designing. This applies mostly to teachers in situations allowing them to develop truly interdisciplinary units—primarily elementary teachers. Therefore, while at some point you need to align standards to your unit plan, the task of unpacking and aligning may be done later if this step is not necessary to fully explore the possibilities of the thematic unit you are writing.

The key to unpacking standards is to pick out key *verbs* and *nouns*, especially looking for where the nouns are connected to verbs in a declarative statement. This can often provide the basis for a use-

DIG DEEPER further into unpacking standards on p. 199

ful essential question (McTighe and Wiggins 2013) and can be completed using the instructions found in Appendix 2: Thematic Unit Scope and Sequence—Unpacking Standards. See Figure 8.5: Biology Unit I Unpacking Standards for an example of some of the standards unpacked for unit I of the example biology curriculum. The example is only a partial list in the interest of providing a concise example.

# Thematic Unit Scope and Sequence – Unpacking Standards

Unpacking the standards is a step that can be done as a means to refine any of the essential questions: BIQ, TQ, sTQ, or GQ. It therefore can be done at any point in the design process when it becomes necessary for further fleshing out and refining the content of the thematic unit.

| Step 1 - List the standards: | Step 2 - Identify the key nouns and verbs of each standard: |
|---|---|
| 9.1.1.2: Understand that scientists conduct investigations for a variety of reasons, including: to discover new aspects of the natural world, to explain observed phenomena, to test the conclusions of prior investigations, or to test the predictions of current theories. | Conduct investigations; discover; natural world; explain observed phenomena; test conclusions & predictions. |
| 9.4.1.2.4: Explain the function and importance of cell organelles for prokaryotic and/or eukaryotic cells as related to the basic cell processes of respiration, photosynthesis, protein synthesis and cell reproduction. | Cell organelle function; prokaryotic; eukaryotic cells; respiration; photosynthesis; cell reproduction |
| 9.4.2.2.1: Use words and equations to differentiate between the processes of photosynthesis and respiration in terms of energy flow, beginning reactants and end products. | Photosynthesis; cell respiration; energy flow |
| 9.4.2.2.2: Explain how matter and energy is transformed and transferred among organisms in an ecosystem, and how energy is dissipated as heat into the environment. | Matter and energy transform; matter and energy transfer; energy dissipation |

*This example is only partial list of standards aligned to this unit.

Step 3 - Revising / Writing Questions:

Use the identified nouns and verbs to initially write (during scope or theme-chunking phase of unit design) or revise the essential questions for the thematic unit during finalizing phase of unit design.

**FIGURE 8.5**   Biology Unit I Unpacking Standards

# Thematic Unit Scope and Sequence—Theme Chunking

Whether utilizing standards as a guide or not, the thematic unit does need to be broken into smaller chunks that will eventually be communicated to students in the form of guiding questions (GQ) and possibly sub-thematic questions (sTQ). Utilizing the KDUs from the unit scope, the next step is to identify any ways the unit KDUs can be grouped into subtopics or chunks. Using the same process of unpacking content standards and objectives, you can convert the theme-chunks into questions. At this point, I advise teachers to not worry about the size of the question and therefore worry about labeling these questions as sub-thematic questions or guiding questions. As you work with the questions you will identify some as being broader and more conceptual, and some as quite specific and then adjust the questions accordingly. This process is completed utilizing Appendix 3: Thematic Scope and Sequence—Theme Chunking. See Figure 8.6: Biology Unit I Theme Chunking for an example of theme-chunking.

Notice that I have identified two thematic areas. Recall that this unit had many KDUs and was slated to last up to six weeks. Therefore, it is likely that this unit will ultimately have two sub-thematic questions which will each be assessed separately as formal formative assessments such as essay quizzes or small projects or papers. Also notice that I did not rewrite every vocab term from the KDUs, but instead identified the processes and concepts that these terms might be used to define and explain. This document is only for my use as the teacher. I'm confident in my background knowledge in this topic and do not need to repeat a list of terms. However, if I was designing a unit I was less comfortable with, I might provide more detailed list of KDUs at this step as well. Notice also that the guiding questions at this point are lots of "how" and "what" questions and not particularly "essential" as defined in Chapter 7. Remember, this is an iterative process and I will revise and refine later.

# Thematic Unit Scope and Sequence—Draft GQs and KDUs

The next step is to refine the wording of the essential questions (TQ, sTQ, GQ) and alignment of the GQs to the KDUs. This can be completed using Appendix 4: Thematic Unit Scope and Sequence: Draft GQs and KDUs.

A reasonable number of guiding questions for a unit might be four to eight questions. If you find that you have more questions than that, you might need to break the theme into smaller sub-themes, and some of the questions you have already generated might actually be a sTQ in scope. A sub-theme might be a "chunk" of KDUs that would be assessed with

## Thematic Unit Scope and Sequence – Theme Chunking

Step 1 – Using Unit Scope KDUs identify potential topical groupings of the KDUs: **These will become sTQs**

Step 2 – Convert the topics into essential questions (potential sTQ and GQ questions): **sTQs**

| Sub-topics for the unit | Draft Questions: |
|---|---|
| Energy capture and transfer<br><br>- Photosynthesis process and equation<br>- Cell respiration process and equation<br>- ATP function and how formed<br>- Tracing energy from sun through living system<br>- Relationship between photosynthesis and respiration | - How does energy flow through an ecosystem as an open system?<br>- What is the process of photosynthesis?<br>- What is the equation (inputs and outputs) of photosynthesis?<br>- What are the various stages of how an organism "burns" glucose for energy with and without oxygen?<br>- What is the relationship photosynthesis and cell respiration?<br>- What is ATP and how is it formed? |
| Matter transfer and recycling<br><br>- Necessary molecules such as CHNOPS<br>- Decomposition process and examples of decomposers<br>- Carbon, Nitrogen, Water cycles<br>- Role organisms play in storing and transferring matter<br>- Trace path of carbon and nitrogen in system<br>- Impact humans have on geochemical cycles | - How is matter recycled through the ecosystem as a closed system?<br>- What is biomass?<br>- How are matter and energy different?<br>- What molecules are necessary for life and where do we get them?<br>- What role do fungi play in an ecosystem?<br>- What relationship do fungi have with plants?<br>- What is the connection between fungi, decomposition, and energy in the Earth system?<br>- How is carbon stored both for long and short term?<br>- What is the impact of humans on the carbon cycle? |

**These will become GQs**

**FIGURE 8.6**   Biology Unit I Theme-Chunking

a formal quiz, writing assignment, lab, presentation, etc., but only focused on one aspect of the larger theme. Look back at the theme-chunking example. Each theme chunk has what is potentially a sTQ and multiple GQs. At this point you have a draft of the unit described through essential questions: the Thematic Question, the sub-Thematic questions (if necessary), and the Guiding Questions and aligned to the KDUs. Consequently, then, at this phase of the design process the final nature of the summative assessment that is most appropriate for the theme should begin to emerge and reveal itself to you like Michelangelo chipping away at the marble to reveal the sculpture inside.

We've now clarified where we are heading with the unit and created an outline of the route we'll be taking with the essential questions. The next step is to finalize the KDUs and align them to the sub-theme (if present) and guiding questions. Depending on the thoroughness of your KDUs for the thematic question, this might be no more than cutting and pasting the KDUs from the unit scope to the specific GQs. A more likely scenario is that you will discover additional KDUs as you think more specifically about each guiding question. Remember, the process is iterative, and this might require you go back and add to the unit KDUs and possibly even adjust your thinking for the potential summative assessment. Just as with the unit KDUs, the amount and breadth of the KDUs (a lot of Ks, very few Us, for example) might also require that you modify the questions. I label this step "draft" because some tweaking of the question wording might occur during the final step of creating the final scope and sequence, but for the most part, this draft should be mostly complete and final. See Figure 8.7: Biology Unit I Draft GQs and KDUs for an example from the biology curriculum. Compare the guiding questions on this list to the guiding questions on the previous theme-chunking document. The number of questions and the wording of the questions have changed so that they are hopefully more intriguing and accessible. This should make them more useful on day one to define that topic, lesson, or activity, and also solicit prior knowledge about the topic, as well as be used again at the end for assessing learning. This is an important characteristic of the questions for using them in a lesson following the CCC learning cycle. Also, notice that many of the original guiding questions that were addressing very specific content, like the photosynthesis equation, have been eliminated. Those memorized science facts and foundational concepts will still be required to be used for the student to adequately and fully answer the guiding, sub-thematic, and thematic questions, but each factoid does not require its own question. The specific location of when these terms are initially taught and then further utilized by the student to complete the Ds and Us of the KDUs will emerge in the specific lesson planning phase yet to come.

# Thematic Unit Scope and Sequence – GQ Draft KDUs

| Guiding Question: | How does an ecosystem capture the sun's energy? |
|---|---|
| **K**now: | • Photosynthesis process and equation resulting in glucose (sugar)<br>• Basics of 1st and 2nd law of thermodynamics<br>• Chlorophyll; producers; spectrum; photons; chlorophyll; chloroplasts; light and dark reaction; Calvin cycle; mono-, di-, poly-saccharide; eukaryotic cells<br>• Cell's structures involved in completing photosynthesis |
| Be able to **D**o: | • Set-up and complete controlled experiment<br>• Trace path of energy from sun into the plants |
| **U**nderstand: | • Role of plants in providing all energy for an ecosystem<br>• Application of thermodynamics to energy transfer<br>• Plants role in maintaining ecosystem homeostasis |

| Guiding Question: | How does an organism (such as yourself) burn and use energy? |
|---|---|
| **K**now: | • Anaerobic and aerobic process and equations<br>• Consumers; ATP; fermentation; glycolysis; chemical energy<br>• Structure and function of mitochondria |
| Be able to **D**o: | • Set-up and conduct controlled experiment<br>• Trace path of energy through living cells |
| **U**nderstand: | • The process of producing ATP<br>• How ATP results in action in a cell |

| Guiding Question: | In what ways do living things "work together to capture and use energy? |
|---|---|
| **K**now: | • Homeostasis; emergent properties; biome; biosphere; community; ecosystem; biotic; |
| Be able to **D**o: | • Trace path of energy from sun through living system and out of system as heat |
| **U**nderstand: | • The role individual organisms play in transferring energy<br>• The most energy is lost to the system as heat<br>• The difference between consumers and producers |

**FIGURE 8.7**   Biology Unit I Draft GQs and KDUs

## Thematic Unit Scope and Sequence – GQ Draft KDUs

| Guiding Question: | How does matter and energy interact in living things to make biomass? |
|---|---|
| **K**now: | • Abiotic; matter; biomass; carbon cycle |
| Be able to **D**o: | • Apply concepts of photosynthesis and cell respiration to the carbon cycle |
| **U**nderstand: | • The difference between matter and energy<br>• The carbon cycle<br>• 1st and 2nd laws of thermodynamics applied to living systems<br>• Human impact on the carbon cycle |

| Guiding Question: | In what ways would an ecosystem change if there were no fungi and bacteria? |
|---|---|
| **K**now: | • Types of fungi; types of bacteria; prokaryotic cells; fungi structure |
| Be able to **D**o: | • Follow path of nitrogen through system<br>• Follow path of carbon through system |
| **U**nderstand: | • The role of fungi and bacteria as decomposers<br>• Difference between eukaryotic and prokaryotic cells<br>• The nitrogen cycle<br>• The relationship between fungi and plants<br>• Human impact on the nitrogen cycle |

| Guiding Question: | In what ways could the essential atoms and molecules in your body be the same ones that were in prehistoric plants and animals? |
|---|---|
| **K**now: | • Carbon cycle; nitrogen cycle |
| Be able to **D**o: | • Describe how living organisms store matter and burn energy |
| **U**nderstand: | • Gaia Hypothesis and how it explains planetary homeostasis<br>• Different ways carbon is stored in the earth's living and non-living systems |

**FIGURE 8.7**   (Continue)

# Thematic Unit Final Scope and Sequence

The last step of designing a thematic unit is identifying the lesson topics to be explored through a variety of formative assessments/learning activities, as well as align content standards to the unit. Once we do this step and create a final document with the essential questions, KDUs, potential learning activities/formative assessments, summative assessment(s), and aligned content standards, we will have the final unit plan. This step can be completed using Appendix 5: Thematic Unit Final Scope and Sequence.

We're getting closer, we aren't lesson planning yet. *Back away from that lesson plan*—it's the piece of cheese in the activity trap at this point. Lesson planning comes next. At this step we are brainstorming types of classroom activities. You will notice that I put the term formative assessment and learning activities together previously. This was purposeful. A teacher working from a constructivist learning theory paradigm will soon recognize that everything the students are doing is a formative assessment, providing feedback loops to you as the teacher, and to your students, as to what comes next on the journey toward mastery of content and skills. Whether you are grading a lab report, writing assignment, quiz, or simply observing and listening during a discussion, you should be taking note and gathering information as to students' progress. Every learning activity has the potential to provide this "data" to you and the student, and every assessment activity should also still be a learning activity requiring reflective thinking on the part of the student. Therefore, they really are one in the same.

As you complete brainstorming for types of assessments/learning activities, you again might need to adjust your KDUs for a guiding question, which might require that you adjust the guiding question. Again, it is an iterative process, not a linear one. When done, you will have a road map for the unit that includes where we are heading (the answer to the thematic question) and the route we will take to get there (the answers to the guiding questions). See Figure 8.8: Biology Unit I Thematic Unit Final Scope and Sequence for an example.

The last step of course (finally!) is lesson planning and the actual act of teaching, which is the subject of next and last section of the book. However, before we dive into those specifics, let's take one last look at the nature of our unit planning process. It is an example of backward design in that we began with our end goal in mind and worked from there (Wiggins and McTighe 2005). Let's go back and review the curriculum design flow chart (Figure 8.1), but now review it backwards from the ending point to the beginning. The lesson plans are the means by which you facilitate students learning the KDUs. This allows students to respond to the guiding questions (and sTQs if necessary) building proficiency with the guiding questions. Students will then possess the KDUs allowing them to answer the thematic question. This ultimately provides the students the means to demonstrate proficiency with the course Big Idea Question.

# Thematic Unit Final Scope and Sequence

Step 1 – Finalize Unit Scope:

Assessed at end of unit with summative assessment

| Planning for a Thematic Inquiry | |
|---|---|
| **Unit Title:** | Matter and Energy |
| **Thematic Question:** | How do you participate in an ecosystems flow of energy and matter? |

| Unit KDUs (By end of unit, students shall…) | | |
|---|---|---|
| Know: | Be able to Do: | Understand: |
| • Photosynthesis process / equation<br>• Cell respiration process / equation<br>• Examples of producers and consumers<br>• Aerobic and anaerobic respiration<br>• ATP production and use by cell<br>• 1st and 2nd law of thermodynamics<br>• The importance of these molecules: C, H, N, O, P, S<br>• The basic structure of bacteria and fungi<br>• Decomposition process and examples of decomposers<br>• Geochemical cycles (C, N, H2O)<br>• Homeostasis<br>• The difference between long-term and short-term carbon sinks<br>• How biomass is formed | • Follow the flow of energy from the sun, through ecosystem organisms, and out of system as heat energy<br>• Design and complete a controlled experiment<br>• Follow the path of carbon and nitrogen as it cycles through the ecosystem<br>• Describe the interaction of organisms (humans/animals, plants, fungi, bacteria) to maintain ecosystem homeostasis | • The relationship between photosynthesis and cell respiration<br>• The process of producing ATP<br>• The application of thermodynamics to organisms energy<br>• The difference between matter and energy<br>• The role that living organisms play in cycling matter through ecosystem<br>• The role humans have on the cycling of carbon and nitrogen |

The KDUs should outline the entire unit

| Unit Summative Assessment Idea and Description: |
|---|
| • Essay response to the thematic question. To get an "A" a student will need to answer the thematic question using a majority of the unit terms and concepts correctly and provide coherent response that explains the connections between those concepts in describing how the writer participates in the ecosystem through those scientific processes.<br>• Complete Extended Investigation: Complete independent project investigating student-generated question. In unit I, the teacher will provide list of potential investigative questions and project outlines. With each subsequent unit, more of the scaffolding is removed until, by Unit VI, all students are completing an investigation entirely of their own design in scope and style of project. |

**FIGURE 8.8**  Biology Unit Final Scope and Sequence

# Thematic Unit Final Scope and Sequence

Step 2 (if necessary) – Finalize unit sub-Thematic Questions Scope:

> **This unit is broken into two halves, each framed by a sTQ.**

| Planning for a Sub-topic of the Theme | | |
|---|---|---|
| **Sub-Theme Title:** | Energy Cycling | |
| **Sub-Thematic Question 1:** | How are you a part of Earth's ability to capture and cycle energy? | |

| Topic KDUs (By end of this topic, students shall…) | | |
|---|---|---|
| **Know:** | Be able to **Do:** | Understand: |
| • Photosynthesis process / equation<br><br>• Cell respiration process / equation<br><br>• Examples of producers and consumers<br><br>• Aerobic and anaerobic respiration<br><br>• ATP production and use by cell<br><br>• 1st and 2nd law of thermodynamics | • Follow the flow of energy from the sun, through ecosystem organisms, and out of system as heat energy<br><br>• Design and complete a controlled experiment<br><br><br>**Notice that the KDUs are taken directly from Step 1** | • The relationship between photosynthesis and cell respiration<br><br>• The process of producing ATP<br><br>• The application of thermodynamics to organisms energy |

| Sub-Theme Formative Assessment(s): |
|---|
| Essay quiz providing a response to the sub-theme question. Students will be prompted to use combination of diagrams and description to describe how energy enters the ecosystem, cycles through the living components (producers and consumers) and leaves the system as heat. To get an A, students will need to correctly use almost all of the appropriate terms correctly in describing the processes. |

> **Each half of the unit framed by the sTQ is assessed with a formal formative assessment, but higher stakes than a typical graded assignment**

**FIGURE 8.8**  (Continue)

# Thematic Unit Final Scope and Sequence

| Planning for a Sub-topic of the Theme | | |
|---|---|---|
| **Sub-Theme Title:** | Matter Recycling | |
| **Sub-Thematic Question 2:** | In what ways are all living things (including humans) part of the movement of matter through an ecosystem? | |

This sTQ frames the second half of the unit.

| Topic KDUs (By end of this topic, students shall…) | | |
|---|---|---|
| **Know:** | **Be able to Do:** | **Understand:** |
| • 1st and 2nd law of thermodynamics<br>• The importance of these molecules: C, H, N, O, P, S<br>• The basic structure of bacteria and fungi<br>• Decomposition process and examples of decomposers<br>• Homeostasis<br>• The difference between long-term and short-term carbon sinks<br>• Geochemical cycles (C, N, H20)<br>• How biomass is formed | • Design and complete a controlled experiment<br>• Follow the path of carbon and nitrogen as it cycles through the ecosystem<br>• Describe the interaction of organisms (humans/animals, plants, fungi, bacteria) to maintain ecosystem homeostasis | • The difference between matter and energy<br>• The role that living organisms play in cycling matter through ecosystem<br>• The role humans have on the cycling of carbon and nitrogen<br>• Explain how matter is transformed and transferred |

| Sub-Theme Formative Assessment(s): |
|---|
| • Essay quiz providing a response to the sub-theme question. Students will be prompted to use combination of diagrams and description to describe how matter recycles in an ecosystem through the living components (producers, consumers, and decomposers). To get an A, students will need to correctly use almost all of the appropriate terms correctly in describing the processes and also describe the role humans play in either the carbon or the nitrogen cycle. |

**FIGURE 8.8** (Continue)

# Thematic Unit Final Scope and Sequence

Step 3: Finalize guiding questions, standards, and sequence of formative assessments/learning activities. Each guiding question is listed separately in one data table.

*if using sTQs, then number GQs in the following manner:

**Numbering system matches the GQ to the larger sTQ.**

o The first GQ of sTQ 1 would be numbered 1.1, the second, 1.2 and so on.
o The GQs for the second sTQ would be numbered 2.1, 2.2, etc.
o If no sTQs, then GQs can be numbered sequentially, 1, 2, 3, etc.

| Planning for Specific Learning Activities: | | |
|---|---|---|
| **Guiding Question 1.1*:** | How does an ecosystem capture the sun's energy? | |
| **Question KDUs** | **Formative Assessment / Learning Activity** | **Standard Alignment** |
| • Photosynthesis process and equation (inputs and outputs) <br> • Set-up and complete controlled experiment | • Lab activity growing plants and measuring change in biomass <br> • Photosynthesis Review Sheet <br> • Reading assignment on Photosynthesis <br> • Journaling assignment about writing lab conclusions <br> • Weekly journaling | • 9.1.1.2.: Scientific method process <br> • 9.4.1.2.4: Cell organelles in photosynthesis |

**Notice these KDUs are taken directly from sTQ 1 KDUs**

| Planning for Specific Learning Activities: | | |
|---|---|---|
| **Guiding Question 1.2 *:** | How does an organism (such as yourself) burn and use energy? | |
| **Question KDUs** | **Formative Assessment / Learning Activity** | **Standard Alignment** |
| • Cell respiration process and equation (inputs and outputs) <br> • The difference between anaerobic and aerobic respiration (and examples of each) <br> • The importance of glucose and other sugars <br> • The production and use of ATP in the cell <br> • Set-up and complete controlled experiment | • Reading assignment on cell respiration <br> • Cell Respiration Review Sheet <br> • Collaborative assignment tracking energy in chemical bonds <br> • Weekly Journaling | • 9.4.1.2.4: Cell organelles in cell respiration |

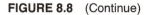

**FIGURE 8.8** (Continue)

# Thematic Unit Final Scope and Sequence

| Planning for Specific Learning Activities: | | |
| --- | --- | --- |
| **Guiding Question  1.3\*:** | In what ways do living things "work together to capture and use energy? | |
| **Question KDUs** | **Formative Assessment / Learning Activity** | **Standard Alignment** |
| • The interrelationship between photosynthesis and cell respiration in plants (and all other organisms) | • Lab activity measuring the carbon dioxide / oxygen changes in solution using snail and *elodea* plant <br><br> • Lab activity / hands-on activity making models of the molecule inputs and outputs of photosynthesis and cell respiration <br><br> • Weekly journaling | • 9.4.2.2.1" Use words and equations to differentiate between photosynthesis and cell respiration <br><br> • 9.4.2.2.2: Explain how energy is transformed and transferred |

**These will become the lesson plans**

**which will be aligned to the standards**

**combined to address the GQ**

| Planning for Specific Learning Activities: | | |
| --- | --- | --- |
| **Guiding Question 2.1\*:** | How does matter and energy interact in living things to make biomass? | |
| **Question KDUs** | **Formative Assessment / Learning Activity** | **Standard Alignment** |
| • Biomass <br> • The carbon cycle <br> • Human's impact on carbon cycle <br> • Apply concepts of photosynthesis and cell respiration to carbon cycle <br> • 1st and 2nd laws of thermodynamics | • Lab activity growing plants and measuring change in biomass <br><br> • Lab activity / research tracing the carbon cycle <br><br> • Whole class simulation activity modeling the movement of carbon in the ecosystem <br><br> • Carbon cycle reading assignment <br><br> • Weekly journaling | • 9.2.1.2.2 Explain how the rearrangement of atoms in a chemical reaction illustrates the law of conservation of mass <br><br> • 9.3.2.3.1: Trace cyclical movement of carbon... <br><br> • 9.3.4.1.2 Explain human activities affecting natural cycles <br><br> • 9.4.4.1.2: ecological risks/impact on ecosystem from human activity |

**FIGURE 8.8**   (Continue)

## Thematic Unit Final Scope and Sequence

| Planning for Specific Learning Activities: | | |
|---|---|---|
| **Guiding Question <u>2.2</u>\*:** | In what ways would an ecosystem change if there were no fungi and bacteria? | |
| **Question KDUs** | **Formative Assessment / Learning Activity** | **Standard Alignment** |
| • Fungi structure<br>• The nitrogen cycle<br>• Human's impact on nitrogen cycle<br>• Inter-relationship between fungi and plants | • Nitrogen cycle reading assignment<br>• Weekly journaling<br>• Fungi Structure and Function mini-research Assignment | • 9.3.2.3.1: Trace cyclical movement of nitrogen...<br>• 9.3.4.1.2 Explain human activities affecting natural cycles<br>• 9.4.4.1.2: ecological risks/impact on ecosystem from human activity |

| Planning for Specific Learning Activities: | | |
|---|---|---|
| **Guiding Question <u>2.3</u>\*:** | In what ways could the essential atoms and molecules in your body be the same ones that were in prehistoric plants and animals? | |
| **Question KDUs** | **Formative Assessment / Learning Activity** | **Standard Alignment** |
| • Role of fungus and bacteria as decomposers<br>• Process of decomposition | • Reading about Decomposition<br>• Mini research project on The Gaia Hypothesis<br>• Bottle Biology decomposition / School garden compost pile investigation | • 9.4.1.2.1: Cells are composed of primarily a few elements (CHNOPS) |

**FIGURE 8.8**   (Continue)

In the end, this really is a *linear* process containing many smaller iterative cycles of development. I have found to do this process successfully, and not get overwhelmed by the complexity of the iterative nature within the linear, organization is the key. This allows me, as the designer, to take on manageable design tasks while keeping the big picture in mind and not falling back into that activity trap. Using the provided worksheets and graphic organizers to track the essential questions, KDUs, summative, and formative assessments, and align content standards will provide you the scaffolding necessary to complete this design process so you can lead students on this learning journey.

## Communicating the Road Map of the Learning Journey with Students

My colleague likes to say there are people that see the whole forest, some who see the trees, and then some who see every individual leaf. I'm a forest guy. I gravitate to seeing the big picture and the connections between the trees to make up the forest (to continue the metaphor). My wife is definitely a leaf person. We make a good team. We've also discovered that we do best when driving a new route if she drives and I navigate. When she navigates, it seems I'm on a "need-to-know" basis. She'll tell me the next turn, but that's it. That's the detail that matters to her so that is all she's looking at in the directions or on the map. Drives me crazy! Being a forest person, I need to be able to visualize the entire route and the destination to be comfortable. We get there when she navigates, but I'm anxious the entire time. So, she drives and I navigate. I give her the details she needs when she needs them, and meanwhile I can gaze at the whole route on the map to my heart's content.

In curriculum planning, I have learned to trust my natural ability to see the forest, and then have developed very specific strategies, organizational tools, and rely on the collaboration of colleagues to force myself to see and attend to all of the details of the "leaves." You will have all kinds in your classroom—students who need to see the big picture first and struggle with the details, and students who will get lost in the leaves and never realize they are even walking in a forest. Your job is to provide a means for all your students to follow the path of inquiry you have worked so hard to develop and put in front of them— whether they need to see the whole route and need help attending to the details, or they couldn't care less about what comes next and are just focused on today's task, but require guidance to see the connection between the pieces and understanding the "big picture."

## Unit Road Map Table of Contents and Outline

Conventional wisdom in teaching is to provide students with as detailed list of what is expected in the coming unit of study, and to explicitly align all of the learning activities to the objectives or goals for the unit. Additionally, since the shift to accountability through standardized testing is pervasive throughout K-12 education, teachers often feel compelled to also explicitly align and communicate how all learning activities and assessments align to a content standard. I agree with the first aspect—students should have as clear of picture as to what is expected of them before they begin a task. However, I do not usually promote the second aspect for K-12 students. Your students don't care about the standards, and shouldn't, because the standards are not written for them. They are written for the teacher by a committee of experts. Therefore, for K-12 students, I leave the standards out of any documents I share with students outlining the learning journey of the unit.

Whatever tool you use to communicate this information to the students should be a living document and resource students will use throughout the unit—not just something they look at on the first day of the unit and then stuff into their backpack or locker to never see the light of day again. This resource, used effectively, will become the scaffolding for the most important, and often overlooked, aspect of the CCC learning cycle: confirming.

The first tool I like to use is the Unit Outline and Table of Contents. Figure 8.9: Biology Unit I Outline and Table of Contents, is an example of one for the high school biology unit shown previously. This is the first unit in course in which students are working toward the BIQ of "What is your role as an individual, and member of the human species, in the biological world?" As you read through these questions on the Table of Contents notice (if you can recall any of your high school biology) that the traditional topics of cellular activity of photosynthesis (how plants make glucose) and cell respiration (how all living things burn glucose) and the study of organisms such as bacteria is all done in the context of a larger topic that relates to a student's role in the cycling of energy and matter in an ecosystem. This is done purposefully to avoid the students feeling this is "random crap" that is only being learned for one purpose—to take a test. It is about themselves and their role, which is the context for all learning in this course.

As you review this example you can identify that the "outline" of the unit is communicated through the essential questions and the vocabulary. The end goal of the learning journey is communicated with a description of the summative assessment. The majority of the document, however, is left for the students to complete. Throughout the unit the students will do the following as a component of "sense making." First, and foremost, they will keep a table of contents of all the assignments completed and topics covered. They will record the score received and they will align that task or topic to one of the guiding questions. Additionally, they will record if corrections and additions were completed—more about the specifics of this process in the next chapter.

If the student properly completes this task, they will have accomplished two things. First, they will know how they are doing in the unit and the class. This is crucial as a means of empowering the student to own their progress in the course. Secondly, they will have a completed study guide for any quizzes or exams. They should know these three things: what

# Unit I Road Map: Outline and Table of Contents

| **Unit I:** Matter and Energy |
| --- |
| **Thematic Question:** In what ways do you participate in the flow of energy and matter on planet Earth? |

| **Sub-Thematic Question 1:** How are you a part of the Earth's ability to capture and cycle energy? | | | |
| --- | --- | --- | --- |
| **Guiding Questions:**<br>    1.   How does an ecosystem capture the sun's energy?<br>    2.   How does an organism (such as yourself) burn and use energy?<br>    3.   In what ways do living things "work together" to capture and use energy? | | | |
| **Vocabulary**<br>*Homeostasis, emergent properties, biome, biosphere, community, ecosystem, biotic, abiotic, Gaia Hypothesis, consumer, fusion, spectrum, carbohydrate, atom, thermodynamics ($1^{st}$ & $2^{nd}$), bonds, glucose, $CO_2$, $H_2O$, light energy, photons, chlorophyll, chloroplasts, photosynthesis, light reaction, Calvin cycle, ATP, NADPH, starch, polysaccharide, monosaccharide, disaccharide, respiration, aerobic respiration, anaerobic respiration, fermentation, glycolysis, mitochondria, Citric Acid cycle,* | | | |
| **Investigations, Activities, & Assignments** | **Guiding Question** | **Score** | **Corrections (Y or N)** |
|  |  |  |  |
|  |  |  |  |
|  |  |  |  |
|  |  |  |  |
|  |  |  |  |
|  |  |  |  |
|  |  |  |  |
|  |  |  |  |
|  |  |  |  |
|  |  |  |  |
|  |  |  |  |
|  |  |  |  |
|  |  |  |  |
|  |  |  |  |
|  |  |  |  |
|  |  |  |  |

**FIGURE 8.9**   Biology Unit I Table of Contents and Outline

# Unit I Road Map: Outline and Table of Contents

| **Sub-Thematic Question 2:** How is matter recycled through the ecosystem as a closed system? | | | |
|---|---|---|---|
| **Guiding Questions:** | | | |
| 1.   How does matter and energy interact in living things to make biomass? | | | |
| 2.   In what ways would an ecosystem change if there were no fungi and bacteria? | | | |
| 3.   In what ways could the essential atoms and molecules in your body be the same ones that were in prehistoric plants and animals? | | | |
| **Vocabulary** | | | |
| *chemical energy, matter, biomass, stoma, decomposers, bacteria, fungi, hyphae, mycelium, sac fungi (ascomycota), club fungi (basidiomycota), imperfect fungi, penicillin, nitrogen (N$_2$), potassium, phosphorous* | | | |
| **Investigations, Activities, & Assignments** | **Guiding Question** | **Score** | **Corrections (Y or N)** |
| | | | |
| | | | |
| | | | |
| | | | |
| | | | |
| | | | |
| | | | |
| | | | |
| | | | |
| | | | |
| | | | |
| | | | |
| | | | |

**Unit I STQ Formative Assessments:** Open-ended essay quiz answering the each sTQ utilizing and applying specific examples, terminology correctly.

**Thematic Question Summative Assessment:** Open-ended essay exam answering the TQ utilizing and applying specific examples, terminology correctly.

**Extended Investigation Personal Project:** Complete an in-depth investigation into one aspect of Unit I content with an individual personal project.

**FIGURE 8.9**   (Continue)

content is expected of them, how it aligns to the essential questions (which can be used as practice exam and quiz questions) and where to find the information (which assignments align to which questions). This then empowers the student to take ownership of their preparation and studying.

You might also have noticed that nowhere on this document are the content standards. This unit is aligned both to Minnesota K-12 science standards and also the Next Generation Science Standards. As stated before, standards are not written for students and they are not your curriculum. The standards should be in the service of you and your teaching, not the other way around. More about this in the next section as well. When teachers use the standards as the reason students are to learn a concept, they invalidate the importance of the concept for the children. The reason to learn becomes that they have to—and it isn't even their teacher that is telling them. Teachers may feel that this allies them and their students with a common purpose. But it isn't a very helpful common purpose. I believe this removes all of the purpose-motive from the learning process. In fact, I think it communicates that we learn this because the government says we have to—so let's just make the best of it. That isn't the way to foster the development of lifelong learners or participatory citizens in a healthy democracy. So keep the standards in the background and use them as a resource to guide your curriculum development.

The example provided (in that format) is clearly only appropriate for secondary students. This document, as designed would not be useful to elementary-aged students. The organizational skills and sense-making tasks that students do when using this document are, however, appropriate for all ages. Therefore, these tasks need to be completed utilizing tools that are not only age appropriate, but also subject/setting appropriate as well. A paper handout to physical education students might be impractical. As would a paper handout to second grade students. One simple solution is to utilize technology such as interactive white boards to project an age appropriate set of essential questions and complete the process of recording and aligning tasks collaboratively with students throughout the unit. Each day the shared document can grow, be modified, adapted, and added to by individuals coming up to the board and adding to it at the conclusion of each lesson in that unit of study.

## Unit Road Map—Learning Maps

The second component of the unit road map is a tool I have adapted from Jim Knight (2013) which he calls learning maps. I have used three different versions of learning maps, but all serve the same function. While the table of contents is a chronological list of topics, the learning map, however, is a thematic notation of topics and more importantly how those topics connect and lead to deep understanding of the unit thematic question.

The first example is a learning map designed as Knight (2013) directs (Figure 8.10). The advantage of this design is that it can be read at the beginning of the unit, literally, reading from the top down utilizing the line connectors to frame the whole unit for the students. This can be quite useful for students understanding the context of everything they are learning (or going to learn). The disadvantage is that it provides possibly too much structure for some students. This has the potential to limit how students use this tool and some end up simply listing again the topics, but at least into categories. While some may utilize this tool to make connections between topics and construct deeper meaning, others may just have a differently formatted table of contents. Notice also that the organization has 3 topics when the outline has 2 topics. This forces students to reorganize the items they put on the map in a slightly different manner, possibly revealing connections between ideas.

## Unit I Road Map – Learning Map

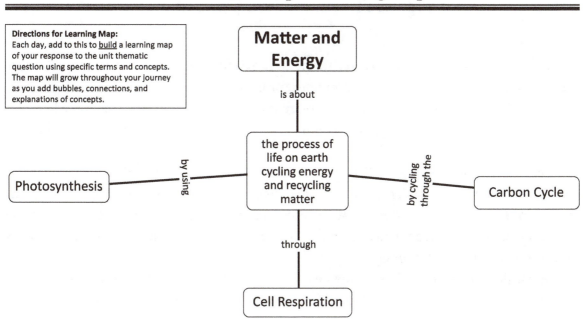

**FIGURE 8.10** Topical Learning Map

The second example (Figure 8.11) is more open-ended and the central focus of the map is the unit thematic question, not a paraphrased summary of the unit theme. In this example, the unit thematic question is in the middle with the sub-theme questions as additional bubbles. This still provides some structure for students, but the focus of what

## Unit I Road Map – Learning Map

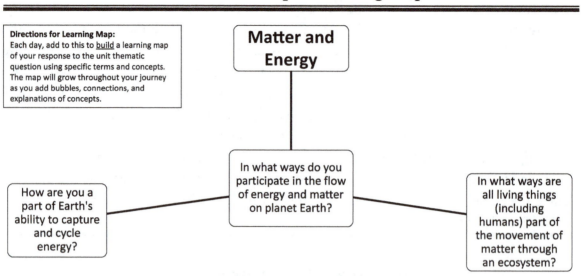

**Directions for Learning Map:**
Each day, add to this to <u>build</u> a learning map of your response to the unit thematic question using specific terms and concepts. The map will grow throughout your journey as you add bubbles, connections, and explanations of concepts.

**Matter and Energy**

In what ways do you participate in the flow of energy and matter on planet Earth?

How are you a part of Earth's ability to capture and cycle energy?

In what ways are all living things (including humans) part of the movement of matter through an ecosystem?

**FIGURE 8.11**   Essential Question Learning Map

students record is connected directly to the unit essential questions. If used with a unit without sTQs, then I would attach a bubble for each GQ to the central TQ. This format does sacrifice requiring students to categorize the content in a slightly new way from the Outline and Table of Contents, but does more directly connect the concepts to the specific questions.

The third variation (Figure 8.12) simply provides the unit thematic question in the center, thus giving the students the task (and freedom) to organize the concepts as they make sense of them. In my working with adult learners (undergraduate students in teacher education courses), I have found this option to be the one that is utilized the most effectively and completed the most thoroughly by students.

Regardless of the model used, the key to the road map is that two tools are provided for students. First is a record of the unit to serve as an organizational guide to the learning and second is a conceptual map of the how specific aspects of the content connect to create a theme. Completed thoroughly, the student ends the unit of study with a literal rough draft for a response to the thematic question. Whether the assessment used is a traditional exam built around the essential questions, an essay answering *the* thematic question, or a project-based/performance assessment aligned to the thematic question, the student should have a resource to approach those tasks with confidence that they

# Unit I Road Map – Learning Map

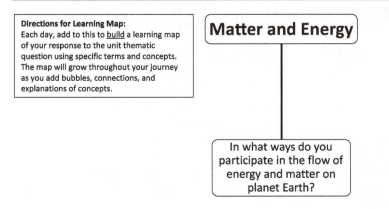

**Directions for Learning Map:**
Each day, add to this to <u>build</u> a learning map of your response to the unit thematic question using specific terms and concepts. The map will grow throughout your journey as you add bubbles, connections, and explanations of concepts.

**Matter and Energy**

In what ways do you participate in the flow of energy and matter on planet Earth?

**FIGURE 8.12** Thematic Question Learning Map

know what will be expected of them in terms of content knowledge. The summative assessment should not be a surprise or catch the students with a trick question. Save that for bar trivia.

These tools would need modification to be age appropriate for younger students and for students in a nonclassroom setting such as a physical education class. In both of these cases, it might be more practical to have a class version of these documents to record what work has been done on one document (creating an outline) and make the connections on the other document (creating the concept map). This could then be done collaboratively with students each day to process and complete the learning cycle for the day—possibly as a document on an interactive white board so students could actively participate in adding components to the document, moving them around and drawing connections. This could also be done with a digital format like a "prezi" presentation that allows for multiple layers of depth of information. The students could continue to dig deeper into a topic and add new layers as you zoom in throughout the unit. This could also be done "analog" on a large bulletin board, white board, or with sticky notes. This overtly big and visual means of recording and connecting topics could also be done with older students as well, serving as a means of whole-class sense making throughout the unit and especially at the end of the unit. If utilized effectively, students should be able to see how *everything* connects and has a purpose to be studied and learned.

# Appendix 1

## Thematic Unit Scope and Sequence – The Scope

Step1 - Briefly describe the topic or theme to be explored by students in this unit of study:

_____

_____

_____

_____

Step 2 - Identify the grade level of study and potential length of unit:

Grade Level:_____   Length of Unit:_____

Step 3 - First draft of thematic question:

_____

_____

Step 4 - Means by which the student will demonstrate/put into use culminating understandings for the unit theme:

_____

_____

_____

_____

Step 5 - Identify that which students will have to Know, Do, and Understand to complete the summative task and demonstrate understanding:

**Know** (vocabulary terms; single concepts; observable facts; rote-learned information; names and dates; formulas; etc.):

_____

_____

_____

_____

_____

**Do** (skills, procedural steps, application of rules, etc.):

_____

_____

_____

_____

**Understand** (Application of concepts; connection between "know" items; cause and effect, etc.):

_____

_____

_____

_____

_____

# Appendix 2

## Thematic Unit Scope and Sequence – Unpacking Standards

Unpacking the standards is a step that can be done as a means to refine any of the essential questions: BIQ, TQ, sTQ, or GQ. It therefore can be done at any point in the design process when it becomes necessary for further fleshing out and refining the content of the thematic unit.

| Step 1 - List the standards: | Step 2 - Identify the key nouns and verbs of each standard: |
| --- | --- |
| | |

Step 3 - Revising / Writing Questions:

Use the identified nouns and verbs to initially write (during scope or theme-chunking phase of unit design) or revise the essential questions for the thematic unit during finalizing phase of unit design.

# Appendix 3

## Thematic Unit Scope and Sequence – Theme Chunking

Step 1 – Using Unit Scope KDUs identify potential topical groupings of the KDUs:

Step 2 – Convert the topics into essential questions (potential sTQ and GQ questions):

| Sub-topics for the unit | Draft Questions: |
| --- | --- |
|  |  |

# Appendix 4

## Thematic Unit Scope and Sequence – GQ Draft KDUs

| Guiding Question: | |
| --- | --- |
| **K**now: | |
| Be able to **D**o: | |
| **U**nderstand: | |

| Guiding Question: | |
| --- | --- |
| **K**now: | |
| Be able to **D**o: | |
| **U**nderstand: | |

# Appendix 5

## Thematic Unit Final Scope and Sequence

Step 1 – Finalize Unit Scope:

| Planning for a Thematic Inquiry | | |
|---|---|---|
| **Unit Title:** | | |
| **Thematic Question:** | | |

| **Unit KDUs** (By end of unit, students shall…) | | |
|---|---|---|
| Know: | Be able to **D**o: | Understand: |
| • | • | • |

| **Unit Summative Assessment Idea and Description:** |
|---|
| |

# Thematic Unit Final Scope and Sequence

Step 2 (if necessary) – Finalize unit sub-Thematic Questions Scope:

| Planning for a Sub-topic of the Theme | | |
|---|---|---|
| **Sub-Theme Title:** | | |
| **Sub-Thematic Question 1:** | | |
| **Topic KDUs** (By end of this topic, students shall…) | | |
| **K**now: | Be able to **D**o: | **U**nderstand: |
| • | • | • |
| **Sub-Theme Formative Assessment(s):** | | |
| | | |

| Planning for a Sub-topic of the Theme | | |
|---|---|---|
| **Sub-Theme Title:** | | |
| **Sub-Thematic Question 2:** | | |
| **Topic KDUs** (By end of this topic, students shall…) | | |
| **K**now: | Be able to **D**o: | **U**nderstand: |
| • | • | • |
| **Sub-Theme Formative Assessment(s):** | | |
| | | |

## Thematic Unit Final Scope and Sequence

| Planning for a Sub-topic of the Theme | | |
|---|---|---|
| **Sub-Theme Title:** | | |
| **Sub-Thematic Question 3:** | | |
| **Topic KDUs** (By end of this topic, students shall…) | | |
| Know: | Be able to **Do**: | Understand: |
| • | • | • |
| **Sub-Theme Formative Assessment(s):** | | |
| | | |

# Thematic Unit Final Scope and Sequence

Step 3: Finalize guiding questions, standards, and sequence of formative assessments/learning activities. Each guiding question is listed separately in one data table.

*if using sTQs, then number GQs in the following manner:

- o   The first GQ of sTQ 1 would be numbered 1.1, the second, 1.2 and so on.
- o   The GQs for the second sTQ would be numbered 2.1, 2.2, etc.
- o   If no sTQs, then GQs can be numbered sequentially, 1, 2, 3, etc.

| Planning for Specific Learning Activities: | | |
|---|---|---|
| **Guiding Question _____ *:** | | |
| **Question KDUs** | **Formative Assessment / Learning Activity** | **Standard Alignment** |
| | | |

| Planning for Specific Learning Activities: | | |
|---|---|---|
| **Guiding Question _____ *:** | | |
| **Question KDUs** | **Formative Assessment / Learning Activity** | **Standard Alignment** |
| | | |

## Thematic Unit Final Scope and Sequence

| Planning for Specific Learning Activities: | | |
|---|---|---|
| **Guiding Question \_\_\_\_\*:** | | |
| **Question KDUs** | **Formative Assessment / Learning Activity** | **Standard Alignment** |
| | | |

| Planning for Specific Learning Activities: | | |
|---|---|---|
| **Guiding Question \_\_\_\_\*:** | | |
| **Question KDUs** | **Formative Assessment / Learning Activity** | **Standard Alignment** |
| | | |

| Planning for Specific Learning Activities: | | |
|---|---|---|
| **Guiding Question \_\_\_\_\*:** | | |
| **Question KDUs** | **Formative Assessment / Learning Activity** | **Standard Alignment** |
| | | |

## Thematic Unit Final Scope and Sequence

| Planning for Specific Learning Activities: | | |
|---|---|---|
| Guiding Question ____*: | | |
| Question KDUs | Formative Assessment / Learning Activity | Standard Alignment |
| | | |

| Planning for Specific Learning Activities: | | |
|---|---|---|
| Guiding Question ____*: | | |
| Question KDUs | Formative Assessment / Learning Activity | Standard Alignment |
| | | |

| Planning for Specific Learning Activities: | | |
|---|---|---|
| Guiding Question ____*: | | |
| Question KDUs | Formative Assessment / Learning Activity | Standard Alignment |
| | | |

# Part 4

## Student-Centered Instruction

In Part 4, we finally get to lesson planning! Most new teachers or students learning to become teachers want to jump into lesson planning right away. Creating quality, inquiry-based, minds-on lesson is crucial to being a great teacher. However, I put this at the end to impress upon you still further the importance of lesson plans purposefully fitting into a unit built around a bigger idea. Therefore, part four starts by revisiting the CCC learning cycle, now applying that structure to lesson planning within the context of a unit plan. We then dig deeper into the actual writing of lesson plans and a resource chapter of teaching methods and techniques to utilize in the creation of student-centered instruction.

# Chapter 9

# Enacting Instruction Based on Constructivist Learning Theory

The term constructivism is used to label a philosophy of education, a learning theory, and also a pedagogical methodology (Colburn 2000). That label has now become most widely used as a synonym for any "student-centered" philosophy or methodology that places student activity at the center of the learning as opposed to the teacher in the active role and students observing and listening to the teacher. Those not proficient in teaching from a constructivist paradigm may consider it too idealistic, inefficient, difficult, or relativistic to be practically applied, expecting it to result in an unorganized or unstructured classroom environment and curriculum. Constructivist teaching is often associated with curriculum built on student-driven questions and interests which does not mesh with the current standards-based climate of education—rooted firmly in an essentialism philosophy of education. To the extreme, a constructivist-based classroom could be one in which all learning emerges from student-generated questions. However, constructivism broken down to the fundamentals of constructivism as a learning theory, is really about how the brain acquires, stores, and utilizes new information. The learner is not simply receiving information, but restructuring existing schema. The learner is adapting existing cognitive structures through his or her actions grounded in objects and the environment with which the learner is interacting (Yilmaz, Constructivism: Its Theoretical Underpinnings, Variations, and Implications for Classroom Instruction Spring 2008). Making meaning occurs when the learner makes multiple links between new information and/or experiences and his or her existing information and/or experiences (Michael 2006). I would argue that any teaching methodology that facilitates learning in this manner is constructivism.

From this paradigm, constructivism can be applied to any subject and any classroom. Still, to many teachers, shifting away from teacher-centered, didactic instruction and assessment is simply too daunting. However, this shift does not have to be overwhelming if one uses the Consider, Construct, Confirm (CCC) learning cycle to design lessons, units, even whole courses that hold true to constructivism.

# Digging Deeper into the CCC Learning Cycle

First, to better understand constructivism applied to lesson design, let's begin with this example. Consider this question: From where does a tree get most of the molecules that make up its mass—the soil or the air? If your answer was "the soil," you would be in agreement with most people. A study of MIT graduates interviewed in the video series *Minds of their Own* confirmed this answer (Schneps 1995). This answer is wrong, however. Most of the mass of a tree (carbon atoms) comes from carbon dioxide the plant absorbs from the atmosphere during photosynthesis. Many people have this misconception because from their lived experience they have created this hypothesis: if you put plants in soil, then water them, they get bigger. This leads them to the theoretical conclusion that plants must be pulling their mass from the soil. What we as learners *truly* know is what we learned from our lived experience. That is knowledge we *own* even if it is wrong. Knowledge told to us even if it is correct, but not experienced, is often only *rented* for a short period of time.

This prior knowledge is difficult to change. Even something totally foreign to the learner gets equated to a lived experience in the form of a metaphor. It is the lived experience that generates knowledge that is owned. I am confident that at some point during their schooling, the misinformed MIT students were told the right answer about photosynthesis and where plants get carbon dioxide, but it did not coincide with their lived experiences. It was also possibly presented to them outside of any bigger context, so it was an isolated factoid of information. After the test, the taught knowledge faded away and the lived experience knowledge came back—like mildew bleeding back through a fresh coat of paint on a damp bathroom wall. Teaching in a process that incorporates the learning cycle can help to mitigate this problem and help students turn that *rented* knowledge into *owned* knowledge. The context, and interconnection between individual bits of information with existing knowledge is necessary for making meaning and the retention of information for the long term, or *owning* it. This is in contrast with information learned simply by rote. Rote knowledge tends to be quickly forgotten, unless greatly rehearsed. Additionally, the learner doesn't have the broader integration of the knowledge to allow him or her to correct faulty ideas (Novak and Canas 2008).

As introduced in Chapter 1, the learning cycle (Figure 9.1) begins with the *consider* phase of a lesson or sequence of lessons. This might involve thinking prompts, engaging stories, questioning, demonstrations, etc. This is nothing new in teaching, however, one aspect of the consider phase often overlooked is purposefully engaging students in exposing their prior knowledge about a topic. Too often, teachers skip this step and simply use the attention grabber to introduce a topic and tell the students the objective. Without exposing the prior knowledge, you have embarked on that linear teaching equation described in Chapter 1, and have eliminated the possibility of the necessary feedback loop to complete the learning cycle.

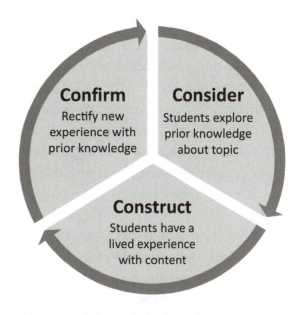

The learning cycle continues with the *construct* phase of the lesson. This is what

**FIGURE 9.1**    CCC Cycle Applied to Lesson Planning

you think of as the actual activity, lecture, demonstration, etc.—what most would consider the entirety of "teaching." But teaching is more than just the activity of the teacher "teaching" something to students. The essential question to ask yourself as the teacher when designing the activity is this: In what way can you provide situations for students to have a lived experience to deepen understanding and build meaning? Deep understanding requires authentic tasks (Fosnot 1996). Methods that actively engage the students are practices such as cooperative learning, authentic learning, project-based learning, minds-on learning, etc. I use the phrase minds-on instead of hands-on. Minds-on can be hands-on, but hands-on is not by default minds-on. Minds-on requires the student to ask questions, ponder, solve problems, and so on. Hands-on can be simply following chemistry lab instructions but not knowing why. It might be active and engaging because there might be the potential for an explosion of some kind (what more could a teenage chemistry student want?), but doesn't require any construction of meaning. To construct knowledge students need to become active learners who, with the facilitation of the teacher, engage in scholarly participation in the learning process (Gordon 2009). For this to occur, this requires more than passive reception of information.

The last phase of the learning cycle, the *confirm* phase, is the feedback loop that completes the cycle. During this phase the teacher purposefully guides students in wrestling with the cognitive dissonance between what they thought initially about a topic and what they experienced in the construct phase. New events, experiences, and understandings are perturbations, causing disequilibrium for the learner which he or she needs to resolve for true learning to occur (Yilmaz 2008). If they began with correct assumptions, these were deepened and confirmed. If they began with incomplete information, more was added filling in gaps in understanding. If they began with misconceptions, the act of dealing with this difference is when the learning is cemented and the student transitions from renting information to owning the information. If you do not facilitate this last portion of the learning cycle, taking them back to a comparison to their initial ideas, the cycle is never completed. If the confirming phase is skipped then often the student's experienced knowledge wins out in the brain in the long run. This is what happened with the MIT graduates regarding plant mass.

For a classroom to look, sound, and feel "constructivist" it needs to be student-centered at least 70% of the time which includes providing experiences such as learning experiences from multiple perspectives, realistic and relevant contexts, student voice in the learning process, learning embedded in social experiences, multiple modes of presenting what is learned and student metacognition about what was learned and how it was learned (Dagar 2016).

I'll use an example to show how a common traditional lesson can be easy adjusted to fit into the learning cycle. Recall from your high school biology, a typical cell lab almost everyone completed during which you looked at a simple plant cell such as the aquatic plant called *Elodea*. Constructed in the linear fashion. This lesson might proceed as follows. Students enter class and the teacher tells them they will learn about the cells that make up all living things. She then to tells them about cells, shows some pictures of cells, and demonstrates how to get the sample, make the slide, and operate the microscope. Students then go and do the lab activity she just described. As they do the lab, they draw pictures in their lab notebook. Often these pictures look more like the diagram used to introduce the lab than the actual object in the microscope (Figure 9.2). I know this because I've graded many of these labs. At the end, the teacher asks, "Did you all see the cell and the nucleus, the cell membrane and cell wall?" They answer, "Yes." If she asked if they could see the mitochondrion like the one in the picture from the book, many would say yes to this as well. They can't see these by the way, unless using better equipment than in most high school

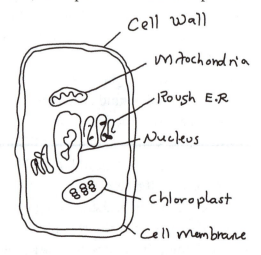

**FIGURE 9.2**   Student Drawing of Plant Cell

science labs. They think they should have seen these parts, so they either trick themselves into thinking the saw it, or believing the correct drawing in their lab notebook should contain this part of the cell, they add it to their drawing based on the diagram from their textbook to make sure that they have the right answer. In this example the teacher has used what I call the, *tell, show, and re-tell* model of teaching. We've gotten really good at this. I was really good at it for a long time teaching high school biology. It is a really good model for short term memorization of the right answer for a test. I produced a lot of good test takers throughout my career. I don't want to even think about how little those students today can remember and apply the biology I taught to their everyday living and decisions.

Now let's consider this same exact lab procedure within the structure of the CCC learning cycle. Instead of telling the students what they will see, the teacher begins with probing questions in order to access the students' prior knowledge about what makes up living things and what is inside those things (McTighe and Wiggins 2013). Then she sends them on their way to experience seeing what those things might be. The actual lab procedure is exactly the same as the first example. However, instead of sending the students into the lab already having stored the expected answer in their short-term memory, she is sending them into the lab activity with their pre-conceived answer, based on their prior lived experience. It's okay if they are starting with the wrong conception of what the cell will look like. During the lab, the teacher is still actively involved, making sure students are seeing actual cells and not air bubbles for example. Since the students don't know what they are supposed to see, they aren't going to guess at what they think the teacher wants them to see and then draw that in their lab notebook. Instead they will draw what they honestly see (Figure 9.3). What they see might be very similar to the expected answer, or it may not. It *is* authentic however. So, when do they actually learn the right answer about cells? After students complete the active learning portion of the lesson is when the teacher now steps in and actually *teaches*. Though of course, by facilitating their inquiry, she was teaching all along.

The confirm phase involves the teacher providing a means for the student to compare what he saw in

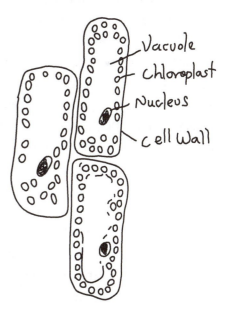

**FIGURE 9.3** Authentic Student Cell Drawing

the microscope to what he or she already thought he or she knew about cells. Instead of lecturing up front about the cells, the teacher lectures on the back end of the lesson. Instead of taking notes on a blank piece of paper, the students then make corrections and additions on their lab report they completed while looking at the cells. In this process the student triangulates (Figure 9.4) the new knowledge with accepted scientific answer about cells (provided by the teacher

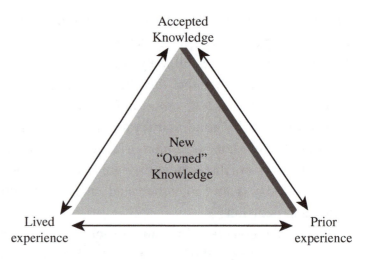

**FIGURE 9.4**   Triangulation of "Owned" Knowledge

or the student's own research or reading of a textbook) with his or her prior knowledge and his or her own lived experience in the lab. By doing this, the teacher is completing the learning cycle and the students are constructing new meaning about the nature of cells based on a new lived experience. This type of reflective activity, built into the curriculum as a normal part of the classroom procedure, is essential for making meaning and construction of knowledge (Kumar 2006). With this step completed, the new knowledge has a better chance of replacing the prior knowledge and therefore becoming the student's new perception of cells they now own instead of renting for the upcoming test. In the end, the activity did not change, but the setup and the closing of the activity were changed, and the traditional lecture was changed from an act of the teacher dispensing information to a discussion and processing of the students' experiences and then comparing and contrasting their observations with the information the teacher presents. The hands-on activity has now been transformed into a minds-on activity as an integral part of the learning cycle. This final segment of the cycle is crucial. Constructing knowledge involves students actively, and purposefully, reconciling the cognitive dissonance between past experiences and new experiences, preferably, in collaboration with other learners or the teacher (Splitter 2008). During that moment when the students recognizes a cell structure they saw under the microscope and labeled in their diagram as the same as the one in the diagram labeled by an expert scientist, they now own it as if they discovered it themselves. That's the "I get it" moment all teachers look for.

If you have truly learned something to the point in which you *own* it, you have participated in constructivism. In the end, this is how the brain works. If you have knowledge that is deep enough to apply and use, you must have constructed meaning. Our top students do this naturally in the subjects that interest them. If you are a teacher, you probably did it also as a student, especially in the subject area you have now specialized in as a teacher. These students (and maybe you as well) were, in essence, teacher proof. All they might require is guidance to tell them what to learn. Once pointed in the right direction, these students often can listen to a lecture, read the text, and then create their own visualizations, metaphors, mnemonic devices, and so on, to move that knowledge from short-term memory and incorporate it into their worldview. That is constructing meaning. That is constructivism. Our top students do this whether or not we provide them a structured means to do so. Unfortunately, didactic, traditional teaching only works for those self-motivated students—those that are already thinking through the lens of that subject. For me it was biology. Many of the rest of the students are bored with that subject (and maybe all of school), and therefore, at best memorize what they need to so they can rent the information long enough for a test and then forget it and move on. No harm, no foul. I think we can do better.

Teaching using a learning cycle of *consider, construct,* and *confirm*, is one way that you can provide for *all* of your students a structured curriculum that gives them *all* the opportunity to make meaning—not just the top 10% to 20%. In the end, that is our job as teachers. To make it as easy as possible for as many of our students as possible to learn as much as possible to the highest level as possible.

# Chapter 10

# Finally, Lesson Planning

"**P**roper **p**reparation **p**revents **p**oor **p**erformance." These are the five P's as quoted by my colleague and friend, Dr. Linda Colburn. No matter how engaging, entertaining, and creative you are, you cannot successfully "wing it" and be a great teacher. You might get by or even have moments of brilliance, but let's set our sights a little higher, shall we? Of course some days you will wing it out of necessity and some days when you wing it, it will be an inspired success. Certainly you should allow the curriculum to emerge and you should be willing to follow the lead of your students' interests, current events, and so on. I've worked with some gifted teachers who could have been great teachers, but were just okay because they did not purposefully plan out their units and lessons. They had moments of brilliance where substantial, inspired, learning happened. But without purposeful planning, these moments were ephemeral, came and went, and often could not be repeated or captured again. Wouldn't it be better if you set yourself up to have multiple lessons that followed a coherent scope and sequence and provided your students opportunity after opportunity for inspired learning to occur?

## Backward Design Applied to Lesson Planning

A lesson plan is the planning for a single learning segment that is completed in one sitting. For secondary teachers, a class period would have a single lesson plan. For elementary teachers, a lesson plan will be the learning segment completed in one sitting about a topic. This could be a few minutes long to an entire school day. Others might consider the five learning segments spread out over five days to complete a learning objective as one lesson with multiple parts or days. I prefer not to, as doing this interrupts the learning cycle. I believe it is important to include in each learning segment some aspect of the three phases of the learning cycle, in that one session with students, even if they are going to continue exploring the topic the next day. Cliffhangers may be good for TV shows, but I don't think so for lesson plans. However, there is no reason the confirming for day one of the lesson cannot get the students thinking about the continuation of that topic that will occur the next day.

Planning lessons, like planning units from a constructivist learning theory foundation, requires backward planning. In unit planning, if you do not begin your planning with the final outcome and assessment in mind, it is nearly impossible to accurately anticipate how long a unit will take, where your students will struggle, or conversely, breeze through the content. Without knowing these two things prior to beginning a unit, the scope and sequence of instruction might wander and meander through the topic, feel disconnected and random to the student, and also create a situation where you cannot anticipate student needs, and therefore, do not provide adequate scaffolding for the learning. The same goes for lesson planning.

The lesson planning process should begin with alignment to one or more guiding question(s) from your unit plan. If not, why are students being asked to complete the lesson? I do not advocate students being burdened with knowing which mandated content standard the lesson may align to—that's your burden as the teacher—but they should be aware of which essential question from the bigger picture of the unit the lesson aligns to. Depending on the nature of the lesson, it's perfectly acceptable to have students begin the lesson with an attempt at answering the guiding question. This, therefore, requires that *you* know the answer to the question! Before designing the lesson activity, you must identify what students will demonstrate at the end of the lesson, to what level they will demonstrate it, and also in what form they will demonstrate their knew knowledge.

Now that you know the question and the answer, this outlines your goal for the lesson. This is different than a learning objective. The goal of the lesson is the central focus of the lesson and part of the context and rationale for the lesson. The context and rationale are the specifics of why students are completing this lesson. It is also an explanation of why they are completing it when they are in the sequence of the unit as well as a description as to how the learning will happen. If the goal of the lesson is for students to memorize steps to completing a task, such as solving a math equation, using a piece of science equipment such as a microscope, or identifying state capitals, a student designed, then, in-depth project-based learning experiences would not be the correct choice. Instead, routinized practice might be the correct approach for such a task. However, keep in mind that the end goal of student proficiency must have a purpose that aligns to a guiding question which builds toward understanding a larger essential question (TQ or sTQ). If not, then why would you take the time to have students memorize that task? Conversely, a goal of students developing deep understanding about the reasoning behind a pattern of historical events, application of a science process or topic, discovering and making sense of an abstract concept or theory, or other such higher order cognitive tasks, might require in-depth student discussion, research, and synthesis best completed through project-based learning activities. Your context and rationale for the lesson should make the case for why you are teaching the lesson the way you are.

With the end goal of the lesson identified, you can use the following three questions to guide the development of lessons to lead the students through the learning:

1. In what way will students uncover their prior knowledge about the topic?
2. In what way will students actively explore and experience the content and skill of the topic?
3. In what way will students make sense of their new experience and build understanding?

Teachers commonly focus instruction entirely on the middle question, therefore, only planning what they will do to teach the students—what the teacher has to cover in the amount of time they have. In addition to not being student-centered, it also results in the teacher skipping the first step entirely and jumping right into telling the students the infor-mation. The lesson, be it an active-learning experience such as a lab activity, or a passive-learning experience such as a lecture, often then concludes when the time allotted for the lesson expires and students turn in the completed assignment, take a quiz, exit ticket, or other formative assessment which the teacher grades to determine how well the student learned the content. The end.

The mistake made in this scenario (beyond the complete absence of the consider phase) is the disassociation of the learning activity and the formative assessment. While at times the lesson might conclude with a specific formative assessment that is not a part of the learning activity of the lesson, such as an exit ticket at the conclusion of a class discussion, it is crucial that everything that students complete throughout lesson *is* a formative assess-ment. Any activity that is providing you (and the student) feedback regarding their progress with the content is a formative assessment. Completing a Know, Wonder, Learn (KWL) chart at the beginning of the lesson, pre-writing, opening discussion, or any other activity to explore prior knowledge is a formative assessment. Participating in an organized class discussion in which you as the teacher makes note of who participates and what they say is a formative assessment. Moving among the students throughout a lab activity and noting, which students are excelling or struggling with the task is a formative assessment. Students comparing and contrasting understandings developed from a discussion, a lab activity, or other such task, as a means of doing "sense-making" at the end of the lesson serves as formative assessment.

While the day's activity may conclude with students turning in an assignment, recognizing that purposefully utilizing all student activity throughout the lesson as formative assessment will not only focus your attention on the important aspect of the lesson, it may also increase efficiency. You might discover that you already have the data you need to determine if the students are understanding the concept without having them complete an additional, separate, assessment after completing the lesson. This can help you break free of the shackles of telling students information, having them work with it, and then separately assessing their progress.

Most of the time, this formative assessment data collected during the learning process is informal and not a "graded" activity recorded in the gradebook. Often times, however, the completed assignment, lab sheet, questions, discussion summary, etc., is something you will collect at the end of the lesson to review and use to inform the next day's lesson. You might grade this for accuracy, participation only, or simply review. It is important to realize that the learning cycle is not complete just because the students turned in an assignment. You might still be in the construct phase and the confirm phase will occur the next day when you return graded work to the students. This does not mean you will entirely skip the confirm phase on day one of that topic. What will happen before they turn in the assignment to do some of the actions of confirming such as comparing what they have learned so far with a peer, evaluate their work thus far, or begin to contrast it with prior knowledge? Then, when you return graded work to students with prompts to correct errors and fill in gaps in the content, and then provide them time to work collaboratively with peers to "make sense" of the content is when they will finish the act of *confirming*. Through the act of correcting errors, filling gaps, and/or making connections to other aspects of the unit, that formal formative assessment now has functioned to cause another round of sense-making and served not only as an assessment tool, but also as a continuation of the learning experience and a confirming activity.

Certainly, formal formative assessments, such as a quiz, which check for specific concept understanding, at a specific point in the learning process, will still need to occur as well. This is crucial for recording data that tracks the student's progress through a unit of study. But this graded formative assessment should occur after students have been properly introduced to new concepts, had time to explore, experience, and practice with those topics, and had the opportunity to complete the entire learning cycle with that concept. In the context of building understanding toward the guiding question aligned to this particular lesson, the students have completed the learning cycle. However, recall that the entire unit is also follows the learning cycle. In the context of building understanding toward the thematic question, the quiz is still a step toward the student building proficiency with a new concept. In this context, it is entirely appropriate to consider the graded task such as a worksheet, lab activity, writing assignment, etc., still as part of the *construct* phase of the lesson which still requires confirming. Even a formally graded quiz that was intended purely to check for understanding and high stakes enough that it is recorded permanently in the gradebook as a record of progress, still might require *additional* confirming when handed back to the student. These formal formative assessments should still be instructive for the student, and not just handed back and stuffed to the bottom of their backpack. These are still checkpoints along the way on their journey to answering the thematic question with the summative assessment.

No matter the specific learning activity, be it something traditionally considered more student-centered such as a student-designed project, to a very traditional worksheet, the key to students utilizing the experience to *own* their own knowledge requires that activity is part of a lesson plan and also a unit encompassing all three aspects of the Consider, Construct, Confirm (CCC) learning cycle.

## Lesson Plan Template

An online search will turn up countless examples of templates for writing a lesson plan. A lesson plan template provides scaffolding for a beginning teacher to ensure that he or she doesn't miss anything in the planning process. Figure 10.1 is an example of a lesson plan template that I like beginning teachers to use. Take some time to read the template and look carefully at the bullet point instructions for each component. This basic Lesson Plan Template has two sections: **Information about the Lesson** and **Lesson Plan Details**. Two components of the first section worth highlighting here are the *Central Focus & Context and Rationale* and the *Misconceptions* components. The first is really getting at the goal and purpose of the lesson. However, one component often overlooked is to purposefully plan not only when you teach a lesson on a concept, but also just as important is to purposefully think about the way it should be taught and basing that decision on sound learning theory and research. It is also very valuable to dig deep into the *Misconceptions* component, as the deeper you explore this before planning the lesson, the more likely you are to include aspects of the lesson that purposefully allow students to uncover and then dispel misconceptions about that concept. Also, review the italicized prompts in the **Lesson Plan Details** section and as you do, identify how those components fit the broad description of the CCC cycle phases described in Chapter 9.

# Lesson Plan Template

| Instructor: | Subject Area: | Grade: | Date: |
| --- | --- | --- | --- |

### Information about the Lesson

Complete each section below to provide the background information about the lesson. Use italicized prompts as a guide but do not answer each separately and explicitly. Type the background information in each section **below** the dotted line.

**Central Focus & Context/Rationale:**

- *Describe the big idea or the central focus of the lesson.*
- *Explain why this lesson is taught when it is in the curriculum and use research and theory to explain why it is being taught the way it is planned.*

**Learning Objective(s)**

- *Using observable language with measurable verbs, identify what students will know and/or be able to do by the end of the lesson.*

**Guiding Question**

- *List the guiding question that frames this lesson.*

**Materials Needed:**

- *List (as if writing for a sub) the materials needed for this lesson.*

**Misconceptions:**

- *Identify common misconceptions you anticipate students may have prior to the lesson about the concepts addressed in this lesson.*

**FIGURE 10.1** Lesson Plan Template

**Prior Academic Learning and Prerequisite Skills:**

- *List the prior knowledge and skills that you anticipate students to have and need to be successful in the lesson.*

**MN Content Standard(s):**

- *List all standards addressed within the content of this lesson.*

## Lesson Plan Details

- Provide a detailed description of what the teacher and students do to complete the lesson objectives written in **outline/bullet-point** format.
- Include instructional strategies, learning tasks, key questions, transitions, student support, student grouping, and **assessment (informal and formal) strategies throughout the lesson**.
- The italicized prompts are reminders of what qualities should exist in these plans. Do **not** answer each prompt as if it is a question.

**Lesson Introduction:** *This is the* **"consider"** *phase which sets the stage, engages the learner while activating prior knowledge and experiences. Make sure your plan accounts for these aspects of a constructivist lesson:*

- *Sets purpose and piques curiosity through the use of prompts and/or guiding questions.*
- *Activates and assesses student prior knowledge and/or experiences.*
- *Introduces and explains the learning task.*

| Minutes | Description of Activity |
|---------|-------------------------|
|         |                         |

**Learning Activities:** *This is the* **"construct"** *phase when students build on prior knowledge and experiences thus building new knowledge and skills through new learning experiences. Make sure your plan accounts for these aspects of a constructivist lesson:*

- *Students are actively engaged with the content knowledge/skills to make meaning as the lesson is relevant to the student's personal experiences, cultural background, or where they live (called community assets in Ed-TPA).*
- *Models skills and allows for practice of skills.*
- *Students engaged with one another to explore the topic.*
- *Supports a variety of learners.*

**FIGURE 10.1** (Continue)

| Minutes | Description of Activities |
|---------|---------------------------|
|         |                           |

**Lesson Conclusion:** *This is the* **"confirm"** *phase when students* <u>complete informal and/or formal assessments</u> *that require them to reflect on what was learned, compare new knowledge and skills to prior knowledge, correct misconceptions, and check for understanding. Make sure your plan accounts for these aspects of a constructivist lesson:*

- *Students show and share what they have learned with you and other students.*
- *Students compare new experience to prior knowledge and experiences.*
- *Students correct any misconceptions.*
- *Students extend ideas and check for understanding.*

| Minutes | Description of Activities |
|---------|---------------------------|
|         |                           |

**Citations:**

- *List any sources used for the lesson idea or activity?*
- *What research, researchers, and/or theories could be used to support the content or methodology of the lesson?*

**FIGURE 10.1** (Continue)

I want to also call your attention to Figure 10.2, the additional components added to the lesson plan template to make it an **Enhanced Lesson Plan Template**. You will notice that this lesson plan template includes additional sections on assessment, academic language, and differentiation. These three components of the Enhanced Lesson Plan, are not additional activities the teacher or student does in some lessons (the ones written using this template) and not in others. These components are behind the scenes aspects of teaching that a great teacher is thinking about and planning for with *every* lesson. Ideally, a teacher would use the Enhanced Lesson Plan for every lesson to ensure proper and purposeful planning for all aspects of the lesson and the issues and situations required for student success with the lesson. I use the Enhanced Lesson Plan as a tool for teacher candidates to learn how to apply concepts of assessment, academic language, and differentiation to their lesson planning, but fully expect that when it comes to daily lesson planning, the reality of a typical teacher's day does not allow for such detailed, precise lesson planning.

---

# Assessment

- Write a **narrative** that explains the choice of, and how different assessment strategies were used in the lesson activities above.
- Include all forms of assessment used, both informal and formal formative and summative (if applicable). Use the italicized statements/questions to guide the writing of the assessment utilized throughout the lesson.
- Do not answer each separately and explicitly.
- Type your narrative below the dotted line to reduce length of document.
- Each assessment strategy described below should be readily identifiable as to how it is implemented in the "Lesson" sections above.

**Assessment Strategies**

- *Describe the assessment strategies and attach copies of appropriate materials.*
- *Identify individual assessments as individual, small group, or whole class.*
- *Describe how the assessments each align to the objective(s).*
- *Identify the kind of evidence that is collected for each assessment strategy and how it is collected.*
- *Describe how students will be provided feedback based on the assessment strategy.*

---

# Academic Language

- Write a short **narrative** for each section below that explains the two components of academic language.
- Be sure that these align to the lesson objectives, activities and assessments used.
- Complete each section below the dotted line.

**Language Demand:**

- *Identify new content vocabulary and any non-content vocabulary used in this lesson.*
- *Describe the syntax (written) and/or discourse (oral) language demands students will need to understand to properly learn and use vocabulary and/or concepts to complete the learning task and/or demonstrate their understanding.*

---

**FIGURE 10.2**  Additional Components for Enhanced Lesson Plan

**Language Function:**

- *Describe one language function essential for students to meet the learning objectives. Sample language functions are: analyze, argue, categorize, compare/contrast, describe, explain, interpret, predict, question, retell, and summarize.*

- *How and where will students use this language function?*

## Differentiation

- Write a short **narrative** for each section below that explains the supports targeted to the subgroups and individual learners within the class so that all of your students have the best opportunity for success.

- Complete each section below the dotted line.

**Building on Personal/Cultural/Community Assets:**

- *Explain how the lesson allows students to link new learning to prior academic learning and personal/cultural/community assets.*

**Grouping Students**

- *Describe how and why students will be divided into groups, or why they will be working individually.*

**Planned Supports**

- *Describe the targeted supports used to allow diverse learners to meet lesson objectives and the academic language demands and function.*

**FIGURE 10.2** (Continue)

Lastly, Figure 10.3 is an example of a completed lesson plan aligned to a guiding question from the previously described biology curriculum using the **Enhanced Lesson Plan Template**. As you review this example, look closely at the italicized prompts for each section of the lesson plan and see if you can identify what in the lesson plan aligns to each italicized prompt for that section.

| Instructor: | Subject Area: | Grade: | Date: |
|---|---|---|---|

## Information about the Lesson

Complete each section below to provide the background information about the lesson. Use italicized prompts as a guide but do not answer each separately and explicitly. Type the background information in each section **below** the dotted line.

**Central Focus & Context/Rationale:**

- *Describe the big idea or the central focus of the lesson.*
- *Explain why this lesson is taught when it is in the curriculum and use research and theory to explain why it is being taught the way it is planned.*

The biology class that this is used for is a biology class in a private school. There are approximately 20 students per class. Within this class there are no students with identified IEPs. There is one student with a 504 plan for written language. There are 6 students identified as ESL.

This is the first lab of the year in biology class. This serves two purposes. The first is to reinforce the scientific method by having the students identify variables and create a hypothesis and introduce the lab report format for the course. The second is to explore the concept of biomass. This lab also requires the students to work for the first time in their cooperative lab groups to design the lab. There are limitations to the design of the lab procedure due to materials provided, and class discussion will lead all groups to similar setups for their experiment. This lesson plan is just the experiment design. The lab will be set up in lesson 2 and the lab report will be completed in a later lesson after the plants have grown enough to collect data.

Students will work in lab groups so that they can support one another in identifying the variables and write a hypothesis in the proper format. This is the first experience of many that will be completed in cooperative learning groups. The cooperative learning is rooted in social constructivism. The lab is designed following constructivist learning theory in that students must first uncover their own misconceptions about plant growth before proceeding with the experiment. At the conclusion of the experiment they will have to support or refute their hypothesis which will complete the learning cycle and require them to reconcile any incongruities between their prior knowledge and their observations in this lab.

**Learning Objective(s)**

- *Using observable language with measurable verbs, identify what students will know and be able to do by the end of the lesson.*

1. Students will write a hypothesis as in "if…, then…" statement.
2. Students will design and set up lab experiment that will isolate and test one variable.
3. Students will accurately identify and use terms "dependent," "independent," and "constant" variables.

**Guiding Question**

- *List the guiding question that frames this lesson.*

How does matter and energy interact in living things to make biomass?

**FIGURE 10.3** Example Enhanced Lesson Plan

| **Materials Needed:** |
| --- |
| • *List (as if writing for a sub) the materials needed for this lesson.* |
| Seeds of fast growing plants such as rye grass; Different growing media; Small pot, flat or cups; Lab report handout—Student; Lab handout—Teacher; Lab Report Guideline |
| **Misconceptions:** |
| • *Identify common misconceptions you anticipate students may have <u>prior to the lesson</u> about the concepts addressed in this lesson.* |
| Common misconception is that plants get mass and "food" from the soil and that plants must be in soil to grow. Students will know/believe that a hypothesis is a "guess" and that a theory is not much more than an educated guess. |
| **Prior Academic Learning and Prerequisite Skills:** |
| • *List the prior knowledge and skills that you anticipate students to have and need to be successful in the lesson.* |
| There are no science content areas that are needed before beginning this activity. Students should have familiarity with the terms variable and hypothesis. Students need rudimentary graphing skills, but if necessary these can be taught while completing the lab report. |
| **MN Content Standard(s):** |
| • *List all standards addressed within the content of this lesson.* |
| 9.1.1.1.2; 9.1.1.2.1; 9.1.3.4.3; 9.3.2.3.1; 9.4.1.2.1 (standard narrative removed for printing space purposes) |

## Lesson Activities

- Provide a detailed description of what the teacher and students do to complete the lesson objectives written in **outline/bullet-point** format.
- Include instructional strategies, learning tasks, key questions, transitions, student support, student grouping, and **assessment (informal and formal) strategies throughout the lesson**.
- The italicized prompts are reminders of what qualities should exist in these plans. Do not answer each prompt as if it is a question.

**Lesson Introduction:** *This is the "**consider**" phase which sets the stage, engages the learner while activating prior knowledge and experiences. Make sure your plan accounts for these aspects of a constructivist lesson:*

- *Set a purpose and pique curiosity through use of prompts and/or guiding questions.*
- *Activate student prior knowledge and/or experiences.*
- *Introduce and explain the learning task.*

| Minutes | Description of Activity |
| --- | --- |
| 8 | Introduce the lab with this 5 minute time lapse video of plants growing from Planet Earth series (https://youtu.be/hn5ghusEN-s) and ask them to discuss in their lab groups the investigative question for the lab: From where does the plant get the mass that accumulates when it grows? |

**FIGURE 10.3** (Continue)

**Learning Activities:** *This is the "construct" phase when students build on prior knowledge and experience and build new knowledge and skill through new learning experiences. Make sure your plan accounts for these aspects of a constructivist lesson:*

- *Students are actively engaged with the content knowledge/skills to make meaning.*
- *Learning experience connects to the student's personal experiences, cultural background, or community assets.*
- *Model skills and allow for practice of skills.*
- *Students are engaged with one another to explore the topic.*
- *A variety of learners are supported.*

| Minutes | Description of Activity |
|---|---|
| 15 | As students work in their groups they will utilize the "stoplight cones" to indicate if help is needed from the teacher.<br><br>In lab groups students will complete the background information (using the projected lab instructions as a guide) in their lab notebook.<br><br>• They will answer these questions (they can discuss in their lab groups, but may not look up answers nor will the teacher give them the answers. The purpose is to have them dig into their prior knowledge.)<br>  1. What element makes up most of the mass of a plant?<br>  2. Where does it get this element, the water, the air or the soil?<br>  3. What other elements are necessary for an organism to grow?<br>  4. Where does the plant get these elements, the water, the air or the soil?<br><br>• Students will identify the variables and write a hypothesis.<br><br>By high school biology, students usually know that a hypothesis is "an educated guess." The goal is to get students beyond that notion, to making a predictive statement that can be evaluated at the conclusion of the lab activity. It is important to get them to recognize the pattern that the "If" part of the statement is what we know, think, or will do, and the "then" part of the statement is what will happen. These two portions of the statement can be linked to the independent variables (the things that will change) and the dependent variable (the change that will be observed or measured).<br>  1. Independent Variable:<br>  2. Dependent Variable: |
| 15 |   3. Constant variables:<br>  4. Hypothesis:<br><br>• Students design this investigation, however, they are given limitations due to time and materials, so they essentially all design the same investigation. You may choose to discuss and brainstorm the procedure as a whole class. The primary purpose of them designing this investigation is to practice identifying variables and writing clear instructions. |

**FIGURE 10.3**  (Continue)

|  |  |
|---|---|
|  | • Provide each group access to seeds (any fast growing plant works—grass, clover, alfalfa, radishes, etc) |
|  | • Provide each group access to at least two substrates to plant seeds in and proper pots or cups to plant seeds in—even paper drinking cups will suffice. |
|  | • Students can also "plant" seeds by sandwiching between two layers of paper towel or filter paper in a petri dish. |
|  | • It is important to remind students to create a method to record the before and after weight of the plant. |
|  | • This can be done by weighing the seeds prior to planting and then removing the plants with the roots and separate from the substrate at the conclusion. |
|  | • It is also reasonable to measure the amount of growth above the ground, disregarding the root growth, as long as the comparison between the different set-ups is equal. |

**Lesson Conclusion:** *This is the "**confirm**" phase when students reflect on what was learned, compare new knowledge and skills to prior knowledge, correct misconceptions, and check for understanding. Keep in mind this may occur after students have completed the assessment task(s). Make sure your plan accounts for these aspects of a constructivist lesson:*

- *Students show and share what they have learned with you and other students.*
- *Students compare new experience to prior knowledge and experiences.*
- *Students correct any misconceptions.*
- *Students extend ideas and check for understanding.*

| Minutes | Description of Activity |
|---|---|
| 10 | • Call the class back together and discuss as a class the three types of variables. |
|  | • Ask each group to briefly share their hypothesis and how they will set up the experiment. |
|  | • After all groups have shared, if time, lab groups can make any changes to their variables, hypothesis, and experiment design. If necessary this will be the first step in day 2 of the lab—setting up the experiment. |

## Assessment

- Write a **narrative** that explains the choice of, and how different assessment strategies were used in the lesson activities above.
- Include all forms of assessment used, both informal and formal formative and summative (if applicable). Use the italicized statements/questions to guide the writing of the assessment utilized throughout the lesson.
- Do not answer each separately and explicitly.
- Type your narrative below the dotted line to reduce length of document.
- Each assessment strategy described below should be readily identifiable as to how it is implemented in the "Lesson" sections above.

**FIGURE 10.3** (Continue)

**Assessment Strategies**

- *Describe the assessment strategies and attach copies of appropriate materials.*
- *Identify individual assessments as individual, small group, or whole class.*
- *Describe how the assessments each align to the objective(s).*
- *Identify the kind of evidence that is collected for each assessment strategy and how it is collected.*
- *Describe how students will be provided feedback based on the assessment strategy.*

- - - - - - - - - - - - - - - - - - - - - - - - - - - - - - - - - - - - - - - - - - - - - - -

- The teacher moves from group to group during the following segments, offering assistance without providing direct answers, and making note of groups struggling with any components of the lab design process:
  - Thinking Prompt discussion
  - Lab background information
  - Experiment design
- During closing discussion, make mental note of how many groups struggled with identifying the variables and developing a hypothesis in the correct format and designed an experiment that will isolate one dependent variable.
  - If time runs short (or concern students struggled more than anticipated), collect one lab report from each group to review work so far and provide written feedback for groups to review at beginning of next lesson.

## Academic Language

- Write a short **narrative** for each section below that explains the two components of academic language.
- Be sure that these align to the lesson objectives, activities and assessments used. Complete each section below the dotted line.

**Language Demand:**

- *Identify new content vocabulary and any non-content vocabulary used in this lesson.*
- *Describe the syntax (written) and/or discourse (oral) language demands students will need to understand to properly learn and use vocabulary and/or concepts to complete the learning task and/or demonstrate their understanding.*

- - - - - - - - - - - - - - - - - - - - - - - - - - - - - - - - - - - - - - - - - - - - - - -

- Vocabulary: Hypothesis; independent variable; dependent variable; constant variable; lab report; biomass;
- Language Demands:
  - Discourse: Listening to instructions; effective communication with lab partner
  - Syntax: Following written instructions (projected); scientific writing on the lab report

**Language Function:**

- *Describe one language function essential for students to meet the learning objectives. Sample language functions are: analyze, argue, categorize, compare/contrast, describe, explain, interpret, predict, question, retell, and summarize.*
- *How and where will students use this language function?*

- - - - - - - - - - - - - - - - - - - - - - - - - - - - - - - - - - - - - - - - - - - - - - -

**FIGURE 10.3** (Continue)

- Hypothesizing anticipated results and expressing that hypothesis in written form, in form of "if, then" statement correctly identifying the three types of variables in an experiment.

## Differentiation

- Write a short **narrative** for each section below that explains the supports targeted to the subgroups and individual learners within the class so that all of your students have the best opportunity for success.
- Complete each section below the dotted line.

**Building on Personal/Cultural/Community Assets:**

- *Explain how the lesson allows students to link new learning to prior academic learning and personal/cultural/community assets.*

- - - - - - - - - - - - - - - - - - - - - - - - - - - - - - - - - - - - - - - - - - - - - - - - - - -

- The planet earth video, followed by the investigative question and background questions are designed to have students figure out and discuss their prior knowledge about plants. This lab will be followed up by further exploration of the link between plant growth and energy for all living things (including them) on the planet as well as the source of oxygen in the atmosphere.

**Grouping Students**

- *Describe how and why students will be divided into groups, or why they will be working individually.*

- - - - - - - - - - - - - - - - - - - - - - - - - - - - - - - - - - - - - - - - - - - - - - - - - - -

- Because this is the first lab of the year, in the first week of class, the students are not known to the teacher. Therefore groups for this first lab are assigned randomly. (groups of 3–4)

**Planned Supports**

- *Describe the targeted supports used to allow diverse learners to meet lesson objectives and the academic language demands and function.*

- - - - - - - - - - - - - - - - - - - - - - - - - - - - - - - - - - - - - - - - - - - - - - - - - - -

- Each table will have a handout with the lab write-up instructions that they follow to write their lab procedure in their lab notebook.
- The teacher will move from group to group. Students will display "stoplight cones" indicating progress (Green = Teacher keep moving, we're good; Yellow = Teacher, check back soon; Red = Teacher stop because we are stuck)
- Students can make changes to lab write-up so far based on closing discussion. If necessary, teacher will collect and provide written feedback and suggestions before day 2 of the lab.

## Citations:

- *List any sources used for the lesson idea or activity?*
- *What research, researchers, and/or theories could be used to support the content or methodology of the lesson?*

- - - - - - - - - - - - - - - - - - - - - - - - - - - - - - - - - - - - - - - - - - - - - - - - - - -

**FIGURE 10.3**   (Continue)

Some may continue to use a template as detailed as the one I provide here. Others develop their own that includes only the most important aspects to record in writing. Others still really don't have a written lesson plan, but simply a list of what activities the students will be completing. Depending on the teacher's situation and experience, any of these approaches may work as long as they realize the lesson is more than just an activity.

Therefore, we will use the Enhanced Lesson Plan as a learning tool, and I encourage you to use the standard Lesson Plan Template as your daily planning tool.

It is crucial that even if you do not write out all of the elements in the lesson plan templates below, it is absolutely crucial that the teacher designing the lesson is accounting for all of the elements of the full enhanced lesson plan template in their planning. Without using a template, many of these elements slowly, fade out of the teacher's planning, and are soon dismissed. The result of that slide however, is more and more of your students slipping down the engagement ladder to level three, two, or even one.

Now that you have reviewed the aspects of a lesson plan that aligns to constructivist learning theory, we'll dig deeper into the specific components of, and how to write quality lesson plans adhering to the CCC learning cycle.

# Planning From Guiding Questions and Formative Assessment

Just as good unit planning begins with the assessment in mind, so too, does lesson planning. Your lesson will incorporate some form of formative assessment. The lesson may include many small informal formative assessments and/or include one or more formal formative assessments. This of course is determined by the purpose and goal of your lesson and where it fits within the scope and sequence you have developed for the unit plan. As stated before, this makes up the central focus and the context and rationale for the lesson, but is worth repeating. Think of the central focus as the big idea of the lesson. Imagine this scenario, you are meeting a colleague for coffee on a Saturday morning, and you want to tell him or her about this great lesson you did that week. How would you describe it? What is your "elevator" pitch for the lesson? That short description is your central focus. As stated before, but again worth repeating, the context and rationale is the description of why you are teaching this topic when you are (in the sequence of the unit), and why you are teaching this lesson the way you are teaching it. Your decision about the method of instruction (be it didactic instruction to student-designed projects) must be based in sound educational theory. Eventually, these are two components that a practiced teacher does not write out with each lesson plan, once they establish their curriculum and specific types of activities used within that curriculum. Initially, however, this is quite important for the novice teacher to take the time to think about and write out to ensure they understand what it means to choose teaching methods purposefully aligned to the lesson goals.

From your unit plan you should be able to identify the guiding question you need to address and the general idea you have already developed for the learning activity/formative assessment aligned to the KDUs for that guiding question. All things being equal, it is likely that one lesson will address only one or part of one guiding question from your unit plan. Avoid the temptation to write out all the leading or hook questions that you will use at some point in the lesson (say in a discussion, on a worksheet, in a lab, on a quiz, etc.) as your guiding questions. Keep the lesson aligned to a single guiding question from your unit plan. It is unlikely a single lesson will answer multiple guiding questions, but it might be likely that multiple lessons will be required to address a single guiding question (depending on the breadth of the question of course).

## Using Objectives Safely

Previously, I have written about the role of learning objectives in teaching. I advocate not sharing learning objectives with students, or if doing so, ensuring that they are written with age-appropriate terminology and

> **DUG DEEPER** Learning objectives from p. 119

language. I prefer using guiding questions to communicate lesson purpose with the students. Table 10.1 compares the purpose of learning objectives with the purpose of guiding questions.

| Learning Objective Purpose | Guiding Question Purpose |
|---|---|
| • State end goal of lesson<br>• Identify the appropriate learning activities and methods for the end goal<br>• Align appropriate assessment(s) with learning activity and lesson goal | • Invite learner into the lesson topic<br>• Communicate the topic to be investigated<br>• Allow the learner to access prior knowledge about the topic<br>• Provide context for the lesson |

**TABLE 10.1**  Compares the Purpose of Learning Objectives with the Purpose of Guiding Questions

Learning objectives are, however, absolutely crucial to great teaching. A great teacher purposefully thinks about what the student will know, do, and understand by the end of the lesson. Therefore, once you know the central focus, context and rationale, and the aligned guiding question from your unit plan, you can identify the specific learning objectives for that lesson. A sound learning objective is one that is observable with measureable results. Well-written learning objectives are: measureable, specific, and focused on the learner. A learning objective is the intended outcome of the lesson and not the activities to achieve the goal of the lesson. So, let's look at the components to sound learning objectives.

1. The content, skill, or understanding of the learning objective. You should be able to identify these as the nouns and verbs in the KDUs aligned to the guiding question for which you are designing the particular lesson.
2. A definition of the level to which students will master this content or skill, and
3. The process, skill, or the assessment activity the learner will be doing when demonstrating achievement or mastery of the objective.

The content of the learning objective is defined by the guiding question and the KDUs for that guiding question. The means by which students achieve that content, and the level to which they master the content or skill is what is defined by the verbs used in the learning objective. Table 10.2 provides a sample list of verbs aligned to Bloom's Taxonomy. The verb that you choose for the learning objective should match your central focus as well as the context and rationale for the lesson.

| Remember | Understand | Apply | Analyze | Evaluate | Create |
|----------|------------|-------|---------|----------|--------|
| choose | ask | adapt | analyze | argue | act |
| define | classify | apply | categorize | arrange | assemble |
| identify | conclude | calculate | compare | criticize | compose |
| list | convert | change | contrast | decide | construct |
| locate | describe | experiment | differentiate | defend | create |
| match | explain | demonstrate | distinguish | evaluate | infer |
| memorize | give example | develop | examine | justify | invent |
| record | interpret | perform | outline | plan | design |
| repeat | recognize | predict | test | prioritize | develop |
| select | summarize | use | survey | support | predict |

**TABLE 10.2** Sample List of Verbs Aligned to Bloom's Taxonomy

The above table provides a list of verbs to use along with the content (usually nouns) of learning objectives. Using verbs such as these can help ensure that your learning objectives are specific and measurable. Table 10.3 is a list of words to avoid in learning objectives, as the use of these verbs often results on learning objectives that are not measurable. The learning objective serves one purpose for you as the teacher, to identify the benchmark you will look for to confirm if students have learned what you wanted.

| Verbs to Avoid in Learning Objectives | | | | |
|---|---|---|---|---|
| understand | appreciate | know | approach | become |
| believe | grow | improve | increase | see |
| experience | learn | think about | comprehend | progress |

**TABLE 10.3**   List of Words to Avoid in Learning Objectives

Some of the words on this list might surprise you, such as understand and know. Of course, the majority of your learning objectives are likely to actually define to what level students build understanding or knowledge, but when these two words are used without a descriptive adverb in a learning objective, the learning objective lacks definition. To what level will the students understand the content? Is a little bit of understanding of new knowledge adequate? What is your definition of a little bit, versus one of your colleagues, or the students? Therefore, a more precise word choice that defines the level of knowledge and understanding serves as a better verb in the learning objective. Table 10.4 provides a comparison of measurable to nonmeasurable learning objectives.

You can see that a good learning objective is built directly on the KDUs identified for the guiding question framing the lesson(s). You can also see that the verbs used in the learning objective defines the nature of the learning activities/formative assessment that students will complete in the lesson. For example, a physical education teacher could assess the students' knowledge of the rules of tennis for the objective above with a verbal quiz or short essay since the objective is asking that they describe the rules of the game. However, if that goal of students knowing the game of tennis was expressed with a learning objective such as: "students will accurately officiate and score classmates playing a game of tennis," that would require a performance assessment in which your physical education students were playing, officiating, and correctly scoring tennis matches. How you write the learning objective, then, should align directly with the nature of the learning activity/formative assessments throughout the lesson.

| Nonmeasurable Learning Objectives | Measurable Learning Objectives |
|---|---|
| Students will know photosynthesis. | Students will correctly list the equation for photosynthesis. |
| Students will understand the game of tennis. | Students will describe the rules of the game of tennis. |
| Students will appreciate 20th century poetry. | Students will critique the impact of Robert Frost on 20th century poetry. |
| Students will increase their proficiency with an overhand serve. | Students will be able to complete an in-bounds overhand serve 50% of the time. |
| Students will become aware of the importance of recycling. | Students will justify the need for a new recycling program in their school. |
| Students will know the parts of speech. | Students will correctly diagram a sentence, correctly identifying the nouns, verbs, adverbs, adjectives, and prepositions. |

**TABLE 10.4**    A Comparison of Measurable to Nonmeasurable Learning Objectives

# Unpacking and Using Standards Safely

In Chapter 8, we learned how to unpack the standards for the purpose of identifying essential questions for a unit plan. In this process, you undoubtedly discovered that all standards are not created equally, and that the questions generated from that process are not all equal as well. Stan-

DUG DEEPER into unpacking standards from p. 124 & 136

dards and benchmarks that are broadly written in scope tend to generate broader, more open-ended questions. Conversely, standards or benchmarks that are very specific in nature tend to result in questions that are closed-ended. When generating your questions for the unit plan, you might have discovered that the broader, more open-ended questions ended up as your TQs, sTQs, or GQs while the closed-ended questions where set aside at the unit planning stage of curriculum design. Those closed-ended questions still have value. They might end up embedded in the lesson plan as leading questions or questions that hook students during the consider phase of the lesson. They might also end up as questions built into the learning tasks and formative assessments used throughout the construct and confirm phase of the lesson.

What we can learn from this is that unpacking the standards is not only useful for helping a teacher to identify the scope of a unit, that same process is also helpful for developing the scope of a single lesson. The scope of the single lesson is precisely defined by the learning objectives for that lesson, which is built off of the nouns and verbs which can be pulled from the KDUs or the standards and benchmarks aligned to that lesson. For example, let's look at a Minnesota third grade social studies standard, 3.3.3.8.1 in Table 10.5.

| Standard | Benchmark | Verbs | Nouns |
|---|---|---|---|
| Process of cooperation and conflict among people influence the division and control of the earth's surface | Identify physical and human features that act as boundaries or dividers; give examples of situations or reasons why have made or used boundaries.<br>*For example:* Physical features—mountains, rivers, bodies of water. Human-made features—fences, hedges, political boundaries. | • Identify<br>• give examples<br>• have made<br>• have used | • physical and human features<br>• conflict among people<br>• earth's surface<br>• boundaries |

| Possible Questions | Possible Learning Objectives |
|---|---|
| • How much space do you need?<br>• How might you resolve a conflict with peers?<br>• How might two countries agree on the border that separates them?<br>• Why are some US states' borders straight while others are jagged and crooked?<br>• What are examples of U.S. rivers forming the border of states? | • Students will label the physical features (mountains, rivers, lakes, political boundaries) on a topographic map.<br>• Students will develop an equitable way to divide up the classroom storage space for their personal belongings. |

**TABLE 10.5**   Unpacked Social Studies Standard

Some things to notice with the above examples. The scope of the questions vary depending on the component of the standard addressed. Some of the questions are of narrow scope, and closed-ended with one right answer. These are suitable to be used during the lesson, such as on a worksheet, in a discussion, or on a quiz. The broader, more open-ended questions, might require the correct use of examples or terms applied to a response that is an opinion, interpretation, or analysis. The more open-ended questions are better possibilities for a thematic, sub-thematic, or guiding question. You can also see that the standard was the foundation for the more open-ended questions, while the benchmark was the foundation for the closed-ended questions. Notice also that the nouns and verbs primarily from the benchmark form the foundation for the learning objectives that are specific and measurable. Lastly, recognizing that these standards are written for a third-grade social studies curriculum, you can see that the standard certainly, and the benchmark mostly, are written using terms and language that would not be very useful to a student in understanding the intent and goal of a lesson. This is a good example of why I do not advocate the use of the actual standard as a means of communicating the goal of a lesson with students.

## Academic Language

The concept of "academic language" as a specific term in education and step in lesson planning is a fairly recent area of research in the field of pedagogy. As we explore academic language, you'll find the concept of academic language has of course always been present in planning, though, not purposefully, and therefore not effectively accounted for in the lesson plans much of the time.

Academic language is the combination of the content specific vocabulary and noncontent vocabulary used by the student or teacher to complete a learning objective or task and also the language skills with which the students will need to be proficient in order to complete the learning objective and/or task successfully. We can break academic language into two components: language demand (including vocabulary) and language function.

Language demand can be defined as the specific ways that academic language is used by students to participate in a learning task through reading, writing, listening, and/or speaking to demonstrate their understanding. Think of language demands as the activities involving some aspect of using language and communicating required of students to successfully complete the lesson. In other words, what will be demanded of them in terms of language usage to complete the lesson? When designing your lesson, pay attention to the means by which students are demonstrating their proficiency in the learning objective (the nature of the final product of the lesson), with words such as *essay, paragraph, sentence, speech, lab report, reflection, play, poem, comic strip, magazine article, poster,* and the like (Denton 2014).

We can further break down the language demands into three components: syntax, discourse, and vocabulary. Syntax are the reading and writing skills that students will utilize in completing the learning objective or task. In what way are students interacting with written language? Discourse is the combination of listening and speaking skills students will need to utilize during the lesson. When will students need to be taking in information by listening and in what ways will students be generating and sharing ideas and learning through speaking? Of course, most lessons involve both syntax and discourse, and neither of these two components of teaching are new. What is new, however, is the purposeful identification of the syntax and discourse demands being made of students. Without purposefully planning for these demands, and then planning how to support students with these demands, it is likely that you will have some students struggle with the task, but, not because they do not understand the content proficiently, instead because they are not able to meet the language demands. This blocks either their ability to learn the content, or maybe even simply communicate their understanding adequately due to a struggle with the means by which you are asking them to communicate their learning.

Recall from my earlier anecdote about my shift in teaching away from objective testing to written essays and projects. In that situation, I was negligent of purposefully accounting for the syntax language demands being put upon my students whose native language was not English. I was frustrated that their test scores on the objective tests did not match my observation through conversation of their understanding of the biology content I was evaluating through traditional testing. If I used a different form of assessment that allowed for adequate time to carefully choose their words, and even use nonverbal forms of communication as well (such as body language and gesturing) many of these students could communicate their learning via discourse or even written (syntax) work if they were given the time and structure to control the written language with an open-ended essay assignment for example. With adequate time, the student learning English could properly think in his or her native language and then accurately write out his or her ideas in an essay format more accurately than he or she could when asked to quickly decode complex multiple choice questions. It was often the case that an example, idiom, or a noncontent vocabulary word resulted in the student misunderstanding the question being asked, leading to a wrong answer. This is an example of student failure caused not by a student's lack of understanding, effort and preparation for a task, but my failure in not recognizing the language demands being made of my students. Without adequate supports the assessment wasn't truly a measure of just content mastery, but also a measure of English reading and writing fluency.

This brings us to the other aspect of language demands, vocabulary, which includes any words the student should be able to define in order to comprehend the content of the lesson. These words may be specific to the discipline (i.e., *artifact* in social studies) or just general words used in school (*rubric, characteristics, infer, analyze*). First, as the teacher you must identify the new content vocabulary that students will need to use or know to complete the lesson. You will also want to identify any links from these new vocabulary words to anticipated background knowledge vocabulary. How will students learn the new vocabulary, and how will you facilitate their connecting that new learning to prior content vocabulary? You cannot assume that your students will see the connections—you must purposefully facilitate this contextual placement of concepts and terms. Secondly, and this was my error with my nonnative English speakers, you must also identify the noncontent vocabulary that may trip up students in completing the lesson. These words are often actually your clue words to the language function. For example, when asking students to compare and contrast two concepts, if you instead ask them to differentiate between the two, will your struggling readers know that word? Many of your students who haven't used that term before might still be able to decode it by its context in the question, but others may not. They might end up not actually comparing and contrasting two concepts that they otherwise understand quite well.

The second component of academic language is language function which describes the use of language by the student to interpret and use the content skill or knowledge. Another way to think about this is to identify the mental or intellectual *processing* that the student will utilize to make sense of what they are learning. These can often be identified by finding the verbs in the learning objectives or standards for the lesson that describe the link between the language demand and the content understanding. These might be verbs such as *identify, analyze, summarize, define, explain, conclude, justify, compare, sort, evaluate, differentiate,* and so on (Denton 2014).

Identifying these aspects of academic language within your lesson is actually the easy part. The next step is to identify the planned supports you will utilize so that students can successfully navigate the language demands and functions inherent in the lesson design. Designing and utilizing planned supports effectively is one aspect of differentiation—the next, and last component of lesson planning.

## Differentiation

Entire books and courses can and should be dedicated to the concept of differentiation. Believe it or not, this is also a fairly new concept in training of educators, really taking hold within the last generation or so, which is a bit of a damning statement for the profession. It is also within that timeframe that constructivist learning theory has taken root, based on an impressive body of research as to how the brain actually processes and makes sense of information, which is then applied to understanding the differences among children regarding how they learn. In fact, student-centered learning (a key component of constructivism) is by its very nature differentiated instruction. By using more student-centered, inquiry-based lessons, even true project-based learning, the student is given the opportunity to have some voice in how they are learning and/or demonstrating proficiency. This is what it means to differentiate instruction.

Two fundamentals are paramount that were not present when I was taught how to be a teacher. First is that true learning only happens in a meaningful context, and that students will not truly learn simply because they are told to do so and it is important. And second, it is wrong to teach and treat all students as a homogenous group and remain ignorant of their individual strengths, weaknesses, and needs as learners. Differentiation really comes down to these three aspects of a lesson: the lesson needs to be culturally/personally relevant; include purposeful grouping (or not) students for cooperative learning; and provide planned supports for students' learning. The purpose of differentiating instruction is as to make learning possible for the variety of all learners in your classroom. After all, your job is to make it as easy as possible for as many as possible of your students to learn as much as possible. No small task, but that is the gig!

The first aspect of differentiation we'll explore is simply creating curriculum that is personally and/or culturally relevant, utilizing the assets you have in the community surrounding your classroom. That sounds more complex than it is. Let's boil it down to an essential question. How will you make your instruction relevant and intriguing to your students so they will sit up and take notice? The ideal scenario would be that when you present a guiding question to your students, they sit up a little straighter and say out loud, or at least think to themselves, "Hmmm, I don't know, that's pretty interesting" or maybe simply, "cool!" We know of course, that for students over the age of 12, even if this was their inclination for an initial response, they will mute it in front of their peers, but that doesn't mean you shouldn't shoot for that response.

This requires some real artistry on your part as the teacher and the developer of the curriculum. The first step is having an intriguing and inviting guiding question (see Chapter 7) that asks something students will want to learn, meaning it has to present a problem or topic that is interesting to the students *as they are right now*. It is not good enough to present the importance of the content and skills you are going to teach as something they will need for their future. What purpose will the child have who doesn't see a future for himself or herself? Do not let the foundation of your lesson further marginalize this child. Of course what you are teaching must be important for their future development, but for students to make meaning and truly learn it, the learning must be real and authentic right now. Second, the question and topic has to be accessible. Not only do your students need to want to learn it, it has to be developmentally appropriate, while stretching their zone of proximal development. Third, the question and topic has to build on prior learning. This requires thoughtfully sequenced lessons as part of a thoughtfully planned unit. What we find as we break down the first concept of differentiation is that by developing thematic, inquiry-based units, utilizing authentic instruction and assessment founded in constructivist learning theory, you have the pieces in place to develop lesson plans that allow for students to link new learning to prior learning and connect that learning to their own personal, cultural, and/or community in which they live.

The second aspect of differentiation is the grouping students for cooperative learning and also the times between the cooperative learning when students must do some work, processing, and thinking on their own which makes the collaborative work more valuable and meaningful. Learning is a social activity and requires that the students are put into the best situations to work collaboratively in a way that benefits all of the learners. What must be avoided is the dreaded group project in which the confident, highly grade-conscious student feels they must take control and do all of the work to ensure a good grade, and the less confident student yields the work and decision-making to the grade-conscious student. While the former student feels taken advantage of, the latter student might often feel marginalized and dismissed. Neither may actually want that dynamic to play out, but over and over again, it does because we teachers create the situation for it to occur with poorly planned group projects. In the context of your lesson planning you must account for why you have students working in the groups they are in (or why they should work individually on this task).

Specifics of how to arrange students into groups, and facilitate effective cooperative learning is explored in more depth in the next chapter, The Teacher Toolkit. Within this section, we will just outline the various types of groupings you may want to use and reasoning behind those choices. Cooperative learning, or learning groups, is something that students should do, not have done to them, requires active learning on their part, and facilitates students working together to achieve a common goal. There are three types of groupings of students: formal, informal, and cooperative base groups (Johnson, Johnson, and Holubec 1994).

Formal groups are purposefully assembled by the teacher requiring students to work together for, from at least 1 lesson, to weeks at a time on a task, resulting in a product of some kind, as opposed to a session of collaborative discussion or processing of a concept or idea.

Informal groups are ad hoc and last from a few minutes to a class session. An example would be a three to five minute turn-to-partner type of discussion. Cooperative base groups are long term, possibly the entire school year or term. Cooperative base groups are heterogeneous with stable group members in which the primary purpose is to allow members to give each other the support, help, and encouragement needed for success. Cooperative base groups involve individuals that are not working collaboratively to complete a shared project or task, but instead are collaborative groups in which the individuals provide support and assistance to one another to complete individual tasks (usually tasks related to the same assignment, but individualized in nature). This is an effective grouping for providing planned supports for students as they complete individual, personal project-based-learning lessons.

The first aspect to consider is the size of the group. Smaller is better, with a range between two to four students. The advantage of larger groups is that there is an increase in diversity of ideas and skills. This can be helpful for completing complex and multi-step tasks. However, the larger the group, the more skills of cooperation are needed for individuals to function within that group. Students working in a pair, must navigate two communication interactions—their communicating to a partner, and interpreting communication from a partner. As the groups grow in size, however, the number of communication interactions increases exponentially. A group of three requires six communication interactions, while a group of four requires twelve communication interactions. The smaller the group, the less likely an individual can "hide" within the group and minimize participation. From the teacher's perspective, it is easier to quickly identify a group struggling with personality conflicts requiring teacher intervention if the group is small.

The third aspect of differentiation is to use planned strategies and supports to allow that all students have access to success whether they have an identified disability and an Individualized Education Plan, are English Language Learners, struggling readers, underperforming students, have gaps in prior academic knowledge, or are gifted and talented students already confident in the content of the lesson you are designing. This requires planned supports, which are instructional strategies, learning tasks and materials, and other resources deliberately designed to facilitate student learning specific to the lesson.

I believe it is a safe bet to always assume you need to provide planned supports for the following three aspects to classroom success (or struggles). Always plan for providing support to students who struggle with reading, writing, and staying on task. Whether you have students with identified learning exceptionalities, or with established Individualized Education Plans, you can always assume you have students who will benefit from support in these three areas. And, a support that is designed to help a student with an exceptionality in writing for example, will often prove beneficial to the student who does not have an identified exceptionality with such skills.

Let's end where we began. "Proper preparation prevents poor performance." To be a great teacher, who provides as many of his or her students with as great an opportunity to learn as much as possible as efficiently as possible, requires very thoughtful planning of inquiry-based lessons that are rooted in thoughtfully planned out thematic units of study. That's the job.

# Chapter 11

# The Teacher Tool Kit

Teaching is a skilled craft. Like any skilled craft, it requires effectively using a variety of tools. This chapter is a teacher tool kit so you can enact your units and the lessons making up those units using techniques to fully engage all of your students. This requires variability in methods you utilize, choosing techniques aligned to constructivist learning theory and appropriate for the goal of the unit and specific learning objectives of the lesson. No matter the lesson or the specific teaching technique utilized in a lesson, two aspects should be ubiquitous throughout all of your teaching. First, you should utilize formative assessments/learning activities that put students at the center of the learning as much as possible. This means that the formative assessments/learning activities should fit within the Consider, Construct, Confirm (CCC) learning cycle, ensuring students' learning involves adequate reflection and community dialogue around prior conceptions, lived experiences, and resolving disequilibrium between the two. "As learners struggle to make meanings, they undertake progressive shifts in perspectives—in a sense, 'big ideas.' These learner-constructed, central-organizing ideas can be generalized across experiences, and they often require undoing or reorganizing earlier conceptions. This process continues throughout development" (Fosnot 1996, 30). Second, your dispositions while teaching should demonstrate intensity and enthusiasm. "When a teacher indirectly communicates, 'This is fun!' or 'This is exciting!' it is contagious for students" (Marzano and Pickering 2011, 4). According to Marzano and Pickering (2011), utilizing a variety of strategies to demonstrate these sentiments, such as using personal stories, dynamics in their presentation and speaking voice, showing passion for the subject, using humor (especially self-directed), or humorous news headlines and quotes.

The goal is to use strategies that put students at the center of the activity and move the teacher off to the side as a facilitator, while establishing a fun classroom culture allowing for sincere passion for learning to emerge, that fosters constructive collaboration among the students.

When the classroom environment in which students spend so much of their day is organized so that student-to-student interaction is encouraged, cooperation is valued, assignments and materials are interdisciplinary, and students' freedom to chase their own ideas is abundant, students are more likely to take risks and approach assignments with a willingness to accept challenges to their current understanding (Brooks and Brooks 1993, 10).

This chapter outlines the basic structure of a variety of teaching techniques that adhere to constructivist learning theory. This is by no means an exhaustive encyclopedia of teaching strategies, but is only a starting point for identifying what might work for you and your classroom. From there, you are of course encouraged to seek and explore deeper knowledge about and specific examples of implementation of such strategies in the classroom.

## Classroom Routines to Build a Safe Learning Community

Unless the classroom is a safe place for students to take risks, explore, inquire, work collaboratively, thinking independently, and freely participate, none of the other tools in your teacher tool kit really matter. The reasoning behind attention to the classroom culture and climate is covered extensively in *Chapter 3: Engaging Students* and *Chapter 4: Co-Constructing Culture and Establishing Norms*. This section builds on what you read in Chapters 3 and 4 and provides specific examples of strategies to purposefully build a positive classroom culture, while specific cooperative and collaborative learning strategies (which of course require routines and a safe learning community) will be covered in a later section in this chapter.

If you are reading this looking for the magic bullet to "dealing with discipline issues," then I'm sorry to disappoint you. The best way to deal with issues is to proactively prevent them from occurring. Easy to say, of course, and hard to implement. Many of us have experienced, and maybe still observe, classroom management strategies rooted in behaviorist philosophy. We've already discussed the problems with using a behaviorist model to engage and motivate students so we don't need to go over that again here and I have previously described the classroom in a more holistic manner (labeling it an ecological approach to classroom culture). The ecological approach, which is in line with classroom management strategies rooted in the growing field of "social curriculum," provides an exciting way of understanding how classroom life

Hmm, this links back to... Active student engagement on p. 37

is jointly constructed and lived by participants within the structures of the classroom environments" (Carter and Doyle 2006, 400).

Managing this "ecosystem" requires careful and deliberate planning, and ongoing vigilance on the part of the teacher. A well-managed classroom exhibits these four characteristics (Wong and Wong 2009):

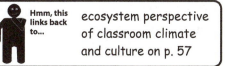

Hmm, this links back to... ecosystem perspective of classroom climate and culture on p. 57

1. Students are deeply involved in academic work,
2. students know what is expected of them,
3. there is little wasted time, confusion, or disruption, and
4. The classroom climate is work-oriented but relaxed and pleasant.

As the teacher, you set the tone, and establishing routines that ensure the above four characteristics is the magic bullet to classroom management. If the ecosystem is functioning well, as described above, there will be little need for discipline. In fact, according to Emmer and Gerwels (2006), the "typical" secondary student responded favorably to simple redirections by the teacher, returning to the assigned tasks 93% of the time.

This highly functioning ecosystem in which students are engaged, on task, and responsive to teacher redirection when necessary requires that you have established the culture and climate through the use of routines. In Chapter 4, I introduced the importance of establishing routines and including the students in the establishment of those routines. Suffice it to say, that the more, you can include students in the establishing of the routines, the more buy-in you will get from the students.

The classroom needs routines for three aspects of the day that coincide with my CCC learning cycle: starting the day (or class), working on academic tasks, and reflecting on the day—what was learned and how it was learned (Wong and Wong 2009). Many elemen-

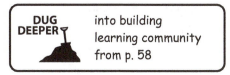

**DUG DEEPER** into building learning community from p. 58

tary teachers (and middle school teachers if the day starts with an advisory) utilize a morning meeting or some kind of "circle time" to start the day. More common in secondary classrooms is to begin the day with the objective, guiding question, or agenda written on the board (or projected) and to begin work after greeting students as they enter.

In either case, greeting students, and in the case of morning meetings or circles, having students greet one another is one means to establish a sense of commitment to the learning community and offer the first

**DUG DEEPER** into inviting students into the classroom from p. 38

entry point for the student into "belonging" to that community. This requires you to be invitational in disposition. Review the chart below (Table 11.1) adapted from Wong and Wong (2009, 62) and evaluate if you are providing an invitational or disinvitational classroom ecosystem for your students.

| Are you Invitational or Disinvitational? | |
|---|---|
| **Inviting Verbal Comments:**<br>• "Good morning."<br>• "Congratulations."<br>• "I appreciate your help."<br>• "Tell me about it." | **Disinviting Verbal Comments:**<br>• "It won't work."<br>• "I don't care what you do."<br>• "You can't do that."<br>• "Because I said so, that's why." |
| **Inviting Personal Behaviors:**<br>• Smiling<br>• Listening<br>• Thumbs up or high five<br>• Holding a door open | **Disinviting Personal Behaviors:**<br>• Sneering<br>• Looking at your watch<br>• Shoving<br>• Letting a door close on a person behind you |
| **Inviting Physical Environments:**<br>• Fresh paint<br>• Living plants<br>• Clean walls<br>• Comfortable furniture | **Disinviting Physical Environments:**<br>• Dark corridors<br>• No plants<br>• Bad odor<br>• Beat-up or uncomfortable furniture |
| **Inviting Thoughts (Self-Talk):**<br>• "Making mistakes is all right."<br>• "I've misplaced my keys."<br>• "I could learn to do that."<br>• "Sometimes I have to think what to say." | **Disinviting Thoughts (Self-Talk):**<br>• "Why am I so stupid?"<br>• "I've lost my keys again."<br>• "I never could do that."<br>• "I never know what to say, I'm so slow to catch on." |

**TABLE 11.1** Invitational versus Disinvitational Classroom

I'm sure as you read those, they seemed perfectly obvious to you, however, you'd be surprised how many of these invitational habits fade from practice as the situation gets more chaotic and the pressures of managing the day-to-day grind of teaching mount. So, be vigilant. Even about those things that are initially obvious.

The more you and your students establish, practice, and continue to utilize routines, the more likely the classroom ecosystem will stay in balance despite the "grind." In a secondary classroom, this requires less explicit teaching, as students bring with them routines of many years of school attendance. For secondary teachers, if your daily classroom operation routines are in line with the rest of the school climate, little purposeful instruction of routines is necessary. I have found in the secondary classroom, explicit instruction of routines is not necessary if you are consistent with the routines and procedures that you utilize. This includes having an established location where the day's goals, objectives, guiding question(s), or activities are listed. Have an established practice of how you get everyone's attention. Have an established practice of how you transition from one activity to another. Will you give a verbal warning, do you use some kind of noise-maker (like chime), or use a nonverbal clue? Establish what it looks like to be ready for class—in seats with books out, homework, out or turned in, etc. Establish how and where work is handed in to the teacher and how and/or where the students get it back. What level of noise is acceptable during different kinds of working situations? The more you can include students in establishing these expectations and routines, the better (see social contract in Chapter 4).

Elementary teachers are much more likely to spend dedicated time at the beginning of the year focused on teaching the routines of the classroom. As stated in Chapter 4, the more you can include students in establishing the expectations and what it looks like when those expectations are being met, the better. To establish these routines, don't be afraid to literally teach the routines and practice them. Model it for the students or have a student model it, and then practice it as a whole class. This means to model, or have students model, even the mundane things such as lining up at the door, coming to the morning circle location, sharpening a pencil, getting into cooperative learning groups, arriving in class, getting out homework, etc. The more these routines are established, the more likely you are going to have a classroom ecosystem that can survive a perturbation or disruption to the balanced nature of it, such as you being absent. The best experience a substitute teacher can have is for the students to show the sub how they do daily routines (respectfully of course—which might also have to be modeled for them!).

Despite all of this effort, students will still have times of misbehavior. Misbehavior is any behavior by a student that is perceived to interrupt the planned directionality of the lesson. These misbehaviors are likely to 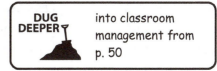 be publicly apparent to the rest of the class and therefore have the possibility of spreading among the rest of the students (Carter and Doyle 2006). They are kids after all!

**DUG DEEPER** into classroom management from p. 50

The routines that you establish as to how you react to such instances are crucial. Recognizing the misbehavior as quickly and quietly as possible is the key to success in proactive classroom management. You do need eyes in the back of your head! This requires that you make frequent eye-contact with students, whether in a didactic instructional situation or students are working independently or collaborative throughout the classroom. Early intervention, emphasizing preventative, collaborative, and instructional strategies are most effective (Emmers and Gerwels 2006). Simple redirections to desist a behavior work almost all of the time. These can be as simple as literally making eye contact, quietly moving to stand near a student, and then placing your hand on his or her desk, maybe tapping the assignment or paper on the desk and then moving on— not standing over the student calling attention of his or her peers to the student. Saying a student's name, is often enough to modify behavior. When students are working independently, the teacher moving around constantly among students is crucial and it is equally crucial that you still can recognize students whose behavior is shifting toward misbehavior right away and intervene. This means that while focused on one student, you cannot ignore the rest of the class. This creates a situation where you are perceived as being unfair, as when you do intervene with a student, he or she will recall when other students did the same behaviors and you didn't intervene. Why are you "picking one me?" will be their response. The fact that you did not see the other students misbehave is not a satisfactory answer to the student being reprimanded. And it shouldn't be. In all of these instances, the preference is that the discussion with the student is discrete, as brief as it can be, and is focused on restoring order and routine. The focus should be on the situation and the behavior, not on the student and his or her identity or personality.

When the quiet nonverbal cues, or incidental, ephemeral verbal cues and actions do not correct a student's behavior then more purposeful behavior management or discipline might become necessary. Disciplinary actions that you take must follow estab-

**DUG DEEPER** into managing misbehavior from p. 61

lished guidelines (either in the social contract, established classroom rules, or school-wide expectations and rules). The disciplinary action should be a logical consequence, follow established hierarchy of escalation of response, and emphasize allowing the student some control for managing how to get out of the situation through choice. All of these should occur with an "emphasis on caring, respect, and trust in interactions with students: collaborative rule making and problem solving; and efforts to help students learn self-management strategies, make good choices, and accept personal responsibility for their actions" (Carter and Doyle 2006, 394).

The purpose is correcting the behavior and doing so in a manner that is discrete as possible so the student does not have to resist to maintain standing among peers, and is instructive for the student for long-term self-management of behavior, and most importantly is viewed by the student as having an instructive purpose, not a punitive purpose. For elementary-aged or middle school students, moving beyond the easy redirection might then involve an individual conferencing session with the student, again with the focus on the behavior, not the personality, and the focus of the conversation being instructive, not punitive. A common approach is to have a routine location for students to utilize take-a-break or think-time strategies. This can be as simple as the student being asked, or removing him or herself to a specific location to refocus his or her activity on the task at hand. For a more severe behavior, the student may be asked to complete a short reflection activity in which the student writes or discusses with the teacher (or maybe a peer mediator) the nature of the misbehavior or conflict, an understanding of why it was a misbehavior, and what corrective action needs to be taken—especially if that corrective action requires something restorative such as an apology or reparation of some kind.

With students who show a continued pattern of misbehavior, then more structured measures will need to occur. The goal is still instructive and ultimately has a goal of the student developing self-

**DUG DEEPER** into using extrinsic motivators safely from p. 44

management strategies. This might often involve establishing individualized expectations for the student, or a behavior contract, between the student and the teacher. This contract should involve the parents so that there is no miscommunication, misunderstandings or mixed messaging for the student between home and school. Often-times a school administrator or counselor will also be involved in this process, either in helping to facilitate if the misbehavior has escalated in nature or frequency, or at least be made aware of the process you are going to undertake with the student and family.

This brings us finally to the use of extrinsic rewards. I've already made the case in Chapter 4 against the long-term efficacy of extrinsic rewards and the potential damage to intrinsic motivation, however, at times, they are necessary. I only advocate contingent extrinsic rewards in the most extreme of situations. As much as you can avoid a "pay for play" situation, where completing a specific action results in a specific reward, the better. Extrinsic rewards that are unexpected, verbal and instructive in nature (not just "good job"), and are positive feedback are least likely to undermine intrinsic motivation (Wentzel 2006). It is clear that extrinsic motivation/reward systems, either routinized monitoring systems such "clip up or clip down" where a clip is moved up or down a behavior scale (for a class or individual) visually representing the teacher's perception of behaviors, good behavior coupons to be redeemed in school or class store, promises of rewards such as extra recess or choice time, or conversely similarly structure punitive measures all can be effective short-term behavior management. If not, we wouldn't have been using them for the past 100+ years in classrooms. Some would argue that these strategies provide scaffolding for teaching proper behavior. It is also possible that well placed, and appropriate extrinsic reward systems can effectively change a student's behavior and the rewards can be removed as the desired behaviors become habitual for the student. It is also possible that the behavior will only last while the behavior

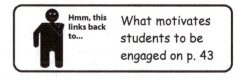

modification is in place, intrinsic motivation will be reduced, or the student becomes a praise junky, becoming dependent on positive feedback to maintain his or her self-esteem. So tread lightly into the world of routinized extrinsic motivation and classroom management strategies. I'll close this section of the chapter with this cognitive evaluation theory flowchart, adapted from Reeve (2006, 653) and encourage its use by you to evaluate specific extrinsic motivational strategies you may be using or considering implementing to determine the potential effect an extrinsic motivational strategy on intrinsic motivation (Figure 11.1).

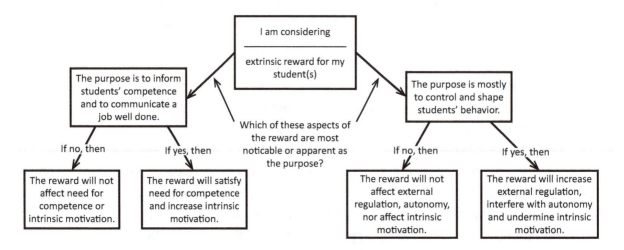

**FIGURE 11.1**    Graphic Representation of Cognitive Evaluation Theory

# Using Thinking Prompts to Uncover Prior Knowledge

Oftentimes a lesson begins with a thinking prompt. Thinking prompts are exactly what the name implies— a means to prompt students thinking about a topic. Therefore, they are primarily used at the beginning of

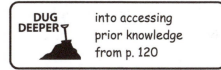

**DUG DEEPER** into accessing prior knowledge from p. 120

a lesson. Teachers, for years, have been using a variety of "attention grabbers" and "hooks." These certainly can be thinking prompts, but a thinking prompt is a bit more than just the mechanism to grab students' attention. It also needs to serve the function of beginning the learning cycle. A good thinking prompt not only grabs the attention of the students, but it also provides a means for the students to consider what they already know about a topic and serves to introduce the topic of the lesson.

One method of getting students thinking about a topic is to use a question that hooks the student. These might be a guiding question from the unit plan you have designed, or a variation of one of the guiding questions. They serve as a "clever opening questions [that] can spark interest, capture imagination, and set up wonder" (McTighe and Wiggins 2013, 12). They may be open-ended questions, or might be more closed ended, to probe at discovering prior knowledge of a specific idea or topic.

Some examples of questions that hook and serve as thinking prompts:

- How might you have showered in dinosaur spit this morning?
- Why do humans tell stories?
- Could history repeat and the U.S. experience another Great Depression?
- Why doesn't a bird's feet freeze in the winter?

Use of multimedia sources can also work well as thinking prompts. Many students would consider themselves visual learners. The use of historical photos, film clips, news stories, etc., can be used effectively in a variety of ways. The most common way to use a visual media as a thinking prompt would be to use it in conjunction with a question that hooks or prompts discussion. The advantage of using a question of teacher design is that the teacher can ensure that the media source will lead to discussion about a specific topic. The disadvantage is obvious. You are taking away the opportunity for the students to generate and ask their own questions. Therefore, a visual thinking prompt can be used in a more open-ended manner and allow students to generate their own observations and questions from the media resource. Through effective Socratic questioning, used to lead the discussion that is generated by the students' observations and questions, the teacher can guide the discussion to the intended learning objective for the lesson.

Some examples of multimedia thinking prompts could include such things as a song about a specific topic, a piece of music, writing, or art from a particular genre or artist, a news report recounting historical or current events, a talk presented by an expert from a reputable source such as TED.com, an established museum, an RSAnimate from the Royal Society for the Arts, or organizations such as National Geographic for Kids.

Print media can also serve as a thinking prompt. This could be such resources as newspaper articles (how quaint—more likely news articles from reputable online news outlets), short stories, poems, single words and metaphors, etc. The use and purpose is largely the same as the visual media. They can be used in conjunction with a hook or guiding question, or can be used in a more open-ended fashion followed by effective Socratic questioning.

Not all thinking prompts have to involve small group or whole class discussion prompted by a visual hook and question. Prompting students to visualize a location, event, or setting, can be an effective means for students to begin thinking about a topic. For example, when opening a discussion about environmental or ecological policy or issues, I like to begin with a simple visualization in which I ask the students to close their eyes and go to their "happy place" by asking them to visualize themselves in the place where they would go to relax and rejuvenate themselves. Almost all students choose an outside, quiet, natural setting. This allows me to use a "hook" question such as, "If these natural places are so important to you (all of us), then why do we continually choose degradation of these spaces for the sake of extracting a natural resource?"

Another, more recent source for audio media is the use of podcasts. You can find a podcast on virtually any subject. One note to keep in mind is that many podcasts do not censor language or content & even the podcast version of regularly broadcast radio shows. Proper previewing is always necessary! Listening to a podcast can present an awkward problem for students in a classroom setting. What do they look at? There is nothing visual and they are surrounded by peers and possible distractions, such as a cell phone. A strategy that I have used is to do a "doodle listen." I have found it effective to instruct students to doodle in a journal or notebook (or maybe a provided sheet of paper) whatever they want while they listen. For many students this serves to focus their listening by engaging their mind in creating images from the auditory description. The doodles can then serve as a starting point for small group or whole class discussion to process what was just heard.

# Cooperative Learning

Effectively implementing cooperative learning requires more planning than one might initially think. Cooperative learning can range from a few-minute exercise to year-long collaborative working groups. Therefore, properly establishing the

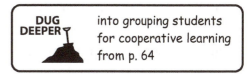

DUG DEEPER into grouping students for cooperative learning from p. 64

membership of cooperative groups is the first step towards effective implementation of cooperative learning strategies. This can be done in a three ways: random, teacher-selected, or student-selected (Johnson, Johnson, and Holubec 1994). The nature of the task should be the determining factor as to which method is utilized. What one must consider is whether or not the groups need to be homogenous or heterogeneous. A complex task requiring a variety of skills, interests, or learning strengths require groups that are academically heterogeneous, whereas a task that is simpler, rote, or prescribed by the teacher may be successfully completed by groupings that are homogenous in personality or skill sets.

One way to form potentially heterogeneous groups is to assign students randomly using systems of simply numbering off. A little more engaging than numbering off is "animalling off." I have utilized this with students by providing an alphabetized list of animals equal in number to the number of students I want in a group divided by the number of students in the class. For example, if I have 32 students in class, and want groups of 4, then I would create a list of 8 animals. My list might include, aardvark, baboon, chimpanzee, dingo, elephant, ferret, giraffe, and hyena. Depending on the age of the students, you could have varying degrees of fun with how they identify in those groups, introduce each other, or simply use it as a means to teach a fact about each animal. The same could be done with historical figures, literary characters, etc. Another means of randomly assigning students into groups is have them pick small piece of wrapped candy such as Starbursts© from a bowl and then assemble by flavor (is it really a flavor, or just a color?). Ok, I have a confession to make about how, when I taught middle school science, I would assign groups that appeared random to students, but wasn't actually random. I would presort a deck of cards so that when I passed them out to the students sitting in their assigned seats I could pre-determine which students would end up with each numbered playing card. The only downfall to this method was adjusting the sequence quickly and surreptitiously as the students took their seats at the beginning of class if I noticed a student was missing.

Another means of grouping is for the teacher to select the groups. This is useful if you want to ensure that each group is heterogeneous with different interests, experiences, or learning preferences, or skills represented (or to simply separate certain individuals who will not work well together). This might require you as the teacher to carefully select every member of every group to ensure the personality, skillset, etc., matches the needs of the groupings. Another method is called stratified randomizing. Stratified randomizing could involve categorizing students by desired characteristic for each group, such as possibly gender, but also, more nuanced attributes or interests, such as ensuring each group has a student who is a strong organizer, reader, drawer, problem-solver, etc. You can first put students into these groups and then randomly select students from those groups and assign to their cooperative learning group.

The final means of grouping students is to allow them to self-select which is least recommended. The advantage to allowing students to self-select is that it is the preference of most students to do so, and they will get to work with their friends. This is also the weakness. Your task is to make it so *all* can learn. Undoubtedly, at least one student will be marginalized and left out, or begrudgingly join a group and then possibly be marginalized within the functioning of that group. For informal group tasks, such as a few minute discussions or sharing of an idea, this may be acceptable as it is usually the least time-consuming process. However, for any group task that is more sustained than a few minutes and/or results in completion of a formal, even possibly graded, task, self-selecting is not recommended for K-12 students.

Informal grouping of students, for short-term collaboration is a common strategy when wanting to provide students a chance to process information more deeply, reflect on what was learned, or complete some sense-making activities. Common approaches are to have students do a think-pair-share during a lesson, where you might ask students to pair up for discussion of a question or topic provided by the teacher and then share out their thoughts with the larger group. You could also have students turn to their neighbor and summarize what the last ten minutes of a lecture was about, to help students process what they have been hearing. Students can be put into round table discussions to do a think-group-share, in which they process an idea, discuss as a group, and then share with the larger class. These types of short-term, processing types of cooperative learning are commonly used as part of a traditional classroom setting—especially in secondary classrooms—as a means to actively engage students in what otherwise might be a quite didactic and passive learning scenario.

Really, what people think about with cooperative learning is the dreaded "group project;" but cooperative learning is an absolutely essential tool in one's teacher tool kit. Multiple studies have shown again and again that cooperative learning is an effective means of instruction and that it can be used at every grade level (Johnson et al. 1994). We've already explored some aspects of when group projects go awry as well as means by which to assign students into groups, so we will focus here on the benefits of cooperative learning and how to execute cooperative learning utilizing formal groupings of students. Effectively implemented cooperative learning results in higher achievement for all students in the group, long-term retention, increased intrinsic motivation, and development of higher level reasoning and critical thinking (Johnson et al. 1994).

For the cooperative learning experience to achieve the above results (in addition to learning content), these essential elements must exist (Johnson et al. 1994):

- *Positive interdependence*: The task must require the students collaborate to complete the task, as opposed to allow one person to do the entire task. They task must require that they must need each other to be successful.

- *Individual and group accountability*: The teacher must have a means by which to evaluate the group and the individual, and the group must have a means by which to safely process and provide feedback to one another about individuals' contribution and participation in the overall group effort.

- *Promotive interaction*: Successful completion of the task must require real work together in a way that they must promote each other's success by helping one another and sharing resources.

- *Interpersonal and small-group skills*: For the group to be successful, they must have to navigate (and therefore practice and develop) skills such as effective leadership, decision making, building trust, communication, and conflict management and resolution.

The effective cooperative learning group will exhibit these components, so let's dig a little deeper into how to facilitate cooperative learning groups utilizing authentic collaboration, resulting in enhanced exploration of content, and the development of crucial social skills. Students must be purposefully grouped (previously discussed) and have a specific task to complete. Students should have autonomy in some aspects of the task such as how to approach and who does what in the group (Knight 2013).

Everyone in the group needs a specific role. For not only purposes of accountability, but also for purpose of learning crucial metacognitive skills. The group must have a safe structure by which to collectively assess progress and group participation towards completion of the task. This requires that students are provided with practiced language to address one another in a group about individual participation and readily available access to the teacher for help with not only content and task completion but also with navigating difficult group dynamics.

Providing a means by which the students can begin the day's work on a project with setting a goal for the day's work can be a first step toward group promotive interaction and positive interdependence. By working together to establish the group goal, they can identify each individual's task for that day's work. Class time allotted for working on the project for the day should conclude with the group processing what was accomplished on each individual's task(s) and how those individual's efforts contributed to the group's progress toward completion of the overall project or task. This should be information that is recorded on daily progress sheets the group uses and turns into the teacher for review. You can then review this written record of progress and monitor the group discussions about the project process. By providing such a regular routine for the class period/day, you are more likely to identify where teacher intervention is needed to help a group distribute work equitably. Through tracking these conversations and the written progress report, you can also then provide feedback to individual members of the group about their collaboration skill development.

For a cooperative learning group to be able to self-structure their approach to an academic task, you have to adequately provide the parameters for the tasks and group processes. The task must be clear and measurable and the students must have access, either from you directly, or from other specified resources to the concepts, strategies of research and task completion, group processing tools (such as daily progress log sheets) and procedures of how to complete the task and work together to do so. Providing the students with a task list, flow-chart, or mind map for them to track progress and see how the individual parts are interdependent is necessary for the group to equitably function.

One means by which to ensure higher-functioning group dynamics is to assign roles, or have the group assign roles (depending on the students' age and the characteristic of the students). Clearly defined roles can help the group distribute work equitably, pulling back the reigns on the over-achieving students and putting some pressure to participate on the student who might otherwise try and lay low and slide by with minimal participation. This creates interdependence among the group members. Roles can be assigned to members to monitor group function, such as monitoring noise, leadership, taking turns, researcher, creative director, art director, clarifier, fact-checker, summarizer, brainstorming manager, etc. (Johnson et al. 1994; TeachingChannel 2018). What they are, and how roles are assigned, is highly dependent on the age of the class, the duration and nature of the task, and the overall climate already established in the classroom. Students can be assigned the role purposefully by the teacher or students self-select into roles (with you serving as arbiter if necessary). For projects where roles may not be skill-dependent, or if part of the purpose is for students to get practice with a variety of learning or social skills, the roles can be assigned by randomly handing out role cards or the roles can be rotated among the group members throughout the duration of the process. What is crucial to effective cooperative learning tasks is that the purpose is clear, the process is structured, and the task is as authentic as possible, and there are safe means for students to be held accountable for participation not just by you but, also by their peers.

Effectively operating cooperative learning groups is a useful means for providing planned supports for students. For a cooperative group to serve as a planned support, requires carefully assigning students to these groups or partnerships so that they can effectively support one another with an anticipated shortcoming of skill or knowledge instead of simply reinforcing the deficiency. Within these groups you might have students providing peer-editing, or pre-writing activities. Another way peers can be grouped to support one another is to pair students up for pre-writing/presentation/project brainstorming. Within pairs, have students take turns describing what they are going to write about (or do presentation or project) about. While the one student is describing their intended writing, etc., the other students take notes. This allows the student to verbally process and organize, while the other records what is said to provide the student doing the talking with a beginning outline for his or her work. Students can also be paired up or put into small groups to work on a reading assignment together. Students can simultaneously read a passage, stopping periodically (or at specifically marked locations in the text) to verbally summarize for each other what they have taken from the reading. This can help any level of reader to better understand and comprehend an assigned text.

Many students will need a variety of supports to complete writing tasks. The teacher can support struggling writers by providing students with an outline for a writing assignment, specific writing prompts, or even sentence starters for a writing assignment. The same strategies can be utilized for scaffolding research tasks or project-based learning tasks to provide a scaffold for struggling researchers.

We'll conclude this section with Table 11.2 summarizing a variety of cooperative learning lesson structures (both informal and formal groupings of students).

| Activity | Task Description |
|---|---|
| Team jigsaw | Divide up among students, articles topics, or portions of a reading to complete individually, and then report back to the group. The group then reports out to the class or teacher their understanding of the topic based on the combination of each group-member's contribution. |
| Note-taking pairs | During lecture/presentation lesson, stop periodically so paired students can share their notes to fill in gaps, seek clarification, make connections, or ask questions. |
| Turn to neighbor | Stop during lecture/presentation and have students discuss a particular topic or answer a specific question. |
| Read and explain pairs | Students paired to collaboratively read passage or text. For learning readers they can read to each other and coach one another. Pairs can also support one another in reading for content, using a similar process as turn to neighbor during a lecture. In this setting, pairs stop at designated points in the reading and explain to one another the content. |
| Writing and editing | Students can peer edit or coach one another with a writing task. Writing pairs can also help one another outline ideas, with one verbally explaining intent and the other recording the steps to provide a written outline for his or her partner while verbally processing intent for the writing project. |
| Student learning cohorts | Students can be grouped to support one another in the research/PBL process. This is not a group task, but like writing and editing pairs in which the group can help individuals to outline research process, peer coach progress, help set goals and hold one another accountable for meeting goals, and even help research by keeping an eye out for sources that might be useful to a cohort's research process. |
| Math learning cohorts | Students can be assigned homogeneously or heterogeneously (and either long-standing or for single lesson) to collaboratively complete a math problem or set of problems. |
| Academic controversies | Choose a topic that has two well-documented, clearly defined sides to the issue. In groups of four, students pair up to cooperatively research a side and develop their position statement. Each pair presents and they now reverse roles and repeat the process. Once all students have researched and argued both sides, they all drop their advocacy roles and work to reach consensus on an opinion and then possibly present to the class. |

**TABLE 11.2**   Cooperative Lesson Structures

# Project-Based Learning (PBL)/Authentic Learning

It should go without saying that as much as possible, we want students doing authentic learning, and nothing is more quintessentially "authentic learning" as PBL. While a PBL exploration can be completed in one day's lesson, PBL usually involves a sustained

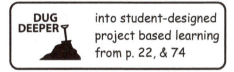

DUG DEEPER into student-designed project based learning from p. 22, & 74

series of tasks or lessons that a student completes over multiple days to answer a question, solve a problem, or deeply explore a topic. Therefore what fits under the umbrella of what could be labeled PBL is broad and to be sure, whole pedagogy books have been written on the variety of ways in which to lead students through PBL. It is safe to say that what I will provide on PBL should be considered a starting point for learning how to implement PBL, but further research, specific to the subject area and/or age that you teach should be explored more deeply as a regular component of professional development, including how entire school structure and curriculum can be built around PBL in such models as in the case Expeditionary Learning Outward Bound (ELOB) schools. It is likely, however, that most teacher candidates and practicing teachers reading this are not in an ELOB or other setting structured around student-designed PBL, so for the rest of this section I will proceed under the assumption that you are implementing PBL in a more traditional school setting and structure.

Numerous research studies in fact demonstrate utilizing significant levels of PBL can increase student and teacher engagement. Additionally, schools utilizing PBL extensively, such as ELOB schools, have recorded increases in academic achievement as measured by basic skills testing as well as advanced skills such as problem solving (Thomas 2000). These findings do not surprise me. PBL, by design, often requires an increase in student-to-student interaction and cooperation. It also quite often involves learning tasks that are interdisciplinary and open-ended enough to allow students the freedom to explore their own ideas in at least in some aspect of the assigned PBL lesson or unit (Brooks and Brooks 1993). Because PBL so often has the potential to tap into the students "purpose motive" instead of relying on the traditional "profit motive" model of motivating and engaging students, students are more likely to take risks and challenge themselves or accept the teacher's challenges to expand their current understanding about a topic or skill.

PBL promotes increased student engagement because it provides students the opportunity to become an expert on something so they can then share or export that knowledge to someone else. It allows them to

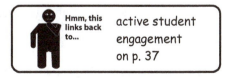

Hmm, this links back to... active student engagement on p. 37

teach something new to others and interact with peers socially as they are exploring and learning (NYC Department of Education 2009). Teaching is fun, right!?

Additionally, PBL lends itself to being easily differentiated by the teacher to meet individual students' abilities, learning styles, interests, and learning differences.

> Project-based learning allows students multiple options for taking in information, making sense of ideas, and expressing what they have learned. It is by definition differentiated as it provides students with multiple ways to acquire content, to process or make sense of ideas, and to develop products that demonstrate effective learning. Students can approach the inquiry process in a variety of ways and build on their own interests and experiences. There is no limit to how deeply students can explore a question, allowing each learning to challenge him or herself to the fullest (NYC Department of Education 2009, 9).

These benefits are predicated on the students having some role in the topic, design, and/ or the method of presentation.

At the beginning of the book I likened teaching and learning to a journey and attempted to shift our paradigm of how we think of these two things as active and ongoing by using the active language of "enacting a story" to describe the process of teaching. PBL has the potential to be the most authentic of learning experiences because by nature, our natural process of enacting the story of our lives and experiencing the world as life-long learners is nothing more than a series of ongoing projects. This is what we do when we learn—we ask questions, we explore, and we discover while enacting our story. Therefore, for PBL to be effectively engaging it must possess many of the following characteristics (NYC Department of Education 2009; Thomas 2000):

1. Prompts student-driven (to some degree) exploration of important ideas central to the class curriculum,
2. Involves student inquiry framed around questions requiring students to explore central concepts of the class curriculum,
3. Requires students acquiring information through independent constructive investigation and independent presentation of ideas,
4. Connected to real world, authentic problems, requiring creative and critical thinking to draw conclusions and generate new ideas about one's on understanding of content.

The key to successfully implemented PBL is student ownership. Therefore it is crucial that students have some level of control over either the content of the project, the method of investigation of the project, or the manner in which they make sense of what was learned and how that new knowledge is presented to peers, the teacher, and parents.

Effective PBL then results in something that has intrinsic value to the student. This can be either in the intrinsic interest in the subject matter or problem being solved, or in the final product that marks the culmination of the project. The final product must be

Hmm, this links back to... authentic learning in the classroom on p. 73

authentic to the student and have a real-life context. This often is a product such as some form of performance assessment like a podcast, exhibition, presentation to stakeholders related to the topic being explored, portfolios of work, etc. PBL should allow students to build on (and therefore improve) their own artistic talents, performance abilities, expertise in syntax (writing) and discourse writing (speaking), and natural inquisitiveness (NYC Department of Education 2009).

It is clear that PBL has a great deal of potential. Even though, a casual observer might think the teacher's role is diminished in a PBL setting, and therefore easier to do, this is absolutely false. In situations where that is the case, PBL is not being effectively implemented and the students' and teachers are likely not enthused by the process, but are fatigued and disengaged by the process. Effective PBL requires careful planning and facilitation on the part of the teacher so the students feel supported and successful. The project students are completing has to be central to the daily operation and structure of the classroom, and the primary means by which they are learning and assessed on the required course content. The project cannot be viewed as an extra assignment to be completed at home.

Let's explore the process of project design and completion. PBL does not involved giving students a push towards completing a project on a student-chosen, or teacher-chosen topic, and then

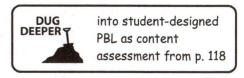

DUG DEEPER into student-designed PBL as content assessment from p. 118

stepping back and letting them run with it. There might actually be a great deal of direct instruction happening throughout the students' completion of the project. The act of completing PBL is a skill, and routinized skills are often best taught using a model of the teacher first showing/doing, students practicing with guidance, and then students practicing and completing with, and eventually without, the scaffolded support from the teacher. Therefore, each step of the PBL process described below, might require that the teacher provide direct instruction for each step, multiple examples, checklists, templates, etc., as the students complete the process. Each of these steps then function not only to move the student closer to project completion and self-assuredness in the process, but also as a formative assessment for the teacher and student, providing data on his or her progress.

The process students follow when designing and then completing PBL is really a scaled down, and individualized version of the process a teacher follows when developing thematic, inquiry-based units. It also closely follows what is taught as the step-by-step process of the "scientific method." The starting point is the topic or theme for the inquiry, and why this is important to the student, and possibly what the goal is, either in what will be learned or what will be produced as the final product marking the culmination of the project.

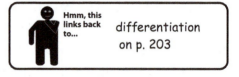

Hmm, this links back to... differentiation on p. 203

The topic of the project will range from the teacher assigning a topic, providing a list of topics to choose from, to the student having autonomy over topic choice. This is dependent on the curricular goal for the PBL experience. If the goal is the process, and PBL is being utilized to teach the inquiry process, but the teacher still has a required agenda (specific content), then the student will not have much autonomy of topic choice. This is risky, as it might not be possible to tap into the students "purpose-motive" in this scenario. At a minimum, in this case, the student must have autonomy over the nature of the final product of the project, and as much as possible, smaller aspects of the content and the process by which to explore the content. Conversely, PBL might be a strategy the teacher is using to teach a specific mode of acquiring and presenting information—such as a research paper. In this scenario the student should have autonomy over project topic choice (within acceptable, age-appropriate parameters of course) if the teacher is prescribing the structure of the final product. The other end of the spectrum is using PBL purely for the purpose of teaching the inquiry process. In this setting, there is no reason the student should not have the autonomy to choose the topic, design the inquiry, and decide on the final product. This doesn't mean he or she gets to do whatever they want. You are still the teacher and responsible for what your students are learning, how they are learning it, and how they present it. Between these two extremes, what is most likely the case in information content-based courses, is for the student and teacher to share ownership of any combination of the topic choice, the nature of the inquiry, or the final product. A common method is for the teacher to provide students with choices of prescribed projects, specific or categories of topics, and/or choices of final products of the project.

This allows the teacher to provide age and developmentally appropriate scaffolding. For example, a teacher may begin the year providing students with a choice of prescribed projects to complete. This does run the risk that none will be appealing to the student, so the teacher still needs to allow for student-generated ideas to have some place in the choice process. As the year progresses, the teacher may remove the number of prescribed project ideas, and slowly shift to more open-ended project choices (in topic or method of presentation), until by the end of the year the students are taking full ownership of the topic, method of inquiry, and final product design. In an information-based content course such as a science or social studies course, it may be necessary for the teacher to provide some limits (or choices) of the parameters of the project, assuming PBL is being used to assess required content mastery.

Whether the choice of topic is partially limited by the teacher or not, the first step to completing a project is choosing the topic. This begins with the student identifying an interest area (even if within a content parameter, such as the Civil War in an American history class). It is natural for students to gravitate towards something they already have an interest in and possibly already have a great deal of knowledge about. After all, they will be graded on this (most likely) and so will want to be successful. Your job is to provide a safe place for the student to challenge him or herself to explore a topic worth exploring that will expand his or her knowledge and skill base.

One way to do this is to guide students to complete a Know/Wonder chart for a variety of topics (see Figure 11.2). In completing these charts, students will catalog what they know and wonder about for a variety of possible project topic choices.

| What I KNOW about _____ | What I WONDER about _____ |
|---|---|
| | |

**FIGURE 11.2** Know/Wonder Chart

The project the student chooses should be one that has more "wonder" questions/statements than "know" statements. If there are more know statements, then there may not be much new ground for the student to explore in that topic. Also, if there are not many wonder statements (regardless of number of know statements), then to what end is the student completing the project? If it isn't a topic of interest, chances are the student will not have much intrinsic motivation to complete the project. That most likely puts the student back into "profit-motive" for completing the project, and will seat them right at step three on the engagement ladder, and most likely ensure a mediocre project that doesn't foster much creativity and critical thinking.

Just as the design of a thematic, inquiry-based unit of study rests on a strong thematic question that is "essential," so too does a student project. This will require that you provide students the necessary guidance to refine his or her question to be one that will

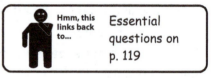

Hmm, this links back to... Essential questions on p. 119

require research on his or her part, and then also requires the student to apply new knowledge or skills to solving the problem or understanding the concept of the question beyond mimetic regurgitation of the topic. It really comes down to this as far as helping a student write and/or choose a question that will foster deep inquiry and engagement: why do they want to know the answer? Challenge the student to provide an answer to *why* they want to know this and find the meaningful connection to him or herself. Just keep asking them "why do you want to know this?" until together you uncover a meaningful reason. Otherwise, it is likely the project will not sustain his or her interest throughout the entire process of completion.

To help students thoughtfully complete the design process, I like to have students propose their project idea to me in a project proposal. This can be done in multiple guided steps for younger students or students inexperienced with PBL, or can be done in one project proposal process step for students more advanced in PBL. It should include these components. Like the unit design process, these steps many be iterative

1. A topic idea/choice and process to determine viability (such as know/wonder chart or explanation as to "why" important)
2. Expression of topic choice in terms of investigative question that is "essential."
3. "Chunking" the investigative question/topic into manageable pieces expressed in the form of guiding questions.
4. The desired outcome of the project. This may involve the student defining what the final product will be, however, it can also be acceptable that the nature of the final product will emerge or evolve as the student continues to explore the essential question.

Successful completion of the project requires that students complete each of the following steps (to age-appropriate degrees of sophistication)

1.   How to find sources for information (including possibly working with a mentor) and/or collect data in the case of primary research
2.   How to cull sources for information,
3.   How to record and catalog information and/or data,
4.   How to prioritize information and data and then apply to answering the investigative question,
5.   How to effectively present the findings.

Each of these steps will undoubtedly require some form of scaffolded support from you as the teacher. Effectively implementing PBL requires that you know your students abilities and interests so that you can actively participate in their successful completion of the project and effectively facilitate completion of each step. This might require recognizing and then providing individualized support and structures for students to complete each task. This is why effectively implementing PBL requires even more active engagement with students and attention to individual needs and ongoing routines and procedures in class than traditional didactic instruction practices.

*Assessing PBL*: In addition to the formative assessment happening during project completion, a final or summative evaluation of the project will most likely occur. How you assess a student's project is entirely dependent on the intended goal for the project, and of course the age of the student and assessment/grading culture of your classroom and school. The final assessment of the project will involve evaluation based on examination of the evidence or artifacts from the project. This could include just an evaluation of the final result, or could include an assemblage of artifacts such as notes, journals, data/research, reflective writing, and self- or group-evaluations that chronicle the entire process. What artifacts are relevant and how those are assessed depend on the original intent of the project.

Assessment isn't just the purview of the teacher. The student should engage in self-assessment, and as much as possible, should also engage in peer coaching and evaluation. These processes should be authentic and necessitate the student using the same grading rubric or checklist as the teacher. This helps to ensure that the student fully understand the expectations on the grading rubric or checklist, which is crucial to both the student meeting any expectations you have, but also then understanding the feedback provided on the rubric so that feedback can become feedforward for the next PBL experience.

In cases, where the project is being utilized to learn and assess content mastery, then the grading rubric or project checklist must provide the student and teacher a means to assess both the content expected to be communicated in the project, the process of completing the project, and the final quality of the presentation of that content. In cases where the entire intent of the project is the process of completing inquiry, then it is important that the grading rubric or checklist is focused on, and using artifacts demonstrating, completion of the steps of inquiry. The content of the project is less important, though certainly it must be accurate. The final quality of the project, while important, must be age-appropriate. If the project process is the primary purpose for the PBL experience, then students (and parents) need guidance to focus on the process and quality of research and information, and not assume a flashy final product is what is important. This is also a challenge when evaluating any project. It is easy and tempting for the teacher to overlook content errors or process gaps if the final product is highly polished—which might be more an evaluation of the parent's involvement than the student's process and engagement. This brings me to my final point, which has been stated before, but requires repeating again. If you are utilizing PBL, then a significant portion of the work needs to be done in the classroom so that you can monitor progress and utilize effective formative assessment of the process and content during the project, and not just the final completed product.

# Formative and Summative (besides PBL) Assessment Examples

The nature of types of formative assessment and authentic learning/PBL summative assessment has been covered in Chapter 5 and previously in this chapter. The purpose of this section is to provide you with

> **DUG DEEPER** into formative assessment strategies from p. 36 & 79

a starting point for identifying a variety of assessment tools and techniques. Also recall that virtually all learning activities you do with students could or should also be considered a formative assessment in a constructivist model. The more a course is developed around authentic project-based learning there is less of a defined line between learning activity and even the summative assessment. This is, at best, a partial list!

- Whiteboard:
    - Students write the answer to a question or problem on a white board and hold it up for the teacher to see. The teacher can monitor the whole classes' progress on a skill set. If all students are facing the teacher, peers should not see one another's

answers and students can then erase their answer to prepare for the next problem or question.

- Traffic Cones:
  - o Used to quickly assess a group's progress on a task or discussion. Use three different colored cups (red, green, yellow), substituting blue if student is red-green colorblind. They can stack the cups so depending on which is showing, this communicates progress to the teacher:
    - Green = Teacher can move along, as we've completed with the task and ready to move on (or participate with the larger group)
    - Yellow = Teacher can keep an eye on us as we are still working, but making progress.
    - Red = Teacher should stop and help us, as we are stuck or confused.
- Peer Coaching and Evaluation:
  - o In addition to peer editing and coaching during writing, reading and research process, peer coaching can also be used when students are completing formal formative and/or summative assessment tasks. Prior to students turning in a paper, project, or other such complex or multi-dimensional task, provide time for the students to peer coach and evaluate one another's assignment. Students use the grading rubric that you will use when evaluating the assignment. They sit down together and go through each other's assignment together, one at a time. As they go through the assignment they have a dialogue about each aspect of the assignment assessed using the rubric provided. The peer completes the rubric as they discuss. Then they go through the other student's assignment. This is much more substantial than simply trading and grading each other's assignment or peer editing a paper. This requires dialogue about the process and content. This is beneficial to both students. The teacher can also unobtrusively listen to these conversations and informally assess the classes' understanding of the content by the content of their conversations and not just what was turned in. The students then turn in the peer-completed rubric with their assignment. This can serve as another piece of data for the teacher to use to assess the classes' general understanding of the concepts, and even individual's by how they peer coached/evaluated their partner. The key is for them to "pair and share" not to "trade and grade."
- Road Map or Learning Log:

o   Unit road maps were presented in Chapter 8 as a tool for students to use to track their progress on the assignments for a unit (the unit outline and table of contents) and their connections between topics (the learning map). This tool can also be used as a component of the summative assessment by having students turn this in with the final summative assessment for the unit. This allows the teacher to see and understand some of the students thinking about the concepts. This is especially useful if the teacher sees a gap that doesn't coincide with their other observations about the student's progress. Referencing the learning map might indicate that the gap is on how it was communicated on the summative assessment, but was accounted for earlier on the learning map. The table of contents portion of the road map can serve as a learning log for the student to track what was completed and what scores or grades were earned on each formative assessment for a unit.

- KWL/OWL Chart:

  o   KWL charts can be used as a class or by individuals to initially record what they already **K**now about a topic, what they **W**onder about a topic to generate investigative questions, and in the end what they **L**earned about a topic. This provides a means for the student to self-assess progress as well and the teacher to see progress as well. The OWL chart is the same, except utilized in an inquiry-based lesson in which the students are beginning with making **O**bservations about an object or phenomenon they can observe.

- Exit Ticket:

  o   An exit ticket is just what it sounds like. It can be graded (like a small quiz) or simply used by the teacher to gauge the classes' understanding of a new concept, which will then inform the next day's lesson. This is usually something that can be completed quickly in the last five to ten minutes of the lesson and asks students to write about, answer one question or describe one concept.

- Entrance Ticket:

  o   An entrance ticket is used to assess students' completion and understanding of an assignment from a previous day, or as a homework assignment allowing the student to be admitted to the class to participate in that day's activity. This is a useful technique to get students to understand that a small task such as a reading assignment needs to be done so they can participate in that days lesson or discussion. By calling it an entrance ticket, the teacher is communicating the value of that assignment for participating in the next activity, and therefore, by not completing it, the student is not only impacting him or herself, but also his or her peers. Consequences for not completing the entrance ticket will depend on the age of the students and the climate and culture of the school and classroom. It's doubtful that you could actually bar a student from entering the classroom without some prior arrangement with administration, but the degree to which the student completed the entrance ticket may impact manner in which they participate in the day's activity in the classroom.

- Clickers:
  - Clickers are used with an interactive white board like an SMART board™. Students can register their response to questions on the board. Their answers are recorded and tabulated for the class and the teacher to see. Alternative to using this dedicated technology, programs such as Kahoot can utilize internet-capable devices to complete the same process.

- Thumbs up, down, to side:
  - This strategy is quite simple. When working with a new concept in whole group, you can ask students to provide thumbs up if they are confident, thumbs down if still do not understand and a thumb to the side if getting it but still not confident.

- Web of Knowledge:
  - This is a variation on an activity used to teach food webs in ecology and also used as a "get-to-know-one-another" activity in advisory settings. Begin with a ball of yarn or string. Students can answer a question about a topic and then toss the ball of string to another student who can answer another question. Alternatively, the students can ask the questions themselves and toss the ball of string. It also doesn't have to be "questions" but instead students expanding on a concept from a larger topic and tossing the string so the next student can expand on that concept or introduce another related concept about the larger topic.

- Gallery Walk:
  - A gallery walk is used as a means for small groups to see the work of other small groups and then learn from those groups and update their work. For example, having students complete a learning map for a unit at the end of a unit on large sheets of paper is a good means for students to complete collaborative sense making. Each group can then post up their completed learning map and then

students walk around the room in their working groups and examine each other's learning maps. When they return to their own map they can make changes or additions to the information on their map.

- QuickWrite:
  - This can be used at the beginning of a class for students to quietly begin thinking about day's topic. This can be a good means of introducing the topic and having students uncover their prior knowledge about the topic. This can also be used as an informal formative assessment later in a lesson in the form of a "few-minute paper" (2–5 minutes) to have students communicate their true understanding at that moment. This is effective at providing the student and the teacher the student's "gut level" understanding of the topic as opposed to what they can look up, or recall by talking with peers.

- QuickDiscuss:
  - This serves the same purpose as a quick write, but is conducted collaborative discussion with a partner or small group of peers.

- Probing Discussion:
  - Sounds like a medical procedure, but not. Probing discussion is purposefully questioning the class with increasingly deeper or more in-depth questions about a topic or concept. To do this properly most likely requires that the teacher has scripted out a number of questions to pull from as opposed to relying on spontaneously thinking of questions that increasingly move from recall of information to application to analysis of a concept.

- Unobtrusive observation:
  - This formative assessment is most appropriate in classes that involve students performing a skill, be it a lab skill in a science class, a skill in a physical education class or other such skill-based activity, or even as an assessment of noncontent-based skills such as collaborative work, leadership, sharing, etc. If done regularly and discretely as a part of the teacher circulating around the room the act of observing should become routine for the students and then not alter their performance.

- Performance Assessment:
  - A performance assessment is self-explanatory by the name. Students are performing something as their summative assessment. This includes such activities that are truly

performances, such as in the performing arts, but is not limited to such a strict interpretation. Students demonstrating how to properly tie their shoes, operate a microscope,

**DUG DEEPER** into summative assessment other than PBL from p. 76

complete a cooking task, or make a formal presentation to a group are all examples of a performance assessment. In all cases it requires that the student adequately complete a task, perform a skill, or present information in an authentic setting.

- Objective quiz and test:
  - These are traditional "pencil and paper" assessments. Much of the time, these are utilized along with a commercially purchased curriculum and textbook which provides a test-bank of questions from which the teacher can pull questions and assemble the test to match the unit essential questions and/or learning objectives. There are some fundamental principles that should be adhered to when constructing such a test.
    - The test should not rely on noncontent academic language that may cause a student to not understand a question despite knowing the content of the question.
    - The test should cover all of the learning objectives for the unit/topic. The test should cover the big ideas and concepts outlined by the learning objectives, not a piece of factoid minutia (think trivia question) that a student may not have had to memorize to have deep understanding of the concept. There should be no surprise or "gotcha" questions.
    - The test should use appropriately selected types of questions to cover all cognitive domains utilized in the unit or topic. Certain types of questions such as matching and fill in the blank are adequate for testing recall but not for cognitive domains higher up on Bloom's taxonomy. Well-crafted multiple choice questions can be written to require students to apply, analyze, and even evaluate concepts, though questions such as this are difficult to write. Short answer and essay questions have the potential to require cognitive thinking higher up on Bloom's taxonomy, but of course, such questions can also be used to test students' ability to recall memorized information.
- Essay Quiz or Exam:
  - An essay quiz or exam is typically one question or a few questions breaking apart a larger concept. The essay quiz or exam can certainly be used to have students

recall memorized information (though not simply terminology) such as recounting the workings of a multi-step process, such as a scientific process, a mathematical process/theorem, or historical event. This form of assessment is also useful for when students are required to apply the use of terminology to the inner-workings of a process or to offer analysis and evaluation of a conceptual idea while properly applying terms and concepts from the unit. An essay quiz or test used in content areas should not be grading the writing, unless students are properly advised and prepared for the fact that a portion of their assessment is the ability to express their ideas in written essay form.

- Long-Form Written Exam or Quiz:

  o This form of assessment is essentially the same as the essay, with the same uses and purposes. The primary difference is opening up the form of writing beyond an "essay" format, thus allowing and even encouraging students to utilize lists, graphics, diagrams, charts, etc., as a component of their response to an exam question.

## Socratic Questioning

Effectively using questions as a teaching tool is difficult. Many teachers who utilize this strategy make some crucial mistakes in implementation. First, they often limit their questioning to the recalling of memorized information. Second, they do not allow nearly enough wait time for students to think about a question and answer. Third, the classroom environment has not been

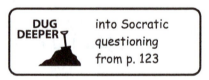

**DUG DEEPER** into Socratic questioning from p. 123

adequately fostered to allow students to comfortably be wrong, or take a guess at answering, therefore, the teacher relies on answers from the select students either willing to take the risk, or who are sure in their response. In either case, it is not an effective formative assessment to gauge the overall classes' understanding of a concept, or to gauge individual's understanding if they aren't willing to respond. It also isn't necessarily an effective teaching strategy if the students only answer to recall information. Those that know the answer, are not required to dig deeper into their thinking and those that don't know the answer, likely will not learn it from hearing another student answer while they are quietly breathing a sigh of relief they were not called upon.

Two of these issues are easy to fix. First, be willing to wait, but, teach students why you are waiting and what you are waiting for. You do not want a student to feel like they have to rescue you or the class with an answer. Instruct students about the strategy of waiting and how questioning can be an effective teaching strategy. Letting them understand your thinking as a teacher provides

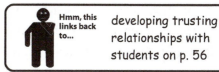

Hmm, this links back to... developing trusting relationships with students on p. 56

an opportunity for the student and teacher to approach learning together, as a relationship built in advocacy, mutual trust, and with a shared purpose, as opposed to an adversarial relationship where the student just hopes to get through the day or class unnoticed and unscathed. The second is creating an expectation that everyone participate. This can be done by calling on students, setting parameters for how often they should participate in a day (literally saying, "I want everyone to answer at least one question during this discussion." can actually work, as simple as it sounds), or devising a systematic way of randomly calling on students such as pulling popsicle sticks with students names written on them from a cup. Ideally, you will create such an engaging collaborative classroom culture that students will feel safe and confident to answer your questions, even if answering with a supposition. So what should this questioning look like?

First let's define three types of questions. The first two are commonly understood: closed-ended and open-ended. Closed-ended questions have one acceptable right answer. "Who was the first president of the United States?" is a closed-ended question. Open-ended questions have multiple possible right answers or even are asking a students' opinion about something. "Who would you say was the most effective president of the United States?" is an open-ended question. I'm going to add a third label for the grey area in-between the two: Limited-open ended questions. These are questions that have multiple components to a right answer or multiple right answers, but theoretically, all could eventually be listed, such as: "In what ways have humans affected the ecological health of the nation's aquifers?" There are multiple answers, but there is a limit to how many answers are accepted by the scientific community. A closed-ended version of this question could be, "What is the human activity that has reduced the nation's aquifers most rapidly?" This still might be a complex answer, but there may only be one accepted answer to the question. An entirely open-ended version might move us to questions about actions, such as "What actions should the U.S. government take to reduce the depletion of the nation's aquifers."

Alright, now let's explore using a variety of questions as an instructional strategy. Using a series of questions to probe a student's or a class's understanding of a concept, and even cause them to think more deeply about a concept requires using a combination of the three types of questions. Through purposeful questioning the teacher can facilitate student exploration of a topic. First, by getting them to think about a subject and recalling what they already know. Then, elaborating on what they already know. Next, then making inferences and conclusions about the concept based on what they already know and have added to their thinking during the discussion by making, hypotheses, predictions, and/or suppositions about the concept based on their prior knowledge and the expansion of their thinking during the discussion. This is how Socratic questioning can be used in a classroom during a lesson in which the goal is to get students to explore complex ideas, explore issues or problems, analyze conceptual ideas, facilitate inquiry-based learning, develop problem-solving skills, construct and deepen knowledge, and uncover assumptions and establish new assumptions based on a logical progression of thought and ideas.

Let's consider four types of Socratic questions that (Carleton College 2016; University of Michigan n.d.):

- Seek clarification
    - Why do you say that?
    - What do you understand to be...?
    - What was the cause of...?
- Probe assumptions
    - What is your assumption...?
    - What is your thinking about...?
    - What was the purpose for why you...?
- Probe reasoning, perspective, viewpoints, and/or evidence
    - What is your evidence for your conclusion that...?
    - What do you think causes...?
    - What would be a good example of...?
- Probe implications and consequences
    - How does _____ affect...?
    - How does _____ connect to what you said before about...?
    - What are you implying?

During a lesson built around Socratic questioning the teacher's job is to provide a situation where all student's attempted responses to questions are respected, honored, and actively utilized to further the discussion. This requires trust between the student and the teacher. Students should be challenged, yet comfortable answering questions honestly and fully in front of their classmates. This requires that the teacher has first established the culture and climate of the classroom for open participation by establishing routines of how individuals add to a discussion, be it completely free-form, or regulated by structures such as raising one's hand or even possessing a talking stick. For Socratic questioning to work, the students have to be willing to participate when called upon (or willing to enter the conversation on their own), be succinct when they do answer, and speak loudly enough so the whole class can hear.

To facilitate a meaningful discussion, first and foremost the teacher must have deep understanding of the concept. From this deep understanding, the teacher can anticipate student misconceptions, prior knowledge, and then plan out questions ahead of time, even sequencing them in the order of the four types of questions listed previously. During the discussion, the teacher must wait. And. Wait. Keep the discussion focused. You can do this by periodically summarizing, even recording key ideas and points on white board. Following up student responses with more questions or an invitation to "say more about…" will also keep the discussion focused. Avoid vague questions or that are beyond the level of the students. Also avoid questions that are too easy, have obvious answers, or are yes/no questions. These are patronizing. Either of these will shut down the conversation. Draw as many students into the discussion as possible, using whatever established routines and expectations already exist for this setting.

Here's an example of a possible series of questions that is Socratic. These sample questions could be used in an upper elementary or middle school science classroom to explore the characteristics of living things to determine if something is scientifically considered to be a lifeform.

- What is life? Describe what characteristics something must have for you to consider it as alive?

- Look at this burning candle. What do you see happening with the flame that makes it appear to be alive?

- Is the flame alive? Why do you think this is so? What evidence can you provide from your observations that matches our assumption about the characteristics of living things?

- If we were to consider the flame as alive, how might that change our definition of "life?"

## Good Old Fashioned Didactic Lecture

"If I want to be a constructivist teacher, can I ever lecture?" The answer is, "Of course!" There are times that it is necessary and valuable for you to conduct a lesson that appears to be a lecture; though, lecturing has been traditionally used for providing students with facts and information and teaching should move beyond this purpose. For one thing, we know that to truly know something and own the knowledge, meaning must be constructed. Second, the world has changed. That method of teaching evolved when individuals, such as Socrates, possessed knowledge that others did not have, and the only means for the students to get that knowledge was from the instructor. This is, of course, no longer the case. And even then, Socrates did not simply drone on about a topic, but he conducted lessons that involved the student and required the student to process, work with, consider prior misconceptions, and ultimately defend their thinking and understanding about a concept. He was a constructivist, even though he may not have used "hands-on" learning, "project-based learning," or "inquiry-based instruction" his students still worked their way through the CCC learning cycle, though it is safe to say it wasn't recognized or labeled as such!

Didactic lecturing is appropriate for presenting and explaining a concept or procedure. Used effectively to present and explain a procedure, didactic instruction is best used in a situation where the teacher can present the steps to completing a skill or process, be it swinging a golf club, drawing a landscape in perspective, solving a math problem, or operating a piece of lab equipment. The didactic lesson would most likely come at the beginning of the sequence of lessons utilizing such a skill or process—often for reasons of safety. The other reason to utilize didactic explanation at the beginning of a sequence of lessons about a skill is when it is important to avoid students inadvertently building bad habits that need to be then corrected. Consider learning to hit a golf ball. Just allowing students to safely explore how to do this in a playful setting which might be in line with inquiry-based instruction, might actually cause students to commit to muscle memory bad habits that then have to be broken. This type of skill instruction often follows a simple, "I do, we do, you do" model. The teacher explains and demonstrates, students collaboratively do with step by step guidance of the teacher and/or peers, and then students continue to practice in small groups or on their own. During this last phase is when students will be making meaning as they progress beyond the basics of the skill and can begin to expand on the skill to deepen proficiency or apply the skill to more complex and divergent situations.

A didactic lesson to deepen understanding about a concept, process or idea certainly has a place in a constructivist classroom as well. Again, this isn't an excuse to talk at students for an hour and tell them a bunch of stuff. Effective didactic teaching has always included opportunities for students to participate verbally with the whole class, small groups, or with a partner, and also require more active participation than simply taking notes. Socratic questioning can be strategically built into portions of a didactic lecture lesson to draw students into the discussion. This requires strong background knowledge, strong understanding of what your students already know, and well-placed and planned questions that will allow the students' answers to bring the lecture to the next planned point in the presentation.

Utilizing methods of cooperative learning described previously that interrupt the monotony of the lecture with small group or partner discussion, summarizing, and questioning can also make the normally passive-learning situation more active for students.

Another appropriate use of didactic teaching in a constructivist classroom is set up so that the students can actively engage in sense making and confirming activities during the teacher's presentation of ideas. This is best conducted in an inquiry-based setting in which the students have had an opportunity to explore an idea, topic, or process. This could be a specific text or piece of art, music, or literature, a scientific lab experience, or any other such situation where students were allowed to explore a topic and draw their own conclusions and understandings from a lived experience. Lecturing after such an experience and utilizing the work students generated during that experience, be they observation notes, a lab report, an analysis of a text, or summary and response to an artistic performance or piece, allows students to juxtapose what they observed and concluded with an accepted, verified understanding or interpretation of that topic. This is a constructivist activity because students are having to rectify any disequilibrium between what they observed and what you are now presenting to them. Or they are confirming their own conclusions with those of "the experts."

In all of these examples, a didactic approach can be acceptable if it fits somewhere in the CCC learning cycle (Figure 11.3) and also allows for students to complete the triangulation around their "owned knowledge" (Figure 11.4) to verify and solidify that understanding.

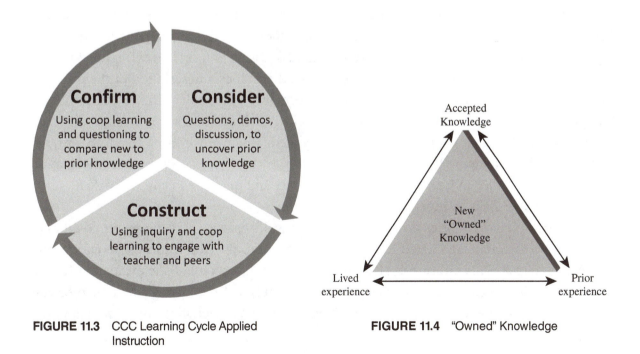

**FIGURE 11.3** CCC Learning Cycle Applied Instruction

**FIGURE 11.4** "Owned" Knowledge

# Grading Rubrics

Grading rubrics were described with some specific examples provided in Chapter 5. A rubric is any tool that a teacher uses to quantify and qualify feedback about student work in a systematic manner. They are an evaluation tool that are used to evaluate (and provide direction) for

DUG DEEPER → into grading rubrics from p. 83

assessments that involve demonstration of a process, usually during a performance assessment or evaluation of a product that is intended to demonstrate a student's proficiency with a concept, topic, or body of knowledge. Rubrics can be a useful tool for allowing a teacher to more efficiently grade these tasks as the teacher can circle items on the rubric, check off boxes, etc., to provide specific feedback to the student without having to physically write out descriptive comments providing that feedback. The more detailed the rubric is, and precisely constructed anticipating what level students will complete work, what that work might look like, and where gaps may occur, the more quickly a rubric can be used during evaluation by the teacher with less individual narrative needed. Conversely a rubric written with less descriptive language and precise examples of student work requires the teacher to provide more individualized narrative to provide adequate feedback to the student. The appropriateness of the specificity of the rubric is situational, with both approaches having merit.

Rubrics can be analytic, holistic, or a combination of the two. Analytic rubrics provide a description for each criterion that is being assessed. This provides the student feedback about individual components of the task and then those individual components are aggregated to calculate a final grade or score for the task. Holistic rubrics (see Figure 11.5) do not itemize each individual component, but instead provides a description of the different levels of the nature of the final product or performance so that the teacher can provide a single score and grade for the entirety of the work. This kind of rubric is certainly faster to use to score a task, but in order to provide adequate instructive feedback (feedforward) for students, this will require the teacher to communicate more specific evaluative information to the student either in written narrative comments and questions or in individual, small group, or whole class conferencing and discussion.

The two types of rubrics can be combined as well. Individual components of a larger task can be described and listed for the teacher to use to provide feedback about specific aspects of a task. This information can then be used to inform a holistic evaluation for the student. I believe this is the most transparent type of rubric. When using a holistic rubric, it is fair to say that the teacher does indeed have certain characteristics he or she is looking

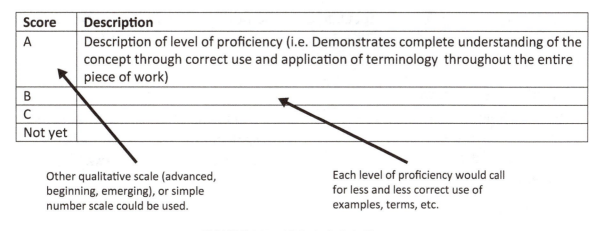

| Score | Description |
|-------|-------------|
| A | Description of level of proficiency (i.e. Demonstrates complete understanding of the concept through correct use and application of terminology throughout the entire piece of work) |
| B | |
| C | |
| Not yet | |

Other qualitative scale (advanced, beginning, emerging), or simple number scale could be used.

Each level of proficiency would call for less and less correct use of examples, terms, etc.

**FIGURE 11.5** Holistic Rubric Format

for in the completed product or performance. Even a checklist of essential elements that the teacher can check off while reviewing the work can be beneficial in informing the final holistic assessment of the work, and also providing a means for quick and efficient feedback to the student.

When designing a rubric, it is crucial that the rubric is aligned to the lesson/unit learning objectives and essential questions and also with the type of instruction that was used in the lesson or unit. It certainly would be unfair to include aspects of quality of writing on a rubric about a content essay, if students were not also instructed that they needed to use a certain writing format to communicate their answer. The rubric must be focused on identifiable attributes that you want to see in the final performance or product. By listing out these attributes and what you anticipate they will look like at different levels of proficiency in the students' work, you will create your descriptive language for the different elements of analytic rubric, or the description of the performance/produce as a whole in the case of a holistic rubric.

There are a variety of graphic designs for completing a rubric. The classic model of an analytic rubric is to be in a grid format. Across one axis of the grid are the levels and across the other axis are the criterion. The teacher can then simply circle or mark the appropriate box. These individual components can then be aggregated to calculate a final score. When designed well, this type of rubric allows for quick grading and specific feedback to the student. The trick is to design it well! When not designed well, some aspects of the students work is not described by any of the boxes. This might require the teacher to circle multiple aspects of multiple levels for a criterion (which might be okay) or to modify the rubric as it is being used to provide accurate feedback to the student. A poorly designed, very detailed, analytic rubric is very difficult to use, requiring considerable additional narrative commenting on the part of the teacher. Figure 11.6 is a template for a grid-formatted analytic rubric.

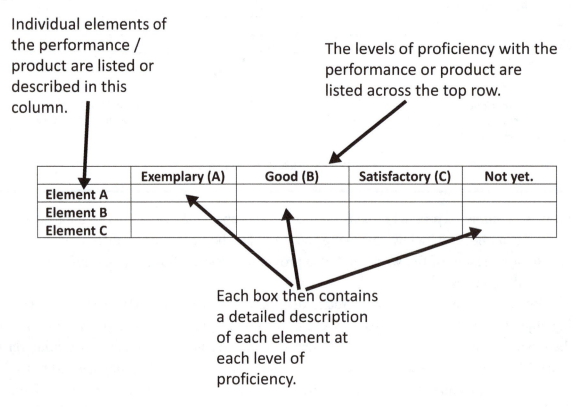

FIGURE 11.6   Analytic Rubric Template

This design of analytic rubric certainly has the advantage of providing a very detailed description of what is expected which can also be its weaknesses. It must be constructed accurately to be effective and therefore takes a long time to create and as we've already seen, is either accurate, making it easy to use, or not. Once created, there isn't much flexibility in how the teacher can use it.

Analytic rubrics do not need to be so rigidly designed. This makes it easier to create and offers more flexibility when being used by the teacher. But, it then does require the teacher to spend more time writing individual comments and questions to provide necessary instructive feedback. Figure 11.7 is a template for an analytic rubric that offers more flexibility. It still describes the attributes the teacher is looking for, but not at varying levels of proficiency. A score for each level of proficiency for each element is still recorded. In the example below, the level of proficiency is not defined, just listed. This is fine if it is

Detailed description
of all components
of each element is
described.

The teacher
circles the score
for each
element.

| Element A described | Exemplary (A) | Good (B) | Satisfactory (C) | Not Yet |
|---|---|---|---|---|
| | Comments/Questions to drive digging deeper: | | | |
| Element B described | Exemplary (A) | Good (B) | Satisfactory (C) | Not Yet |
| | Comments/Questions to drive digging deeper: | | | |
| Element C described | Exemplary (A) | Good (B) | Satisfactory (C) | Not Yet |
| | Comments/Questions to drive digging deeper: | | | |
| Final Score calculated | | | | |

Teacher uses the
individual
component grade to
calculate a final
grade for the task.

Teacher uses space
to provide comments
and or questions
communicating gaps
in that element as
described on the
rubric.

**FIGURE 11.7**  Open-Ended Analytic Rubric

understood what each level means. If not, then, each level of proficiency should be defined as well. This could be done in a row across the top of the rubric, and would then not need to be listed for each element separately.

Both of these rubrics do not list any points, and therefore still would be used in a holistic nature, with the teacher assigning a final grade based on an average of the components—which could be a calculated average or a visual average. Conversely, these rubrics can easily be made "quantifiable" by assigning point values to each level of proficiency and simply adding up the points (Figure 11.8). One could even simply replace the separate boxes defining proficiency levels and replace each of those rows with a point scale. The teacher would then circle the points awarded for that element on the scale for each element. This would allow the teacher to quantifiably weight each element differently if desired. The two can even be combined.

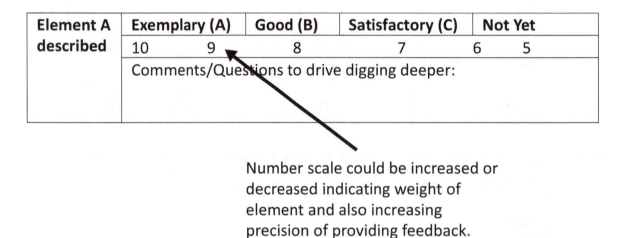

| Element A | Exemplary (A) | Good (B) | Satisfactory (C) | Not Yet | |
|-----------|---------------|----------|------------------|---------|---|
| described | 10            9 | 8 | 7 | 6 | 5 |
| | Comments/Questions to drive digging deeper: | | | | |

Number scale could be increased or decreased indicating weight of element and also increasing precision of providing feedback.

**FIGURE 11.8** Analytic Rubric with Points

In all three of these examples, the same levels of proficiency were used. These can be modified to match the grading scheme being utilized in the class or school. One could add additional levels, or reduce the levels all the way done to one: completed. The proficiency level labels could be eliminated entirely and each element could simply have a point-value scale assigned to it.

A rubric can also be designed to be both analytic and holistic (Figure 11.9). This requires that each element is evaluated separately (in either of the two formats shown above) and then adding a thorough narrative description that describes the performance or product as a whole at each level of proficiency. The teacher would then use the individual criteria to inform his or her decision about how well the performance or product fits the available narrative holistic descriptions. Again, the rubric could have the desired number of levels of proficiency described or labeled—from multiple listed to simply one for each element: completed. The teacher could then check off each element and then provide a final holistic score informed by the checklist. These rubrics can then either be quantified with a number point value or simply be assigned a descriptive grade or letter grade (matching the grading scheme being utilized in the class).

| | Exemplary | Satisfactory | Not yet |
|---|---|---|---|
| **Element A (*either listed or described in detail*)** | | | |
| **Element B** | | | |
| **Element C** | | | |
| etc. | | | |

| Score | Holistic Description: |
|---|---|
| A | *Narrative description of each level of proficiency* |
| B | |
| C | |
| D | |
| F | |

Letter grades could be replaced with a point scale.

Teacher checks off the appropriate box for each element.

**FIGURE 11.9** Combined Analytic and Holistic Rubric

Rubrics can be used for both formative and summative assessments. It is possible to have generalized, standard rubric for a formative assessment that is done regularly and following the same format, such as a reading assignment, lab report, graded discussion, etc. No matter which type of rubric and which formatting used, it is important to provide consistency. Using the same language for describing proficiency levels, and similar formatting will make it more likely students can decipher your feedback so that it can be used for feedforward.

There is one other purpose for the rubric that will impact how descriptive and task-specific language you use to define each element on the rubric. The rubric can be a very useful tool for the student to use to help guide the completion of the product and then be also used for self-evaluation and peer coaching. Therefore, the more descriptive the rubric can be, the more useful for the student. The one exception of this is to not include "answers" to content information in the description. If one aspect of the assessment is to evaluate students' knowledge of content, as in memorization of it and knowing where to use it, then those key terms should not be listed in the description. However, if the assessment is asking them to apply the understanding of key terminology to a larger question or concept, then listing the terms so you (and the student) can check them off as used in the final product or performance would be acceptable.

In the end, the rubric should be a tool that makes it easier to provide the maximum feedback to students in the most efficient manner as possible, and for students to understand that feedback to use as instructive feedforward as well as use to complete self-evaluation.

# Emergent Curriculum

Part of the challenge of utilizing student-centered practices in the current climate of public education is that you have to balance meeting a required curriculum with allowing student questions and interests to drive the learning. There are ways to manage this, though some might say this is a compromise. It may be, but that is the reality of balancing student-centered teaching in an essentialist system.

One method is to allow for time for students to explore ideas and generate topics. This can be done in the context of skill development aspects of the curriculum. From grades Kindergarten all of the way through 12th grade it is valuable for students to complete personal projects of

their own design and own area of interest. The aim of personal projects generally is not content acquisition, but skill acquisition. It's the process that matters, not the topic. Within the framework of personal projects students are learning (developmentally appropriate) life-long learning skills such as researching, organizing information, writing, presenting, problem-solving, etc. All of these skills are important, and many of these skills are written into state and national standards. Therefore, allowing students to complete personal projects is a means of allowing them some autonomy over the content of exploration, while the teacher provides structure for the development of life-long learning skills—both academic and dispositional.

Another form of independent investigation and inquiry students can complete is as a structured component of a content curriculum. Used as a component of a unit's formative and or summative assessment where and how can you provide as much student choice as possible in completing a task. Usually, it is possible to provide choice in either how information is attained or presented. Additionally, it may be possible to provide students with a menu of content investigation subjects that fall within the larger parameters of a unit, but allows for some student choice in what aspect of the content to explore. This isn't completely "emergent" but it is an attempt to provide some student autonomy.

This provision for autonomy can also be done at the whole class level and does not have to be only present during independent student projects. It is also possible to present a class with a required topic to be explored and then have the class collectively decide how to explore that topic, what kinds of activities to do, participate in generating the expectations for projects, and assign teams to complete specific aspects of the research and larger class project. Essentially, this is using the personal project model and applying it to the classroom. This does require a truly creative, and gifted teacher at engaging and motivating students as well as managing student behavior and daily routines to implement this type of collective inquiry-based learning so that all students actively participate and are properly challenged so as to maximize their learning.

# Finding Additional Resources

The purpose of this chapter was to introduce a variety of techniques a teacher can use in his or her tool kit to implement thematic, inquiry-based learning. This chapter just scratches the surface. A couple of reasons I have loved being a teacher is first, it has always required me to continue learning, and second, teaching is a very collaborative profession. Teachers love to share their ideas. For many teachers, when they come across a lesson that really works, they want as many kids as possible to experience it, so, many teachers are even a bit offended if you don't take their ideas! This means it is now easier than ever to find ideas. Countless books are written about very specific teaching techniques and tools and a virtually unlimited resource of teaching ideas are available on the internet. The trick isn't finding resources. The trick is finding resources that hold true to providing students an opportunity to construct meaning and develop truly "owned knowledge" through lived experiences.

Therefore, as you explore all of the available resources for lesson ideas, it is crucial to ask yourself the following questions:

- Who is doing the work in the lesson, the teacher or the student?

- In what way is this activity prompting students to conduct inquiry?

- In what way is this activity allowing my students to have a lived experience?

- In what way is this lesson facilitating students to make a paradigm shift in understanding from their prior knowledge and (mis)conceptions about a topic to newly "owned knowledge."?

- In what way does the student have as much autonomy as possible to tap into the purpose motive?

- Why will this be important to my students? Is it authentic?

If you find an activity that you can see all of these questions accounted for in the design of the lesson, then you've found a great activity rooted in constructivist learning theory to build into a lesson. More likely, however, it will be that you will find an activity that aligns to your learning objective but will require that you make some modifications to fill in the gaps illuminated by answering these above questions.

# Chapter 12

# Conclusion: Developing Your Own Template

Throughout this book, my agenda has been clear. I want to influence teachers so that they know how to provide as student-centered classroom setting as possible. My goal is for students to have as many authentic experiences as possible to prepare them to become life-long learners. I believe this is best done through a variety of strategies that do two things: first provide students as much autonomy as possible in their learning, and second facilitate students making meaningful connections between what they are learning and their daily lives and to make meaningful connections between subjects to develop the ability to analyze complex issues and the complex interconnectedness of the issues the next generation will face. Fair or not, the weight of the world is on the shoulders of the next generation. That's how societies progress. I suppose one might say this is my vision and mission statement as a teacher. This reminds me of a quote attributed to California Indian pedagogy from *Liberal Education* (Van Dorn 1943). "When you teach someone something, you've robbed the person of the experience of learning it. You need to be cautious before you take that experience away from someone else."

Do you know the children's book, *If You Give a Mouse a Cookie* by Laura Numeroff? A boy gives a cookie to a mouse. Then the mouse needs a glass of milk. Then a litany of requests: a straw (to drink the milk), a mirror (to avoid a milk mustache), nail scissors (to trim his hair), and a broom (to sweep up). After that he wants to nap, which requires a story to be read to him, which prompts the mouse to want to draw a picture, and then to hang the drawing on the refrigerator. Looking at the refrigerator of course makes him thirsty, so the mouse asks for a glass of milk. And what goes better with milk, than a cookie?

If you give a child the love of learning….

Except children already have a love of learning. As they grow and go to school, we manage to take that away from many of our students. I had a recent conversation with a teacher when to start having students investigating their own questions and doing their own inquiry. I got the answer I so often get. "We can't do that until we get the basic skills down first—then in more advanced classes students get to do that kind of learning."

No. No. No. No! This is backwards. Children are naturally active learners who should be given opportunities to construct their own frames of thought. Students need to be put in learning situations where they are doing the work of learning, not the work of listening to and memorizing the teacher's understanding of a topic. They need to be free to infer and discover their own answers to important questions. They need to enjoy learning.

There is a notion among many educators that we can't do progressive or constructivist education until we have "taught" them the basic skills. Do you see the contradiction here? This is especially the practice with students who are disengaged or disenfranchised from school and worse, from a life of learning. It is especially true that as these students get older we need to use these methods. Why does the learning in school look less and less like how children learn—asking questions, making mistakes, seeking guidance, exploring, and play?

Ask most teachers how they learned something complex, say for example how to teach, and they won't cite a great lecture where they were told how to teach, or even this book unfortunately! They will cite doing it and figuring it out, hopefully with the help of a good mentor. Why do they then assume their students can't do this until they are "taught" the basic skills? I'm not saying there aren't times for teacher-centered, direct instruction. But, it should be the exception, not the norm. Students would learn the basic skills much better if they weren't memorizing another's understanding of those skills and basic content, but instead were applying those skills and concepts as they were investigating something that had meaning, with the help of a good mentor. That's where the teaching comes in. Don't lecture about a topic, then have them look at it, and then tell them again what they saw. Instead have them consider what they already know, explore it to construct some meaning, and then lecture, or better yet dialogue with them, to allow them to confirm what they saw and deal with the cognitive dissonance with what they thought would happen.

The problem isn't that we have gone away from or quit teaching the basics. The problem is that is predominantly *all* we are doing—especially for students on the wrong end of the achievement gap. I think we don't so much have an achievement gap, but instead a learning gulf that we have created. It mirrors our countries economics. The rich get richer. The poor get poorer. Those engaged with school, get the fun learning. Those behind get the boring learning. If this was you, would you want to keep learning? Why take students that haven't succeeded in learning the basics through teacher-centered models and slow them down even more and continue to do more of the same that didn't work the first time? How will that catch them up?

Instead of decreasing the amount of inquiry, exploration, and play, our students are doing, we need to increase it to keep them loving learning. For Pete's sake, give them a cookie. Who knows what will happen next? Well, maybe that is what scares many teachers.

Teaching is more than just a job or something to do until something better comes along. For one thing it is too hard to approach with that attitude and be successful, and for another thing, it is too damn important. We teachers share a portion of that burden we are putting on the shoulders of the next generation. So, what role do you see K-12 education (both public and private) playing in the next steps our society will take? And then, what is your role in making that a reality?

In the end, there is no one right way to teach. I have provided for you a template to use that I believe will provide you the best opportunity to implement methodologies founded in constructivist learning theory through the Consider, Construct, Confirm learning cycle and utilizing thematic, inquiry-based units of study. But teaching is as much art as it is scientific application of prescribed techniques and methods. The artistic nature of being a great teacher is that you can take all of the available ideas about how to teach, and all of the available ideas about how to build trusting and meaningful relationships with students and make your own template for writing curriculum and lessons, delivering content, and assessing students. That is the art form—how you make it your own. So own it!

Therefore that leaves us where we started.

Then, how will you enact your story as a teacher?

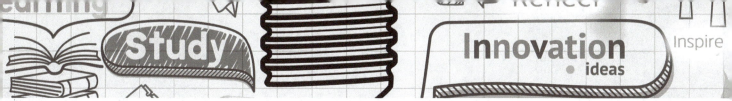

# Bibliography

Ashoka's Start Empathy Initiative. *Rules of Kindness: A Back-to-School Empathy Toolkit.* GenerationON. n.d. http://rulesofkindness.generationon.org/sites/default/files/empathy_toolkit.pdf.

Beaty-O'Ferrall, Mary Ellen, Alan Green, and Fred Hanna. "Classroom Management Strategies for Difficult Students: Promoting Change Through Relationships." *Middle School Journal* 41 (March 2010): 4–11.

Bronfenbrenner, Uri. *The Ecology of Human Development: Experiments by Nature and Design.* Cambridge: Harvard Press, 1979.

Brooks, Jacqueline, and Martin Brooks. *In Search of Understanding: The Case for Constructivist Classroom.* Alexandria: ASCD, 1993.

Bruhn, Allison, Shanna Hirsch, and Kari Vogelgesang. "Motivating Instruction? There's an App for That!" *Intervention in School and Clinic* 52, no. 3 (2017).

Cappella, Elise, Ha Yeon Kim, Jennifer Neal, and Daisy Jackson. "Classroom Peer Relationships and Behavioral Engagement in Elementary School: The Role of Social Network Equity." *American Journal of Community Psychology* 52 (December 2013): 367–379.

Carleton College. *Starting Point: Teaching Entry Level Geoscience.* 2016. https://serc.carleton.edu/introgeo/socratic/second.html (accessed March 14, 2018).

Carter, Kathy, and Walter Doyle. "Classroom Management in Early Childhood and Elementary Classrooms." In *Handbook of Classroom Management*, edited by Carolyn Everton and Carol Weinstein, 373–406. Mahwah: Larwence Erlbaum Associates Inc., 2006.

Colburn, Alan. "Constructivism: Science Education's "Grand Unifying Theory." *The Clearing House* 74 (2000): 9–12.

Colburn, Linda. "Personal Contact." September 2017.

Dagar, Yadav. "Constructivsm: A Paradigm for Teaching and Learning." *Arts Social Science Journal* 7 (2016).

Dass, Pradeep. "Teaching STEM Effectively with the Learning Cycle Approach." *K-12 STEM Education* 1, no. 1 (January–March 2015): 5–12.

Davies, M, and R. Shanker-Brown. "A Programmatic Approach to Teaming and Thematic Instruction." *North Carolina Middle School Association Journal* 20 (2011): 1–17.

Denton, David. *Academic Language.* 2014. http://www.passedtpa.com/hello-world/ (accessed March 4, 2018).

Dewey, John. *Democracy and Education: An Introduction to the Philosophy of Education.* New York: The MacMillan Company, 1916.

Doyle, Walter. "Ecological Approaches to Classroom Management." In *Handbook of Classroom Management*, edited by Carolyn Evertson and Carol Weinstein, 97–125. Mahwah: Lawrence Erlbaum Associates, Inc., 2006.

Dunbar, Robin. "Necortex Size and Group Size in Primates: A Test of the Hypothesis." *Journal of Human Evolution* 28 (1995): 287–296.

Dweck, Carol, and Ellen Leggett. "A Social-Cognitive Approach to Motivation and Personality." *Psychological Review* 95, no. 2 (1988): 256–273.

Emmer, ET, and LM Stough. "Classroom Management: A Critical Part of Educational Psychology, with Implications for Teacher Education." *Educational Psychologist*, 2001: 103–112.

Emmers, Edwin, and Mary Claire Gerwels. "Classroom Management in Middle and High School Classrooms." In *Handbook of Classroom Management*, edited by Carolyn Everton and Carol Weinstein, 407–438. Mahwah: Lawrence Erlbaum Associates Inc., 2006.

Fosnot, Catherine Towmey. "Constructivism: A Psychological Theory of Learning." In *Constructivism: Theory, Perspectives and Practice*, edited by Catherine Towmey Fosnot, 8–33. New York: Teacher's College Press, 1996.

Fosnot, Catherine Twomey. *Enquiring Teachers Enquiring Learners: A constructivist approach for teaching.* Columbia NY: Teachers College Press, 1989.

Furrer, Carrie, Ellen Skinner, and Jennifer Pitzer. "The Influence of Teacher and Peer Relationships on Students' Classroom Engagement and Everydat Motivational Resilience." *National Society for the Study of Education* (Teachers College, Columbia University) 113, no. 1 (2014): 101–123.

Goncalves, Bruno, Nicola Perra, and Allesandro Vespignani. "Modeling Users' Activity on Twitter Networks: Validation of Dunbar's Number." *PLOS One* 6, no. 8 (August 2011): e22656.

Gordon, Mordechai. "Toward a Pragmatic Discourse of Constructivism: Reflections on Lessons from Practice." *Educational Studies* 45 (2009): 39–58.

Hendrickx, Marloes, M. Tim Naubhard, Nerike Boor-Klip, Antonius Cillessen, and Mieke Brekelmans. "Social Dynamics in the Classroom: Teacher Support and Conflict and the Peer Ecology." *Teaching and Teacher Education* 53 (January 2016): 30–40.

Horton, Myles, and Paulo Freire. *We Make The Road By Walking: Conversations on Education and Social Change.* Philladephia: Temple University Press, 1990.

Horton, Todd, and Jennifer Barnett. "Thematic Unit Planning in Social Studies: Make It Focused and Meaningful." *Canadian Social Studies* 41, no. 1 (Fall 2008).

Johnson, Dave W., Roger, T. Johnson, and Edythe Johnson Holubec. *The New Circles of Learning: Cooperation in the Classroom and School.* Alexandria, VA: Association for Supervision of Curriculum and Development, 1994.

Johnson, David W., Roger, T. Johnson, and Edythe J. Holubec. *Cooperative Learning in the Classroom.* Alexandria, VA: Association for Supervision of Curriculum Development, 1994.

Jorgensen, Cheryl. "Essential Questions: Inclusive Answers." *Educational Leadership* 52, no. 4 (1994): 52.

Kerlin, Steven C., Scott P. McDonald, and Gregory J. Kelly. "Making a Science Inquiry Unit." *Journal of Classroom Interaction* 43, no. 2 (Winter 2008): 4–13.

Knight, Jim. *High-Impact Instruction: A Framework for Great Teaching.* Thousand Oaks, CA: Corwin, 2013.

Koyczan, Shane. "To This Day . . . for the bullied and beautiful." *TED2013: The Young. The Wise. The Undiscovered.* Long Beach: TED conferences LLC, 2013.

Kumar, Muthu. "Organizing curriculum based upon constructivism: what to teach and what not to." *Journal of Thought*, 2006: 81–93.

Maclellan, E., and R. Soden. "The Importance of Epistemic Cognition in Student-Centered Learning." *Instructional Science*, 2004: 253–268.

Macy, Joanna, and Chris Johnstone. *Active Hope: How to Face the Mess We're in Without Going Crazy.* Novato, CA: New World Library, 2012.

Markham, Thomm. *Project Based Learning 2nd edition: A Guide to Standards-Focused Project Based Learning for Middle and High School.* Buck Institute for Education, 2003.

Marzano, Robert, and Debra Pickering. *The Highly Engaged Classroom: The Classroom Strategies Series.* Bloomington, IN: Marzano Research Laboratory, 2011.

McLaren, Brian D. *We Make the Road by Walking: A Year-Long Quest for Spiritual Formation, Reorientation, and Activation.* New York: Jericho Books, 2014.

McTighe, Jay, and Grant Wiggins. *Essential Questions: Opening Doors to Student Understanding.* Alexandria, VA: ASCD, 2013.

Michael, Joel. "Where's the Evidence That Active Learning Works?" *Advanced in Physiology Education* 3, no. 4 (December 2006): 159–167.

Milne, A. A. *The House at Pooh Corner.* E. P. Dutton & Company, 1928.

Moyer, Courtney D. "A Thematic Instruction Approach to Teaching Technology and Engineering." *Technology & Engineering Teacher* 76, no. 3 (November 2016): 8–12.

Noddings, Nel. *Philosophy of Education.* Cambridge: Westview Press, 2007.

Novak, Joseph, and Alberto Canas. *The Theory Underlying Concept Maps and How to Construct and Use Them.* Pensacola: Institute for Human and Machine Cognition, 2008.

NYC Department of Education. *Project-Based Learning: Inspiring Middle School Students to Engage in Deep and Active Learning.* New York: NYC Department of Education, 2009.

Osoweicki, Aaron. "The 4-3-2-1 Assessment Grading System." *NSTA National Conference.* Minneapolis, 2009.

Piaget, J., and B. Inhelder. *The Psychology of the Child.* New York: Basic Books, 1971.

Piaget, Jean. *Success and Understanding.* Cambridge MA: Harvard University Press, 1978.

Pierson, Rita. *Rita Pierson: Every Kid Needs a Champion.* May 2013. https://www.ted.com/talks/rita_pierson_every_kid_needs_a_champion.

Pink, Daniel. *Drive: The Surprising Truth About What Motivates Us.* New York: Riverhead Books, 2009.

Quinn, Daniel. *Ishmael.* 1994.

Reeve, Johnmarshall. "Extrinsic Rewards and Intrinsic Motivation." In *Handbook of Classroom Management*, edited by Carolyn Everton and Carol Weinstein, 645–664. Mahwah: Lawrence Elbraum Associates Inc., 2006.

Rifkin, Jeremy. *The Empathic Civilization: The Race to Global Consciousness in a World in Crisis.* New York: Penguin Books Ltd., 2009.

Sanchez, Ray, and Keith O'Shea. *Mass shooter Dylann Roof, with a laugh, confesses, 'I did it'.* December 10, 2016. http://www.cnn.com/2016/12/09/us/dylann-roof-trial-charleston-video/index.html (accessed December 7, 2017).

Schneps, M. H. *Minds of Our Own.* Annenberg Learner. Burlington, VT, 1995.

Singer, Florence Mihaela, and Hedy Moscovici. "Teaching and learning cycles in a constructivist approach to instruction." *Teaching and Teacher Education* 24 (2008): 1613–1634.

Sizer, Ted. *Horace's Compromise: The Dilemma of the American High School.* Boston: Houghton Mifflin, 1985.

Splitter, Laurance. *Authenticity and Constructivism in Education.* New York: Springer Science+Business Media, 2008.

TeachingChannel. *Structure Groups: Making Group Work Work.* 2018. www.teachingchannel.org (accessed March 12, 2018).

Thomas, John W. *A Review of Research on Project-Based Learning.* March 2000. http://www.bobpearlman.org/BestPractices/PBL_Research.pdf.

University of Michigan. *University of Michigan.* n.d. http://www.umich.edu/~elements/fogler&gurmen/html/probsolv/strategy/cthinking.htm (accessed March 14, 2018).

Van Dorn, Mark. *Liberal Education.* New York: Henry Holt and Company, 1943.

Virgin, Robb. "Connecting Learning: How Revisiting Big Idea Questions Can Help in History Classrooms." *Social Studies* 105, no. 4 (Jul/Aug 2014).

Virgin, Robb. "Connecting Learning: How Revisiting Big Idea Questions Can Help in History Classrooms." *The Social Studies* 105, no. 4 (May 2014).

Wentzel, Kathryn. "A Social Motivation Perspective for Classroom Management." In *Handbook of Classroom Management*, edited by Carolyn Everton and Carol Weinstein, 619–644. Mahwah: Lawrence Elbraum Associates Inc., 2006.

Wiggins, Grant, and Jay McTighe. *Understanding by Design.* Alexandria, VA: Association for Supervision and Curriculum Development, 2005.

Wilhelm, Jeffery. "Essential Questions: The Secret to Teaching may be as Simple as Asking Students good Questions-and then Giving them the opportunity to find the Answers." *Scholastic Instructor*, 2012.

Wong, Harry, and Rosemary Wong. *The First Days of School: How to be an effective teacher.* Mountain View, CA: Harry K Wong Publications, 2009.

Yilmaz, Kaya. "Constructivism: Its Theoretical Underpinnings, Variations, and Implications for Classroom Instruction." *Educational Horizons* 86, no. 3 (Spring 2008): 161–172.